CHILDREN AND YOUTH AS 'SITES OF RESISTANCE' IN ARMED CONFLICT

SOCIOLOGICAL STUDIES OF CHILDREN AND YOUTH

Series Editor: David A. Kinney (from 1999)
Series Editors: David A. Kinney and Katherine Brown Rosier (2004–2010)
Series Editors: David A. Kinney and Loretta E. Bass (from 2011)
Outgoing Series Editor: Loretta E. Bass (from 2012)
Incoming Series Editor: Ingrid E. Castro (from 2024)

Previous Volumes:

Volume 22:	2016 Loretta E. Bass, Series Editor; Ingrid E. Castro, Melissa Swauger & Brent Harger, Guest Editors
Volume 23:	2017 Loretta E. Bass, Series Editor; Patricia Neff Claster & Sampson Lee Blair, Guest Editors
Volume 24:	2019 Loretta E. Bass, Series Editor; Magali Reis & Marcelo Isidório, Guest Editors
Volume 25:	2019 Loretta E. Bass, Series Editor; Doris Bühler-Niederberger & Lars Alberth, Guest Editors
Volume 26:	2020 Loretta E. Bass, Series Editor; Anuppiriya Sriskandarajah, Guest Editor
Volume 27:	2020 Loretta E. Bass, Series Editor; Sam Frankel & Sally McNamee, Guest Editors
Volume 28:	2022 Loretta E. Bass, Series Editor; Agnes Lux & Brian Gran, Guest Editors
Volume 29:	2022 Loretta E. Bass, Series Editor; Adrienne Lee Atterberry, Derrace Garfield McCallum, Siqi Tu & Amy Lutz, Guest Editors
Volume 30:	2022 Loretta E. Bass, Series Editor; Sabina Schutter & Dana Harring, Guest Editors
Volume 31:	2023 Loretta E. Bass, Series Editor; Marcelo S. Isidório, Guest Editor
Volume 32:	2023 Loretta E. Bass, Series Editor; Rachel Berman, Patrizia Albanese & Xiaobei Chen, Guest Editors
Volume 33:	2023 Loretta E. Bass, Series Editor; Katie Wright & Julie McLeod, Guest Editors

EDITORIAL BOARD

Lars Alberth
Leuphana University Lüneburg, Germany

Sampson Lee Blair
The State University of New York, USA

Doris Bühler-Niederberger
Universität Wuppertal, Germany

Ingrid E. Castro
Massachusetts College of Liberal Arts, USA

Patricia Neff Claster
Edinboro University, USA

Tobia (Toby) Fattore
Macquarie University, Australia

Sam Frankel
King's University College at Western University, Canada

David Kinney
Central Michigan University, USA

Valeria Llobet
Universidad de Buenos Aires, Argentina

Sandi Nenga
Southwestern University, USA

Kate Tilleczek
York University, Canada

Yvonne M. Vissing
Salem State University, USA

Nicole Warehime
University of Central Oklahoma, USA

Katie Wright
La Trobe University, Australia

SOCIOLOGICAL STUDIES OF CHILDREN
AND YOUTH VOLUME 34

CHILDREN AND YOUTH AS 'SITES OF RESISTANCE' IN ARMED CONFLICT

EDITED BY

TAMANNA M. SHAH
Ohio University, USA

OUTGOING SERIES EDITOR

LORETTA E. BASS
The University of Oklahoma, USA

INCOMING SERIES EDITOR

INGRID E. CASTRO
Massachusetts College of Liberal Arts, USA

United Kingdom – North America – Japan
India – Malaysia – China

Emerald Publishing Limited
Emerald Publishing, Floor 5, Northspring, 21-23 Wellington Street, Leeds LS1 4DL.

First edition 2025

Editorial matter and selection © 2025 Tamanna M. Shah.
Individual chapters © 2025 The authors.
Published under exclusive licence by Emerald Publishing Limited.

Reprints and permissions service
Contact: www.copyright.com

No part of this book may be reproduced, stored in a retrieval system, transmitted in any form or by any means electronic, mechanical, photocopying, recording or otherwise without either the prior written permission of the publisher or a licence permitting restricted copying issued in the UK by The Copyright Licensing Agency and in the USA by The Copyright Clearance Center. Any opinions expressed in the chapters are those of the authors. Whilst Emerald makes every effort to ensure the quality and accuracy of its content, Emerald makes no representation implied or otherwise, as to the chapters' suitability and application and disclaims any warranties, express or implied, to their use.

British Library Cataloguing in Publication Data
A catalogue record for this book is available from the British Library

ISBN: 978-1-83549-371-7 (Print)
ISBN: 978-1-83549-370-0 (Online)
ISBN: 978-1-83549-372-4 (Epub)

ISSN: 1537-4661 (Series)

INVESTOR IN PEOPLE

To my son, Qais
and
to the children who are our future

CONTENTS

List of Figures, Tables and Appendix	xi
About the Editor	xiii
About the Contributors	xv
Acknowledgments	xix

Children and Youth as "Sites of Resistance" in Armed Conflict
Tamanna M. Shah   1

Chapter 1   "We Became One Family": Hardship, Interdependence, and Resistance Among the Lost Boys and Girls of Sudan
Myriam Denov and Régine Debrosse   15

Chapter 2   Humanizing and Amplifying Voices of Displaced Children: A Narrative of an Eight-Year-Old's Journey and Integration
Roxanna M. Senyshyn   35

Chapter 3   How Memories and Narratives Influence Youth's Perceptions of Conflict and the "Out-Group"
Natia Chankvetadze   55

Chapter 4   The Problems of Rural Youth: A Case Study on Conflict, Justice, and Resilience in Sindh, Pakistan
Abdullah Khoso   73

Chapter 5   The Child Quilters of World War I: Bringing Hope and Comfort to Casualties and Survivors of War
Aisha Manus   91

Chapter 6   Unveiling Sudan's Youth: Humanitarian Tales and the Unfolding Rights Agenda in Sudan
Sonali Jha   113

**Chapter 7   Beyond the Frontlines: A Case for Gendered
Peacebuilding and Intervention in Kashmir**
Aksa Jan, Lakshya Kadiyan and Sanjoy Roy   *133*

**Chapter 8   AI's Role in Enhancing Humanitarian
Efforts for Children in Armed Conflict**
Tamanna M. Shah and Javed M. Shah   *145*

LIST OF FIGURES, TABLES AND APPENDIX

Figures

Fig. 2.1	Border Crossing and First Day in Poland: "It Was the Worst Day!"	40
Fig. 2.2a	Veronika's Explanation for the Reason for Fleeing Ukraine (Original).	41
Fig. 2.2b	Veronika's Explanation for the Reason for Fleeing Ukraine (with Annotations).	41
Fig. 2.3	About the First Day: "... It Was Stressful ... All Students Welcomed Me with Pictures."	44
Fig. 2.4	Peers' Welcoming Veronika on the First Day of School.	46
Fig. 2.5	Peers' Welcoming Veronika on the First Day of School.	46
Fig. 2.6	Describing a Poster: "This Cat Is So Cute. She Is Like Ukraine. She Makes Veronika Happy."	49
Fig. 2.7	Dreaming of Time with Family in the Carpathian Mountains of Ukraine.	51

Tables

Table 1	Volume I: Thematic Overview.	10
Table 3.1	Youth Across Different Backgrounds and Their Perceptions.	66

Appendix

Table A3.1	Information about Research's Participants.	71

ABOUT THE EDITOR

Tamanna M. Shah is an Assistant Professor of Instruction in the Department of Sociology and Anthropology at the Ohio University, USA. She serves as an Experiential Learning Community-of-Practice Fellow at Ohio University and is the Book Reviews Editor for *Sociological Research Online*. She earned her Ph.D. in Sociology from the University of Utah and holds a Master's degree in Sociology from Kansas State University and a Bachelor's degree in Economics. She has conducted field research in Kashmir, India, and East Timor. Her interests include comparative political sociology, gender and race, social change, and inequality. She has authored several publications, including "Adjustment to Divorce (Spouses)" for the *Wiley Blackwell Encyclopedia of Family Studies*, and "Chaos and Fear: Creativity and Hope in an Uncertain World" in *International Sociology*. She is currently editing a book on *Gendered Identities in the Media* for Vernon Press. She has collaborated with the Asian Development Bank on water and sanitation policy papers. (ORCID: 0000-0001-9609-0191)

ABOUT THE CONTRIBUTORS

Natia Chankvetadze is a Ph.D. candidate at the Carter School for Peace and Conflict Resolution, George Mason University (GMU). She also holds AAUW International Fellowship at the Davis Center for Russian and Eurasian Studies, Harvard University (2023–2024). She has been a Teaching Fellow at Social Studies Program (Harvard University) and a Graduate Lecturer at GMU's Carter School. She has led and implemented research projects on everyday peace, conflict transformation, trade facilitation, youth engagement, trauma narratives, track I dialogue within Georgia's context. She worked as Non-resident Scholar for Frontier Europe Program within the Middle East Institute and taught the post-graduate course "Peace Policy Analysis" at the Ivane Javakhishvili Tbilisi State University (2017–2021). She co-authored a book *Women During and After War* as well as handbook on *Peace and Conflict Transformation in Georgia*. She has MA in Peace and Conflict Studies from the University of Manchester.

Régine Debrosse is an Assistant Professor and William Dawson Scholar at McGill University. Her program of research focuses on the experiences of Black, Indigenous, and people of color and notably focuses on how hardships and stigma transform relationships (ORCID: 0000-0002-7929-9521).

Myriam Denov is a Full Professor at McGill University and holds the Canada Research Chair in Children, Families and Armed Conflict (Tier 1). Her research interests lie in the areas of children and families affected by war, migration, and its intergenerational impact (ORCID: 0000-0001-7963-1136).

Aksa Jan is a Ph.D. Scholar at the Delhi School of Social Work, University of Delhi, India.

Sonali Jha is a Ph.D. candidate in the School of Media Arts and Studies at Ohio University. She holds a Bachelor's and a Master's degree in English Literature. She has two years of experience in the marketing industry working as a content writer. She focuses on unraveling media and social media usage inequalities, examining how it could help impact society such as human trafficking. She explores the subjective nature of people's tech relationships, along with the significance of comedy in raising awareness. She is passionate about interpersonal communication, media's impact on daily life, digital inequalities and international media.

Lakshya Kadiyan is a Ph.D. Scholar at the School of Social Work, University of Illinois-Urbana Champaign, USA.

xvi ABOUT THE CONTRIBUTORS

Abdullah Khoso is an Assistant Professor at the Centre for Public Policy and Governance, Forman Christian College (A Chartered University). He earned a Ph.D. in Sociology and Cultural Studies from the University of Malaya (UM), Malaysia. During and after his Ph.D., he taught various courses at the Faculty of Arts and Social Sciences, UM. He has an M.Sc. in Anthropology from Quaid-e-Azam University, Islamabad. He has also taught at the International Islamic University, Islamabad, and in different capacities worked with Save the Children International and other organizations. He was honored to help the Ministry of Human Rights Pakistan draft Pakistan's fifth periodic report submitted to the Committee on the Rights of the Child in Geneva. Recently, he has served as an Advisor at the Civil Services Academy, Pakistan Administrative Services, Lahore, specializing in the Midcareer Management Course.

Aisha Manus is an Independent Historian in the United States. She has a Master's in U.S. History, a Bachelor's in History, an Associates in Intelligence, and an Associates in Communication. She is the author of several journal articles on WWI and WWII textiles and homefront studies and has spoken both nationally and internationally on the topic of WWI quilters. A disabled veteran of the United States Air Force, she is also the author of a children's book, *Annabelle the Brave*, about a military child.

Sanjoy Roy is a Professor and Head at the Delhi School of Social Work, University of Delhi, India.

Roxanna M. Senyshyn is an Associate Professor of Applied Linguistics and Communication Arts and Sciences and Coordinator of the English as a Second Language certification program at Abington College, Pennsylvania State University, where she teaches courses in second language education, applied linguistics, and intercultural communication. Her current research focuses on transformative intercultural learning and development in preservice teacher education and the ongoing professional development of educators of culturally and linguistically diverse learners. Her work has been published in academic journals including *Intercultural Education, Journal for Multicultural Education,* and *Journal of Transformative Education,* among others. Beyond academia, she engages with school districts to provide critical professional development for in-service teachers, including supporting students affected by Russia's war against Ukraine. She is also an Advocate for Bilingual Education and served on the Pennsylvania Department of Education Task Force that brought the Seal of Biliteracy to Pennsylvania. Additionally, she is actively involved in Ukrainian heritage language community-based education programs.

About the Contributors xvii

Javed M. Shah, University of Illinois, Chicago, USA, has over 20 years of experience building software products for startups. He is currently pursuing a Master of Science in Computer Science from the University of Illinois, Chicago. He holds a BS in Computer Engineering from the University of Pune and an MBA from the University of California, Berkeley. He is passionate about research in permissionless systems, incentive design, computational science, and machine learning. His work on the multifaceted role of agency in shaping political landscapes has been published in the *International Political Science Abstracts*. He is a versatile technologist and researcher with deep empathy for building socially responsible innovation.

ACKNOWLEDGMENTS

This volume is curated to serve as a resource for scholars and practitioners dedicated to advancing policies for the rights of children and youth. I want to applaud the authors and the reviewers for their unwavering commitment to bringing the narratives and experiences of children to the forefront. A heartfelt thank you goes to the contributors who painstakingly documented and analyzed the stories of children and youth embroiled in conflict. While it brings us joy to share this volume with the world, it was no small feat. As we wrote the chapters, we lived through the adversities faced by these young individuals. I am also grateful for the support and encouragement from the Editorial Staff at Emerald Publishing, particularly Katy Mathers and Lauren Kammerdiener, whose guidance was invaluable throughout this project. A special note of thanks to Professor Loretta E. Bass from the University of Oklahoma, the Series Editor of *Sociological Studies of Children and Youth.*

As the editor, I am inspired by a collective sense of hope and dedication to advocating for children's experiences.

Lastly, I want to acknowledge all those who helped me assemble this volume which gives voice to the struggles of millions of children worldwide. I extend my sincere appreciation to our reviewers, whose thorough and timely feedback significantly enhanced the quality of our chapters.

Dr. Holly Ningard, Ohio University (Special thanks for your support and encouragement).

Sonali Jha, Ohio University.

Dr. S. A. Welch, Professor Emerita University of Wisconsin-Whitewater.

Dr. Jodie Jones, Salt Lake Community College.

Dr. Kazim Tolga Gurel, Independent Researcher.

Nikhil Reddy, Ohio University.

Dr. Mary-Magdalene N. Chumbow DAB-CoVAc 2024 Project Assistant Manager.

Cameron Graham, University of Tennessee-Knoxville.

CHILDREN AND YOUTH AS "SITES OF RESISTANCE" IN ARMED CONFLICT

Tamanna M. Shah

Ohio University, USA

ABSTRACT

This volume transcends the traditional portrayal of children and youth as mere victims or combatants, highlighting their participation as agents of change and resistance. Through compelling narratives and empirical studies, the contributors examine ways in which children and youth engage in, and influence, the socio-political landscape in armed conflict. Emphasizing resilience, contributors to this volume detail how young people navigate the complexities of armed conflicts, contributing to peacebuilding and community reconstruction efforts. Through case studies spanning different geopolitical regions – including Sudan, Ukraine, Georgia, South Ossetia, and Pakistan – scholars highlight the multi-faceted experiences of these young people. With a focus on these intersecting aspects, this volume amplifies the voices of affected children and youth, informing policies, and implementing programs that prioritize their well-being and rights in post-conflict societies.

Keywords: Children in conflict; youth activism; sociopolitical agency; peacebuilding; resilience; resistance

---

Children and Youth as 'Sites of Resistance' in Armed Conflict
Sociological Studies of Children and Youth, Volume 34, 1–13
Copyright © 2025 by Tamanna M. Shah
Published under exclusive licence by Emerald Publishing Limited
ISSN: 1537-4661/doi:10.1108/S1537-466120240000034001

INTRODUCTION

In the fell clutch of circumstance

I have not winced nor cried aloud.

Under the bludgeonings of chance

My head is bloody, but unbowed …

~ William Ernest Henley (n.d.)

Amidst the chaos and devastation of armed conflict, children and youth often emerge as powerful agents of change and resilience. "Children and Youth as 'Sites of Resistance' in Armed Conflict" is a compelling exploration of their roles as active participants, who often function as catalysts for change within the complex dynamics of warfare. They stand amid ruins and regrowth, not merely as silent witnesses but as formidable agents of change. The current conflict climate is brutal for the people within these spaces. As this volume of *Sociological Studies of Children and Youth* was coming together, issues of children's safety and well-being were at the forefront of global conversations with the rising tensions in Ukraine and Palestine. This volume underscores the urgency of addressing these pressing concerns through international dialogue and action, aiming to foster environments where children can thrive despite the adversities they face.

Save the Children reports that approximately 468 million children worldwide live in armed conflict. This figure includes children affected by the crises in Palestine and Ukraine, highlighting the broader issue of child casualties in conflicts across Afghanistan, Yemen, Syria, Myanmar, Haiti, Sudan, Mali, Niger, Burkina Faso, the Democratic Republic of the Congo, Kashmir, and Somalia. Last year alone, out of the 8,630 children reported killed or maimed in conflicts, as many as 4,000 were denied access to humanitarian aid (*End the killing of children in armed conflict*, 2023).

This book marks a departure from the dominant renderings of children in such contexts, often reduced to either victims or instruments of war – child soldiers. Instead, it shifts the discourse to celebrate the agency of youth – revealing stories of survival, resistance, and the indomitable human spirit. The scholarship within these pages is emblematic of a methodological shift, one that seeks to underscore the interconnectedness of youth-led movements and their substantial influence on global conversations and policymaking. Here, the contributors shed light on the vibrant resistance movements led by youth, movements that resonate with power and hope. Through their nuanced research and empathetic narration, these scholars unveil the realities of these young lives, portraying them not as passive entities but as dynamic actors in their narratives of resilience.

Crucially, this book delves into the role of children and youth as catalysts for peace and justice in conflict and post-conflict settings. It examines their significant contributions to reconciliation, community rebuilding, and addressing the root causes of conflict. Incorporating intersections of age, gender, ethnicity, and socio-economic factors, enriches our understanding of the varied experiences of children and youth in conflict zones, spotlighting their roles in forging a more just and peaceful future.

Exploring these lived realities, this collection explores themes of trauma, the role of memorialization, and the implications for human rights within these challenging environments. Detailed case studies from regions like Sudan, Israel-Palestine, Ukraine, Kashmir, and Kosovo provide deep insights into the resilience and coping mechanisms of young individuals confronting the aftermath of traumatic events. The significance of memorialization is underscored, serving not only to honor and commemorate the losses suffered but also as an essential step toward healing and reconciliation. Through these explorations, the contributing scholars elevate the voices of affected children and youth, guiding policies and shaping programs that safeguard their well-being and rights in the wake of conflict.

CHILDREN AND YOUTH AS RESILIENT ACTORS

Children and youth living in conflict zones often carry the heavy burden of trauma due to exposure to multiple traumatic events. Finkelhor et al. (2005) introduced the term "polyvictims" to describe such deeply affected children. Ethno-political violence notably disrupts their cognitive and emotional processing of experiences (Barber & Schluterman, 2009; Betancourt et al., 2010; Cummings et al., 2010), leading to challenges such as an inability to adapt, antisocial behavior, and various negative mental health outcomes (Huemer et al., 2012).

Schick (2019) suggests a deeper self-reflective examination of the *self* and the other to foster an imagination where emotions merge with political realities, leading to an alternative understanding of a political community (Zhang, 2022). Everyday culture plays a crucial role in shaping the emotional narratives of citizens toward the state, influencing their affective engagement with politics (Wolak & Sokhey, 2022), or even resisting dominant structures by establishing "sites of contestation" (Adler-Nissen et al., 2020; Bilgic & Gkouti, 2021; Koschut, 2019). Scholars place significant emphasis on the non-linear characteristics inherent in the analysis of emotions (Beattie et al., 2019). It involves a complex, multi-layered process in which interactions at various levels either strengthen or limit specific emotional narratives and understandings. Emotions are integral to our "common-sense structures" (Beattie et al., 2019, p. 138) and significantly shape our perception of the world.

It is within the overt expression of emotions that a narrative of resilience emerges. The resilience displayed by children and youth transforms potential vulnerabilities into sources of strength, enabling them to navigate and overcome the challenges of their environments. This shift from vulnerability to resilience underscores the importance of recognizing and supporting the inherent capabilities of children and youth as active agents in their communities, capable of contributing meaningfully to peace and recovery in post-conflict settings.

Resilience is traditionally defined as the capacity of a system to adapt and recover from disturbances that threaten its stability and development (Masten, 2014). Alternatively, resilience is also depicted as "competence" (Masten, 2014), "constructive change" (Ridgway, 2001), or as "capability" (Bartley, 2006). Resilience, as an observable phenomenon, is key to understanding children's trauma and how they rebound from such events. Yet, viewing resilience merely through "objective measures of health" (Ungar, 2004) can sometimes miss the rich diversity of cultural interpretations and personal meanings.

This volume seeks to challenge and expand the conventional understanding of resilience, which often relies on a predominantly Western framework (Ungar, 2006). It argues that resilience should be seen not just as a personal trait but as a complex construct that emerges from social suffering and is deeply embedded in community and cultural contexts. For instance, in various conflict zones, resilience takes on locally specific meanings: in Palestine, it is expressed through *sumud* – a term that conveys steadfastness and a profound connection to the land (Nguyen-Gillham et al., 2008). In Kashmir, it manifests as *Tehreek*, symbolizing the struggle and movement for freedom (Shah, 2020, 2021, 2023). These examples illustrate that resilience is more than an individual's ability to bounce back; it is a collective expression of endurance and adaptability. It is (re)constituted across communities as a social representation, reflecting broader narratives of survival and resistance. Understanding resilience thus requires a dual perspective that appreciates both the individual and communal dimensions, acknowledging how cultural, societal, and political factors collectively shape the resilience of children and youth in conflict zones.

We emphasize the *thickness* of individual narratives and experiences to explore how children and youth construct meanings from their traumas and engage in resilient behaviors. In conflict zones, children's resilience is intricately woven with acts of resistance (Massad et al., 2018), stemming from their proactive mobilization of resources and skills to safeguard their psychological well-being (Veronese et al., 2018). Within such violent contexts, children break away from the conventional, static image of passive suffering to emerge as active agents deeply embedded within their social environments (Veronese & Cavazzoni, 2020).

The concept of childhood agency has attracted significant scholarly interest, highlighting several critical aspects such as social interaction (James, 2009), competence, self-determination, and practical action (Shah, 2024b; Stoecklin & Fattore, 2018). However, there remains a critical need to focus more on the significance of place. The local environment is a foundation for children's well-being and a fundamental structure shaping their lived realities (Hart, 2002; Jack, 2010). Acknowledging this dimension can provide richer insights into how these young lives navigate and influence their worlds, particularly in contexts of adversity.

CHILDREN AND YOUTH AS "SITES OF RESISTANCE"

The significance of *place* is fundamental to identity formation (Proshansky et al., 1983), as it serves as a conduit linking individuals with their ancestors and communities. Places — land, homes, or specific locations – forge connections that extend from the past through the present and into the future (Low, 1992). Agency manifests as a powerful expression of individual and collective capability (Giddens, 1984). Children are not passive in this process; they actively shape the spaces around them (Oswell, 2013), and their agency is realized through their engagement in socio-spatial activities such as play, participation in educational and religious institutions, and their connections to the land and family dwellings (Ergler et al., 2017; Moore, 2017). In disrupted environments, the interactions that children engage in with schools, homes, places of worship, community centers, and outdoor spaces, where they explore and play, can be seen as a tangible manifestation of their agency and resistance within their social contexts (Harker, 2005). These interactions also contribute to the formation of a therapeutic landscape (Sampson & Gifford, 2010).

The notion of *situated agency* deepens our understanding of how children's development is influenced by the dynamic interplay between their actions and their environment (Oswell, 2013). This concept reveals how places contribute to more than just well-being; they also shape experiences of trauma. The capacity of locales to act as channels for healing and as arenas of resistance significantly impacts youth and adults (Sousa et al., 2019). Places not only forge our identities but also define the potential for our physical and social existence. At the same time, through our engagement with these spaces - what might be termed our *spatial agency* - we not only navigate but also actively reconstruct these environments and their influences on our lives.

Marshall (2013) observed that children's interactions with their environment enable them to perceive and appreciate the esthetic qualities of their daily activities, thus reclaiming a degree of autonomy over their conditions. This engagement facilitates the mobilization of both personal and communal resilience strategies, allowing them to navigate the unpredictable settings characterized by political and military conflict. Furthermore, Marshall (2015) interprets children's playful activities in zones controlled by military forces as deliberate acts of resistance. Resistance displayed by children can take many forms and strategies. Indirect forms of resistance, through actions, expressions, and responses, are manifest within the everyday realm of emotional politics. Here, individuals, groups, and institutions, often considered peripheral to global politics, exert their agency (Schick, 2019). Some scholars understand agency to constitute emotions of the individual and the collective, and its relationship with the structures of political power (Šadl, 2021). At the basic individual level, emotions are the subjective, conscious reactions to specific circumstances, projected outward as personal feelings (Shah, 2012, 2024c).

Young people mobilize through social movements as well and in doing so claim the public and political space. From the Arab Spring protests to global Occupy protests, young people joined others and were often leaders in responding to injustice (Shah, 2013, 2019). Beyond mobilization is yet another strategy – peaceful "performed" resistance – that often transpires in the form of poetry, art, and music. These activities oppose the oppressive conditions and contribute to the children's subjective well-being and life satisfaction. Such "wounded" environments (Till, 2012) transform into *sites of resistance* and defiance, shaping significant aspects of their developmental pathways in these conflicted landscapes. These spaces, therefore, are not merely backdrops but active elements in the resilience and resistance narratives of children living under such extreme conditions.

CHILDREN AND YOUTH IN PEACEBUILDING

Children's participation in development programs is a central component of numerous United Nations initiatives (UNICEF, 2022). Globally, children and youth are crucial stakeholders in peacebuilding efforts, from planning to evaluation. Their involvement is considered essential for the effective formulation and implementation of peace and humanitarian aid strategies. Acknowledging their roles contributes to knowledge production that can lead to their emancipation (Jabri, 2007). This perspective places young people at the forefront of crafting solutions that directly impact their lives and underscores their role in shaping sustainable peace processes.

The concern here is that the contributions of young people are often "perennially overlooked or viewed with suspicion" (Berents & McEvoy-Levy, 2015, p. 119). This oversight extends into the fields of International Relations (IR) and conflict resolution, where there is a notable scarcity of theoretical engagement with youth (Berents & McEvoy-Levy, 2015). Frequently, young individuals are burdened with the responsibility for emancipation and breaking the cycles of conflict. At the grassroots level, there is a need to integrate the voices of children and youth into the master narrative of peacebuilding and humanitarian initiatives. Too often, young people are categorized as "damaged," "inexperienced," and "victimized" and thus perceived as incapable of contributing to peace (Berents & McEvoy-Levy, 2015).

However, locally, they participate in efforts that aim to restore some measure of peace. Viewing them solely as victims and sufferers of violence diminishes and negates their varied experiences as peacebuilders who navigate complex systems of risk and oppression to advocate for peace at local, national, and international levels. Such delegitimization of youth often relegates them to private spaces, such as the home, further isolating them from public and political engagement. This exclusion from active participation in peace processes undermines their potential roles as agents of change and perpetuates their marginalization within broader societal and political contexts.

Hart's distinction between instrumental and transformative participation is crucial for understanding the roles young people can play in peace initiatives. Instrumental participation typically focuses on achieving predefined objectives, often dictated by external agendas, without aiming for wider societal impact. In contrast, transformative participation, as Hart describes, seeks not only to achieve certain outcomes but also to empower marginalized groups and catalyze significant structural changes within society (Hart, 2002, p. 9). This form of participation recognizes the agency of young people, valuing their input as vital to the process and outcome of peacebuilding activities.

To genuinely enhance the impact of peace programs, they must be deeply embedded in the everyday realities of young lives. This approach involves integrating their experiences, perspectives, and aspirations into the design and implementation of these programs. It acknowledges that young people are not just recipients of aid but critical contributors to the peacebuilding process. By doing so, programs can move beyond mere engagement to actual empowerment, enabling youth to take on leadership roles and advocate for changes that address the root causes of conflict in their communities.

Embedding peace programs in youth realities ensures that these initiatives are responsive to the challenges and opportunities of the unique conflict contexts. It allows for the development of more tailored, effective strategies that resonate with the needs and goals of young participants. By fostering an environment where young people can contribute meaningfully, such programs enhance their immediate effectiveness and contribute to the long-term sustainability of peace efforts, building a resilient foundation for future generations.

This integration of Hart's theoretical framework into practical applications underscores the need for a shift from traditional top-down approaches to more inclusive, youth-centric strategies in peacebuilding. Such a shift not only enriches the programs but also amplifies the transformative potential of young people as key agents of change within their societies.

SCOPE OF CONTRIBUTIONS

In moving beyond the treatment of children and youth as subjects to central figures – both as sites of resistance and as creators of knowledge about conflict and peace, this volume brings together diverse perspectives. Each chapter draws from rich, field-based insights involving youth from regions as varied as Sudan, Ukraine, Georgia, South Ossetia, and Pakistan. Beyond mere narration, some contributors advocate for a dynamic, action-oriented approach to peacebuilding and humanitarian efforts, integrating human rights considerations in Sudan and weaving gender identities into peace processes in Kashmir. A particularly evocative chapter revisits the historical significance of child quilters during World War I, extracting valuable lessons applicable to contemporary conflicts. Collectively, these contributions elevate the often-overlooked voices of youth in global dialogues about conflict and peace, especially resonant amid the ongoing crises in Ukraine and Palestine. The narratives compiled here not only spotlight the diverse forms of violence and marginalization these young individuals endure but also celebrate their remarkable resilience in liminal spaces. These children and youth emerge not just as survivors but as formidable agents of resistance, actively shaping the politics of peace at both local and global levels.

In the opening chapter, Myriam Denov and Régine Debrosse examine the hardships endured by the Lost Boys and Girls of Sudan during their arduous journey to the Global North (Chapter 1). The authors delve into the kinship and mutual support that developed among these unaccompanied minors, underscoring their resilience and agency as they navigated the challenges of flight and resettlement. The narrative redefines the experiences of these children through the lens of their evolving relational dynamics and community bonds. Denov and Debrosse advocate for a nuanced approach to peacebuilding and intervention, stressing the importance of addressing the relational needs of unaccompanied youth – a facet frequently neglected by organizations and government bodies tasked with supporting these individuals. They argue that such entities must extend their focus beyond the immediate survival needs to include the social and emotional support systems that are essential for the long-term well-being and successful integration of unaccompanied youth into new communities.

Children's resistance and adaptability are further explored through the current lived realities of displaced Ukrainian children like Veronika, as they navigate integration within new educational systems amidst the disruptions caused by conflict. Roxanna M. Senyshyn's detailed analysis of the narrative highlights the critical role of supportive educational environments that cater to the unique needs of displaced children (Chapter 2). These environments facilitate language learning and integration and contribute to their healing process. This focus on children's individual experiences, coupled with the advocacy for educational strategies that prioritize personal development and emotional well-being, embodies the essence of children as active participants in shaping their destinies despite the adversities imposed by conflict. The chapter contributes to the broader discourse on how displaced children leverage their agency in navigating new social and educational landscapes, thus echoing the volume's overarching narrative of youth as *sites of resistance* in conflict zones.

Chapter 3 delves into the world of memory and its influence on the youth of Georgia and South Ossetia amidst their ongoing conflict. Natia Chankvetadze outlines how young people from these conflict-divided regions hold conflicting memories shaped by their societies' dominant narratives. This internalization of collective memories often fosters negative perceptions of the opposing community, known as the "out-group," complicating conflict resolution efforts. Chankvetadze's work underscores the urgent need for interactive, inter-community dialogues to bridge these perceptual divides. This alignment reinforces the necessity of addressing the causes of conflicts through informed and empathetic youth engagement.

The intersection of tribal conflicts and the youth of rural Sindh, Pakistan is the setting for Chapter 4. Through the case study of Safeer, a young man entangled in enduring tribal disputes, Abdullah Khoso provides a vivid description of the impact of conflict on children and youth. Safeer's narrative illustrates the direct consequences of violence on the rural youth in Sindh. Additionally, Khoso describes how youth actively participate in resistance, negotiating social, economic, and political pressures. Khoso's detailed exploration of the socio-political fabric of rural Sindh through the experiences of its youth highlights their critical role as agents of change and underscores the importance of local contexts in discussions about children and youth in conflict settings.

Aisha Manus, an independent historian from Georgia, effectively integrates the concepts of resilience and resistance through the historical lens of the Junior Red Cross during World War I (Chapter 5). In a powerful example, the author reveals how children, particularly through the act of quilting, actively participated in the war effort, demonstrating significant agency despite their young ages.

Children and Youth as "Sites of Resistance"

Manus details how these children, referred to as the child quilters, contributed to the war economy and provided comfort to soldiers and orphans affected by the war, showcasing their ability to impact change that transcends time and geographical boundaries. Manus's chapter presents a compelling portrayal of children's agency, highlighting how their active involvement aids peace efforts during conflicts and contributes to broader societal healing and rebuilding. This shift emphasizes their capacity to effect positive change, moving beyond traditional narratives of vulnerability.

Sonali Jha highlights the severe impacts of political and socio-economic instability on Sudanese children and youth (Chapter 6). Against a backdrop of prolonged civil unrest and economic crisis, Jha underscores the daily realities faced by young Sudanese, who are often swept into the currents of displacement and conflict. This narrative enriches our understanding of youth as active participants in conflict, emphasizing the critical need for protective measures and rights-based frameworks to support their journey toward empowerment and healing. Chapter 7 extends the discussion to include the intersection of gender and armed conflict in Kashmir, highlighting the role social work interventions play in addressing gender-specific challenges. Aksa Jan, Lakshya Kadiyan, and Sanjoy Roy explore the violence endured by women, men, and gender nonconforming individuals in Kashmir, stressing how gendered norms and societal expectations shape both resistance and resilience in these settings. Emphasizing the critical need for gender-focused approaches in social work, the chapter argues for a comprehensive strategy that not only acknowledges but also actively incorporates the perspectives and needs of all gender identities in peacebuilding initiatives. The insights from this chapter underscore the importance of integrating gender sensitivity into the broader discourse on youth and children as agents of change in conflict zones, highlighting the transformative potential of inclusive social work practices.

After a comprehensive treatment of children's resistance in Sudan, Ukraine, quilt workers of World War I, Georgia and South Ossetia, Pakistan, and Kashmir, we wanted to account for the future of conflicts within the growing talk around Artificial Intelligence (AI). Chapter 8 presents an overview of the innovative integration of AI with humanitarian efforts to support children and youth affected by armed conflicts. Exploring ways to leverage AI tools such as empathetic computing and Natural Language Processing to address the emotional and psychological needs of young individuals in armed conflict, the authors argue that technology can amplify the voices and aid the healing processes of affected youth. AI also has the potential to enhance traditional humanitarian operations, thereby supporting the broader goal of empowering young individuals and communities in conflict settings.

These chapters treat the political arena as a dynamic space of contestation and resistance, where the struggle for belonging takes center stage. By emphasizing the voices of children, this work underscores their resilience, activism, and well-being, positioning them as survivors and effective participants in shaping their realities and advocating for their rights (see Table 1).

Table 1. Volume I: Thematic Overview.

Themes	Country/Region	Details	Recommendations
Sites of Resistance – Resilience and Agency	Sudan (Chapter 1)	Narrative of the Lost Boys and Girls, focusing on kinship and mutual support.	Enhance community-based support networks to bolster the social and emotional resilience of youth.
	Ukraine (Chapter 2)	Struggles of displaced children adapting to new educational systems.	Implement tailored educational programs that recognize and integrate the cultural backgrounds of displaced youth. Secure safe and accessible educational environments that promote continuity in learning despite conflict.
	Pakistan (Chapter 4)	Emphasizes youth activism and resistance against political strife, tribal honor, serving as potential actors during conflicts.	Support youth-led initiatives and educate the police and enhance public's trust in formal justice, especially courts.
	World War I Child Quilters (Chapter 5)	Contributed to the war economy and provided comfort to soldiers and orphans affected by the war.	Provides evidence that children and youth are key actors in the rebuilding process in armed conflict.
	Kashmir (Chapter 7)	Gendered norms and societal expectations shape both resistance and resilience.	Incorporates the perspectives and needs of all gender identities in peacebuilding initiatives
Psychological Impacts	Georgia and South Ossetia (Chapter 3)	Internalization of collective memories fosters negative perceptions of the opposing community complicating conflict resolution efforts.	Need for interactive, inter-community dialogues to bridge these perceptual divides.
	Sudan (Chapter 6)	Children's daily experiences shape their psychological resilience.	Support and advocacy of the internal organization and civil bodies to advocate for peace and provide support. Provide continuous access to mental health services that cater specifically to children affected by conflict.
Ethical Use of Technology	AI and conflict (Chapter 8)	AI assisted adaptive therapy can empower and amplify voices of children and youth in conflict spaces.	Advocate for ethical technological interventions that integrate youth experiences and voices of activism to rebuild conflict-torn societies.

A CALL TO ACTION ...

In the explorations of cases from different conflict settings, the contributors to this volume reveal how boundaries of belonging are continuously constructed and deconstructed. Children and their childhoods are shaped within the liminal political space they occupy and are victims of. Yet, they find ways to negotiate their young self at the individual and the collective levels, across these contested spaces closely intertwined with the processes of conflict and peace. These narratives extend beyond the familiar territories of war zones to examine the everyday spaces – schools, communities, and public squares – where young people experience and influence the phenomena of conflict and peacebuilding. This exploration does not just recount their involvement as victims or bystanders but redefines them as critical participants in shaping peace and defining conflict across diverse landscapes.

The insights garnered emphasize the importance of challenging traditional perspectives about children and youth to inform ways in which they are recognized as active agents within the dominant discourse of peace negotiations and conflict resolutions. By venturing into critical contexts, where the voices of children are often unheard or overlooked, this volume enhances our understanding of their roles as political subjects. It challenges the prevailing narratives that portray them as symbols of vulnerability or resilience, urging a reconsideration of their contributions to and impacts on global security practices.

As we reflect on these varied and intricate roles, it is critical to call for further research that listens to and prioritizes these young voices in both policymaking and community engagements. As a group of scholars, we call for solutions that are informed by lived experiences, narratives, and methodologies embedded within this volume for a bottom-up approach to peacebuilding. Therefore, this volume of *Sociological Studies of Children and Youth* serves as a call to action: to deepen our exploration of the untapped potential of youth as architects of peace and to reimagine the frameworks within which we view their participation in global dialogues about conflict and reconciliation. This reimagined engagement can lead to more effective strategies that mitigate the impacts of conflict and enhance the prospects for lasting peace.

May peace find its architects in the voices of our youth.

REFERENCES

Adler-Nissen, R., Andersen, K. E., & Hansen, L. (2020). Images, emotions, and international politics: The death of Alan Kurdi. *Review of International Studies*, 46(1), 75–95.

Barber, B. K., & Schluterman, J. M. (2009). An overview of the empirical literature on adolescents and political violence. In B. K. Barber (Ed.), *Adolescents and war: How youth deal with political violence* (pp. 35–61). Oxford University Press.

Bartley M. (2006). *Capability and resilience: Beating the odds.* UCL Department of Epidemiology and Public Health on behalf of the ESRC Priority Network on Capability and Resilience, London.

Beattie, A. R., Eroukhmanoff, C., & Head, N. (2019). Introduction: Interrogating the 'everyday' politics of emotions in international relations. *Journal of International Political Theory*, 15(2), 136–147.

Berents, H., & McEvoy-Levy, S. (2015). Theorizing youth and everyday peace (building). *Peacebuilding*, 3(2), 115–125.

12 TAMANNA M. SHAH

Betancourt, T. S., Borisova, I. I., Williams, T. P., Brennan, R. T., Whitfield, T. H., De La Soudiere, M., Williamson, J., & Gilman, S. E. (2010). Sierra Leone's former child soldiers: A follow-up study of psychosocial adjustment and community reintegration. *Child Development*, *81*, 1077–1095.

Bilgic, A., & Gkouti, A. (2021). Who is entitled to feel in the age of populism? Women's resistance to migrant detention in Britain. *International Affairs*, *97*(2), 483–502.

Cummings, E. M., Schermerhorn, A. C., Merrilees, C. E., Goeke-Morey, M. C., Shirlow, P., & Cairns, E. (2010). Political violence and child adjustment in Northern Ireland: Testing pathways in a social-ecological model including single- and two-parent families. *Developmental Psychology*, *46*, 827–841.

End the killing of children in armed conflict, UN Committee urges | Ohchr. (2023, November 20). OHCHR. https://www.ohchr.org/en/statements/2023/11/end-killing-children-armed-conflict-un-committee-urges

Ergler, C. R., Kearns, R., de Melo, A., & Coleman, T. (2017). Being connected? Wellbeing affordances for suburban and central city children. In C. R. Ergler, R. Kearns, & K. Witten (Eds.), *Children's health and wellbeing in urban environments* (pp. 189–203). Routledge.

Finkelhor, D., Ormrod, R. K., Turner, H. A., & Hamby, S. L. (2005). Measuring poly-victimization using the JVQ. *Child Abuse & Neglect*, *29*, 1297–1312.

Giddens, A. (1984). *The constitution of society: Outline of the theory of structuration.* University of California Press.

Harker, C. (2005). Playing and affective time-spaces. *Children's Geographies*, *3*(1), 47–62.

Hart, J. (2002). Children's Clubs: New ways of working with conflict displaced children in Sri Lanka'. *Forced Migration Review*, *15*, 36–39.

Henley, W. E. (n.d.). *Invictus by William Ernest Henley.* Poetry Foundation. https://www.poetry foundation.org/poems/51642/invictus

Huemer, J., Edsall, S., Karnik, N. S., & Steiner, H. (2012). Childhood trauma. In W. M. Klykylo & J. Kay (Eds.), *Clinical child psychiatry* (2nd ed., pp. 255–273). John Wiley & Sons.

Jabri, V. (2007). *War and the transformation of global politics.* Springer.

Jack, G. (2010). Place matters: The significance of place attachments for children's well-being. *British Journal of Social Work*, *40*(3), 755–771.

James, A. (2009). Agency. In J. Qvortrup, W. A. Corsaro, M. S. Honig, & G. Valentine (Eds.), *The Palgrave handbook of childhood studies* (pp. 34–45). Palgrave Macmillan UK.

Low, S. M. (1992). Symbolic ties that bind: Place attachment in the plaza. In I. Altman & S. M. Low (Eds.), *Place attachment* (Vol. 12, pp. 165–185). Springer Science & Business Media.

Koschut, S. (2019). Can the bereaved speak? Emotional governance and the contested meanings of grief after the Berlin terror attack. *Journal of International Political Theory*, *15*(2), 148–166.

Marshall, D. J. (2013). 'All the beautiful things': Trauma, aesthetics and the politics of Palestinian childhood. *Space and Polity*, *17*(1), 53–73.

Marshall, D. J. (2015). 'We have a place to play, but someone else controls it': Girls' mobility and access to space in a Palestinian refugee camp. *Global Studies of Childhood*, *5*(2), 191–205.

Massad, S., Stryker, R., Mansour, S., & Khammash, U. (2018). Rethinking resilience for children and youth in conflict zones: The case of Palestine. *Research in Human Development*, *15*(3–4), 280–293.

Masten, A. S. (2014). Global perspectives on resilience in children and youth. *Child Development*, *85*(1), 6–20.

Moore, R. C. (2017). *Childhood's domain: Play and place in child development.* Routledge.

Nguyen-Gillham, V., Giacaman, R., Naser, G., & Boyce, W. (2008). Normalizing the abnormal: Palestinian youth and the contradictions of resilience in protracted conflict. *Health & Social Care in the Community*, *16*(3), 291–298.

Oswell, D. (2013). *The agency of children: From family to global human rights.* Cambridge University Press.

Proshansky, H. M., Fabian, A. K., & Kaminoff, R. (1983). Place-identity: Physical world socialization of the self. In J. J. Gieseking, W. Mangold, C. Katz, S. Low, & S. Saegert (Eds.), *The people, place, and space reader* (pp. 77–81). Routledge.

Ridgway, P. (2001). Restorying psychiatric disability: learning from first person recovery narratives. *Psychiatric Rehabilitation Journal*, *24*(4), 335.

Šadl Z. (2021). Emotions and affect in political discourse. *Teorija in Praksa, 58*(2), 370–390 [Abstr. 72.866].

Sampson, R., & Gifford, S. M. (2010). Place-making, settlement, and well-being: The therapeutic landscapes of recently arrived youth with refugee backgrounds. *Health & Place, 16*(1), 116–131.

Schick, K. (2019). Emotions and the everyday: ambivalence, power and resistance. *Journal of International Political Theory, 15*(2), 261–268.

Shah, T. M. (2012). *Collective memory and narrative: ethnography of social trauma in Jammu and Kashmir* [Doctoral dissertation, Kansas State University].

Shah, T. M. (2013). Chaos and fear: Creativity and hope in an uncertain world. *International Sociology, 28*(5), 513–517.

Shah, T. M. (2019). Social justice and change. In S. Romaniuk, M. Thapa, & P. Marton (Eds.), *The Palgrave encyclopedia of global security studies* (pp. 1353–1355). Springer International Publishing.

Shah, T. M. (2020). Children of Kashmir and the meaning of family in armed conflict. In S. Frankel, S. McNamee, & L. E. Bass (Eds.), *Bringing children back into the family: Relationality, connectedness, and home* (pp. 213–216). Emerald Publishing Limited.

Shah, T. M. (2021). Women as "sites of gendered politics". In D. Aikat, B. Beamer, M. K. Biswas, B. Bowen, L. F. Brost, S. Fatima, ... & S. Srivastav (Eds.), *Misogyny across global media*. Lexington Books.

Shah, T. M. (2023). *Global patterns of decolonization and the right to self-determination: A comparative-historical analysis of East Timor and Kashmir* [Doctoral dissertation, The University of Utah].

Shah, T. M. (2024b). Decolonization and peacebuilding: The case of Timor Leste and Kashmir. In P. Pietrzak (Ed.), *Dealing with regional conflicts of global importance* (pp. 262–278). IGI Global.

Shah, T. M. (2024c). Emotions in politics: A review of contemporary perspectives and trends. *International Political Science Abstracts, 74*(1), 1–14.

Sousa, C. A., Kemp, S. P., & El-Zuhairi, M. (2019). Place as a social determinant of health: Narratives of trauma and homeland among Palestinian women. *The British Journal of Social Work, 49*(4), 963–982.

Stoecklin, D., & Fattore, T. (2018). Children's multidimensional agency: Insights into the structuration of choice. *Childhood, 25*(1), 47–62.

Till, K. E. (2012). Wounded cities: Memory-work and a place-based ethics of care. *Political Geography, 31*(1), 3–14.

Ungar, M. (2004). A constructionist discourse on resilience: Multiple contexts, multiple realities among at-risk children and youth. *Youth & Society, 35*(3), 341–365.

Ungar, M. (2006). Nurturing hidden resilience in at-risk youth in different cultures. *Journal of the Canadian Academy of Child and adolescent Psychiatry, 15*(2), 53.

UNICEF. (2022). *Effective, representative, and inclusive child participation at the local level. Child-friendly cities initiative.* https://www.unicef.org/childfriendlycities/documents/effective-representative-and-inclusive-child-participation-local-level

Veronese, G., & Cavazzoni, F. (2020). "I hope I will be able to go back to my home city": Narratives of suffering and survival of children in Palestine. *Psychological Studies, 65*(1), 51–63.

Veronese, G., Cavazzoni, F., & Antenucci, S. (2018). Narrating hope and resistance: A critical analysis of sources of agency among Palestinian children living under military violence. *Child: Care, Health and Development, 44*(6), 863–870.

Wolak, J., & Sokhey, A. E. (2022). Enraged and engaged? Emotions as motives for discussing politics. *American Politics Research, 50*(2), 186–198.

Zhang, C. (2022). Contested disaster nationalism in the digital age: Emotional registers and geopolitical imaginaries in COVID-19 narratives on Chinese social media. *Review of International Studies, 48*(2), 219–242.

CHAPTER 1

"WE BECAME ONE FAMILY": HARDSHIP, INTERDEPENDENCE, AND RESISTANCE AMONG THE LOST BOYS AND GIRLS OF SUDAN

Myriam Denov and Régine Debrosse

School of Social Work, McGill University, Canada

ABSTRACT

The Lost Boys and Girls attempted to escape from the war in Sudan on foot, most often traveling together, separated from their families, and they survived extreme conditions by taking care of each other. However, limited research has focused on their relationships with one another during both flight and resettlement. This chapter explores the connection between the hardships faced by Lost Boys and Girls, alongside the relational experiences forged and the sense of community they developed with one another. To do so, we examine a set of qualitative interviews and a focus group with Lost Boys and Girls who resettled in the Global North and analyze them under the light of the kinship hypothesis, which connects hardships and interdependence in relationships. Drawing upon young people's direct narratives and voices, our data reveal that the bonds that Lost Boys and Girls forged with one another during flight often remained strong after resettlement, highlighting agentive forms of resistance, resilience, and capacity. Findings further reveal high mutual support and high willingness to sacrifice for one another. The significance of these findings for how the experiences of unaccompanied minors are understood, especially for children and youth affected by war and displacement, is discussed.

Children and Youth as 'Sites of Resistance' in Armed Conflict
Sociological Studies of Children and Youth, Volume 34, 15–33
Copyright © 2025 by Myriam Denov and Régine Debrosse
Published under exclusive licence by Emerald Publishing Limited
ISSN: 1537-4661/doi:10.1108/S1537-466120240000034002

Keywords: Unaccompanied minors; war; youth; Lost Boys and Girls of Sudan; resistance; migration; mutual support; willingness to sacrifice

INTRODUCTION

The Lost Boys and Girls of Sudan – a group of unaccompanied, war-affected children and youth, mostly from the Nuer and Dinka ethnic groups, who fled war-torn Sudan – illustrate some of the most extreme circumstances of unaccompanied minors affected by war and displacement. Committee on the Rights of the Child (2005) defines unaccompanied minors and unaccompanied children as those "who have been separated from both parents and other relatives and are not being cared for by an adult who, by law or custom, is responsible for doing so." The Lost Boys and Girls of Sudan courageously fled their home country, unaccompanied, and traversed several countries on foot, braved starvation, dehydration, and deadly wild animals, often not knowing if the families and loved ones they left behind were alive (McKinnon, 2008). For many of these youth, these devastating hardships lasted for years, sometimes spanning for more than a decade. Eventually, many made their way to refugee camps or resettled elsewhere (Chanoff, 2005). The perils of migration posed an immense challenge to these children and youth, amplified by their intersecting experiences of marginalization and stigmatization associated with their age, migration status, and racialized bodies, particularly as many eventually resettled in countries in the Global North (Geltman et al., 2008; Zink, 2017).

Like the Lost Boys and Girls, many war-affected unaccompanied children and youth face acute difficulties associated with ongoing and profound forms of structural, physical, sexual, and psychological violence in the context of war and migration (Denov & Fennig, 2024; Morland & Kelley, 2024). In the current context of growing global upheaval due to war, armed conflict, climate change, the COVID-19 pandemic, and other health crises, examining the experiences of forced migration and displacement among children and youth, particularly those unaccompanied, is vital. It is imperative not only to explore how young people cope, survive, and thrive despite immense hardship but also to examine the relationships among unaccompanied children and youth, how they may rely upon one another to navigate the challenges of flight and resettlement, as well their experiences of community building, agency, and resistance. Indeed, for unaccompanied minors, social relationships that provide support during the migration journey may take on a special importance. Many unaccompanied children and youth have found that leaning on relationships was one of their best coping strategies (Behrendt et al., 2022; Sierau et al., 2019), including some Lost Boys and Girls (e.g., Bates et al., 2013; Luster, Qin, et al., 2009). A recently proposed *kinship hypothesis* that links hardships with interdependence suggests that the quality and characteristics of these relationships deserve greater attention (Debrosse, 2023). The kinship hypothesis suggests that going through

"We Become One Family" 17

hardships is associated with a tendency to forge relationships with other people who share the same plight and that the resulting relationships are marked by strong mutual support and a willingness to sacrifice for one another. Because they have faced stigmatizing hardships, the kinship hypothesis could be particularly relevant to analyzing the experiences of unaccompanied youth like the Lost Boys and Girls.

This chapter examines the migration and resettlement experiences of the Lost Boys and Girls of Sudan regarding shared hardships and relational experiences that follow from bonding over similar difficulties (Debrosse, 2023). In doing so, we highlight not only the challenges faced by Lost Boys and Girls but also the positive forces and supports that appeared to protect them, and the ways in which they actively sought to protect themselves and each other, demonstrating powerful forms of resilience and capacity. The chapter begins by outlining the realities of the Lost Boys and Girls of Sudan and presents three core ideas at the heart of the kinship hypothesis. Then, drawing on the perspectives of a sample of Lost Boys and Girls, we connect their relationships with one another to the multiple challenges they faced fleeing Sudan and migrating to North America, before discussing the implications of our findings. The unique experiences of the Lost Boys and Girls and their modes of connection, mutual support, collaboration, resistance, resilience, and agency can shed new light and offer lessons on the flight and resettlement needs of other groups of children and youth affected by war, violence, and migration.

THE REALITY OF THE LOST BOYS AND GIRLS OF SUDAN

The Lost Boys and Girls of Sudan represent an estimated 18,000 children and youth, mostly from the Nuer and Dinka ethnic groups, who escaped war-torn Sudan at the onset of the second Sudanese civil war in 1983. Under gunfire and fear of death, children and youth urgently fled their homes, and courageously walked miles across countries, often without shoes, in search of safety and refuge (McKinnon, 2008). Orphaned or separated from family and loved ones, the group of youngsters – some as young as three, while others were adolescents – fled the violence of Sudan, and traveled on foot to Ethiopia, where they remained in displaced camps for years (Chanoff, 2005). When war broke out in Ethiopia, they were compelled to flee war on foot yet again – this time to Kenya. These children and youth thus spent years, and in some cases decades, marginalized, impoverished, and stateless, in legal, spiritual, and psychological limbo, and in situations of protracted displacement, waiting to be resettled (MacDonald, 2015). In the early 1990s, UNICEF attempted to reunite many of these children and youth with their families. Later, in the early 2000s, through initiatives coordinated by the United Nations High Commission on Refugees (UNHCR) and international governments, thousands of these children and youth, mostly boys, were resettled to the United States, Canada, and other European countries (see Denov & Bryan, 2012; Luster et al., 2008). Healthcare and NGO workers in refugee camps used the name of the *Lost Boys and Girls* to refer to the group; subsequently, the youth took on this name to refer to themselves.

Gendered power relations have played an important role in conceptualizing and implementing policies, programs, and services for this unique group. The scholarly and practice literature have mostly paid attention to the *Lost Boys*, who have dominated historical narratives and accounts of the group's realities and experiences (Luster et al., 2008). In comparison, the *Lost Girls* have been marginalized and often ignored (El Jack, 2010; for exceptions, see Bassoff & DeLuca, 2014; Grabska, 2010). Importantly, the war in Sudan profoundly affected women and girls – often in different ways than men and boys (Harris, 2010). In particular, wartime sexual violence was rampant and used as a weapon of war, alongside girls and women being sold as slaves or coerced into trafficking situations, where it became extremely difficult for families to later locate them. Among girls who made their way on foot in search of safety and refuge, given gendered conceptions of female vulnerability, many were placed with surviving family members or were adopted. Many of these girls were exploited and used for domestic work which, while providing some form of security, posed obstacles to attending school in the camps. Many were physically and sexually abused and sometimes sold as brides for profit (Bassoff & DeLuca, 2014; Harris, 2010).

When resettlement programs began, a key requirement was that the children must be orphans. Given that many girls had been living within a foster family – the majority for more than a decade – they were no longer considered "orphans." Harris (2010), however, highlights the conditions and context in which these girls were living within these foster families:

> While the girls were placed in foster families who were supposed to be caring for them, more often it seems that the girls were available unpaid servants who were also sexually vulnerable. In addition, there is some evidence that the girls were shielded from UNHCR eyes in order to bring the substantial bride-price that could provide much needed financial aid to the most destitute of the displaced families. (p. 45)

Few Lost Girls were able to benefit from resettlement programs and "the girls simply disappeared" [from view] (Harris, 2010, p. 45). In contrast, boys largely remained in refugee camps and had greater opportunities for resettlement. Among the 4,000 Sudanese refugees approved for resettlement in 2000, only 89 were female (El Jack, 2010). Thus, subsequent research and practice focused primarily on the Lost Boys who resettled in the Global North.

Under the harsh circumstances they faced, walking thousands of kilometers to flee armed conflict, often with no possessions but the clothes on their backs, and facing starvation, dehydration, and disease, the Lost Boys and Girls may have strongly desired to forge ties. Yet, despite the seeming importance of relationships and kinship structures for the Lost Boys and Girls, their relational experiences with each other have garnered little research attention (for exceptions, see Luster, Qin, et al., 2009). We propose to re-examine their experiences under the light of the kinship hypothesis of hardships and interdependence.

THE KINSHIP HYPOTHESIS

In the context of the present research, hardships are persistent challenges that can undermine one's ability to feed, secure shelter, and protect one's physical integrity – such as dire economic difficulties, or war and displacement. When people face hardships, they often desire to connect with other people. Forming community bonds can provide relief and support when overcoming challenging circumstances such as natural disasters (Matsuyama et al., 2016). The kinship hypothesis examines further and attempts to unpack relational processes triggered by people's experiences of stigma – socially constructed labels that are used to set some people apart from others, that are associated with negative stereotypes and discrimination, and that rely on and reproduce power differences (Link & Phelan, 2001).

The core idea behind the kinship hypothesis is that people will actively seek bonds when facing difficulties associated with stigma difficulties, and that bonding through similar difficulties may connect people more deeply than people who bond over other similarities (Debrosse, 2023). To further unpack the kinship hypothesis, this chapter will focus on three of its key ideas which can particularly shed light on the experiences of Lost Boys and Lost Girls of Sudan. First, because profound hardships can generate a desire for deep social connection, they can encourage the formation and strengthening of bonds with people facing similar hardships. Second, relationships forged during shared hardships may be akin to *kinship ties* – ties that are presumably reserved for family members and marked by deep loyalties, a sense of shared fate, mutual support, and a sense that the relationship is irreplaceable. Third, as people mutually support each other through hardships and as these relationships grow over time, they are also likely to be characterized by a strong willingness to sacrifice for one another.

An implication underlying the kinship hypothesis is that connections people make with one another in the context of hardships provide strength not only to cope and demonstrate resilience but also to regain some agency and eventually build capacity to bring meaningful change. Therefore, the idea behind this hypothesis builds on the principle that people connect over similarities – a principle highlighted before by prominent theorizing (Byrne, 1997; Campbell, 1958; McPherson et al., 2001), and demonstrated empirically (Balietti et al., 2021; Gehlbach et al., 2016; Higgins et al., 2021; Sels et al., 2020; Walton et al., 2012). In fact, the three ideas described below illustrate how the kinship hypothesis extends and moves beyond previous research on similarities.

First, when people face hardships, they often desire for strong connections with others. Turning to others is a common strategy for people whose experiences are stigmatized (e.g., Kraus et al., 2012), which makes sense to facilitate survival (e.g., Rimé & Páez, 2023). In fact, when facing hardships, a strategy can consist of turning to other people in a similar situation, who face similar challenges and are similarly motivated to forge supportive relationships (Debrosse, 2023). This is because people enduring hardships may desire social support and thus particularly seek connections, but may also be weary of rejection, exploitation, and misunderstanding and thus prefer avoiding certain opportunities to connect with others (e.g., Chaudoir & Fisher, 2010; Pachankis, 2007; see also Murray, 2005). Having faced some of the most extreme forms of hardships that humans can endure, the relationships of the Lost Boys and Girls may, in some ways, embody this idea, particularly if they turn to one another. In that sense, it is possible that Lost Boys and Girls pulled toward one another because of the immense difficulties that they faced.

Second, mutual support generally characterizes relational bonds formed between people who share hardships (e.g., Hooker & Algoe, 2022; Jacob et al., 2023). This may be, in part, because support provided by close relationships helps to cope with life's adversities. For people of color and stigmatized communities, relying on each other can bring healing from hardships in addition to help coping from them (French et al., 2018; see also Breder & Bockting, 2023; Jacob et al., 2023), and experience more well-being in relationships with close loved ones who share their marginalized experiences (Debrosse et al., 2022). As for many people facing many other difficult circumstances, support can play a protective role for people who have been displaced or have a refugee status (e.g., Iraklis, 2021; Sierau et al., 2019). Yet, research focused on displacement and forced migration has often highlighted the key role played by the support provided by family or by organizations and host communities who do not share their hardships (e.g., Luster, Saltarelli, et al., 2009; Mabeya, 2015; Raithelhuber, 2021). While these sources of support matter greatly, the role of mutual support may be underestimated, particularly for unaccompanied youth. In the case of life-threatening and profound hardships like the ones experienced by the Lost Boys and Girls, mutual support can work to bridge a critical gap – between sustenance and starvation, between security and danger.

Third, over time, relationship bonds forged by people who face hardships are likely marked by a strong willingness to sacrifice for one another. Readiness to sacrifice captures an aspect of relationships that builds on and extends beyond support. Sometimes termed as "communal strength," it reflects the precedence of some relationships over others, and the tendency to experience distress when it is impossible to guarantee that loved ones' needs will be met (Mills et al., 2004). When people have invested highly in close relationships, they tend to commit particularly to them in the future (Rusbult & Van Lange, 2003).

Enduring hardships during devastating times likely encourage people to invest more deeply in the relationships they are developing, particularly with those who have experienced similar situations. As a result, relationships forged through hardships may become imbued with a sense of irreplaceability, where people grow to feel responsible for one another and deeply loyal to each other, like many familial ties. For unaccompanied youth like the Lost Boys and Girls, this readiness to sacrifice could develop from initial encounters when, rapidly, they started mutually supporting one another and helping each other survive through dire circumstances. As a result, they may continue sacrificing for one another even when the immediate dangers of war and displacement have receded, by giving up opportunities for one another and sharing resources to ensure each other's well-being. We further elaborate on these ideas below, and specifically, explore kinship structures and relationships among a sample of Lost Boys and Girls who were resettled to North America.

METHODOLOGY

The present examination of the flight and resettlement realities of Lost Boys and Girls of Sudan and its links to kinship relationships was part of a larger qualitative research project by the first author addressing the experiences of war-affected youth (from a variety of war-affected countries) living in Canada and the United States, who had arrived unaccompanied. The research ethics board of McGill University approved the study. Given this chapter's focus on the lives and resettlement experiences of the Lost Boys and Girls of Sudan, only those participants who fled South Sudan unaccompanied are addressed here. This subgroup represents 12 participants, who ranged between 18 and 33 years of age at the time of data collection, which occurred between March 2008 and September 2010. Participants were recruited through local social workers who provided information about the study to their clients and those who were interested contacted the first author. The first author conducted in-depth interviews and one focus group with a total of 11 Lost Boys and one Lost Girl living in the Canadian provinces of Alberta, British Columbia, Manitoba, Ontario, and one living in the United States. Participants had fled war-torn Sudan between the ages of 3 and 17 (the participant who was aged three reported being carried and taken care of by other older children during flight and migration). For six of the participants, a focus group was used in lieu of in-depth interviews. While in-depth interviews were initially arranged with these youth, on the day of the scheduled interviews, the six participants arrived together. Highlighting their sense of collective and mutual trust, they indicated that they would prefer to be interviewed together. Given that these youth had known each other since childhood, and many were currently living together, they explained that they felt very comfortable conveying their personal journeys in a group context. Responding to their wishes, a focus group was carried out with these six youths in lieu of individual interviews. The focus group and interviews were all conducted in English and audio-recorded with permission and subsequently transcribed. During data collection, participants were asked to recount their stories of flight and the meaning that such experiences had for them. A key aim was to gain not only "thick descriptions" (Geertz, 1973) of young people's experiences during and following flight but also their reflections and interpretations of these experiences.

Analysis of the data transcripts involved careful reading and annotation. Through an inductive analytical process, patterns in the data emerged, particularly, the family-like and kinship structures and interdependence that appeared to encapsulate the experiences of these youths, which are described in the next section. Key themes that emerged from the data included mutual support and building community during flight and resettlement, the importance of family ties, the realities of racism and social exclusion, and financial challenges in the context of resettlement, as well as participants' inherent resourcefulness, agency, resilience, and resistance, all which are explored in greater depth below.

The present research is limited in several ways. First, as with all self-report data, the interviews and focus groups were invariably affected by participants' willingness to divulge personal information and experiences, particularly given the sensitive nature of discussing war, flight, and the challenges associated with sharing their early life histories and experiences. In addition to the sensitive nature of our inquiry, other factors that may have affected the validity and scope of the young people's recollections of their experiences were possible limitations of memory and lack of familiarity with the interviewer. As such, the potential flaws of self-disclosure must therefore be considered when examining the young people's stories. Second, themes pertaining to relationships, kinship, and sacrifice were not explored as extensively with participants during the original data collection as they might have otherwise. At the same time, the spontaneous emergence of these themes during data analysis and clear demonstration that their relationships with each other were precious, supports our idea about the significant and vital role of relational ties for Lost Boys and Girls. Third, the small sample limits the scope of the study, though their depth provides a clearer picture of the life histories and realities of Sudanese youth who fled the civil war.

RESULTS

Hardship and the Experiences of War-induced Flight

Hardship in the form of constant physical threats and violence followed these young people for years. This occurred throughout their migration journeys, first on their journey to Ethiopia, in Ethiopia, on their way to Kenya, and on an ongoing basis within the context of life in the Kakuma refugee camp in Kenya. These youths explained the multiple and complex forms of violence and deprivation they experienced during flight:

> When the war started my parents weren't at home – I was with some other little kids I didn't know. And when the war began, we ran into the forest and that's where I found some of the Lost Boys. One of them took me, and we left Sudan walking on foot to Ethiopia. I was carried by another Lost Boy. When we went to Ethiopia, we stayed there for a couple years, I think 3 [years], and then the government of Sudan make a deal with the government of Ethiopia, and we had to leave the country to go back to Sudan. But we didn't want to leave so the soldiers started killing some of the Lost Boys. So we start to run again – there is a river between Ethiopia and Sudan, most of us there, they died. I was carried by one of the Lost Boys to cross the river. We were being shot at by Ethiopian soldiers. And then we ran. We walk all the way to Kenya.

> [O]n our way a lot of people died too because it was the rainy season, and a lot of people don't know how to swim. They drowned in the water. A lot of people were eaten by crocodiles. A lot of people were eaten by lions. Sometimes diseases, some were exhausted so they remain there. Because you cannot help them, carry them. Because we were young. We tried but ... we were like 20,000 and only 16,000 reached Kenya. Four thousand died on the way there.

Participants reported enduring extreme violence, deprivation, and insecurity, whether physical, psychological, economic, or social. These youths described these experiences and the ways in which they remained in their memories, decades later:

> It was bad what happened on my journey from Sudan to Ethiopia and then from Ethiopia to Kenya. It's hard when you see someone dead. I grew up with these people they were like my brothers and sisters. Most died because there was no food, no water, and we survived by drinking urine.

"We Become One Family" 23

> Not a lot has changed. You know, whenever I talk about it, like, I would want to forget about the pain, it's something that happened, it's stuff that happens, stuff that I went through –I would love to just forget it, concentrate on now and just forget about the past. But it's still there – I try to ... but it's still there.

The devastating physical, personal, spatial, spiritual, political, and health insecurities experienced by these children occurred within extreme conditions of chaos, and deprivation and consequently generated profound fear and uncertainty. These passages reveal that as they fled, youth who were interviewed faced terrible conditions of hardship, which mirror other reports on Lost Boys and Lost Girls difficult experiences. Although such constraining realities may limit children's capacity to protect themselves, as we address below, the children nonetheless attempted to negotiate these challenges with agency, resourcefulness, and resistance. The descriptions of hardships warrant further examination, particularly whether the kinship hypothesis resonates with the young people's realities and experiences.

Building Community During Flight

Within the context of flight, whether from Sudan to Ethiopia, or from Ethiopia to Kenya, the importance of building relations and, with time, forming a supportive community was vital. Tasks such as collecting firewood, building shelter, and preparing food required communal effort and constant collaboration. Lost Boys and Girls regarded community building, alongside temporarily "forgetting" about the loss of family and loved ones, as essential to survival:

> If you think too much about your father and mother, then you're not going to survive. All the people who died [during flight] were really young. They were thinking about their [parents] ... if you don't just go with it, you're not going to survive. You just put it away. Later on, if [our families] are alive we will find them, but first we establish ourselves so we can survive. We take the responsibility of managing ourselves, and maybe later we can find our families.

In addition, demonstrating their agency and resourcefulness, youth collectively chose group leaders, and created structures not only to ensure order and efficiency, but also to provide the necessary encouragement, support, ultimately creating family-like structures. While they did not know each other before flight, survival depended on mutual support. As these youth explained:

> There was a huge number of us. We survived as a group when we selected leaders. They came up with the rules, what we could do, they would tell us to be strong, to not give up.

> They became family. We didn't even know each other before, but when we came together as a group, we became one family.

Forming supportive communal structures was a necessity to survive. Therefore, in line with the kinship hypothesis, the Lost Boys and Lost Girls interviewed in the present research leaned on other youth facing the same hardships. These bonds were deep: in fact, youth referred to and treated each other as "family." These bonds played a role to ensure their survival, in a way that is qualitatively different than support they might have received from other sources (e.g., other people helping them along the way). These bonds were also key to ensuring safety, security,

24   MYRIAM DENOV AND RÉGINE DEBROSSE

and well-being during resettlement to Canada and the United States, which is
addressed further in the next section.

Community Hardships During Resettlement: The Importance of the Collective

Upon resettlement to Canada and the United States, participants experienced
a sense of relief. They no longer had to endure the scourge of war, displacement, and their devastating consequences. However, new challenges reportedly
emerged. These included finding appropriate and affordable housing, education,
employment, financial security, and a sense of belonging in a new social and cultural context. However, their needs were undermined by racial oppression and
social exclusion.

Racism and Social Exclusion

While economic hardships were salient themes articulated throughout interviews
and the focus group, nearly all the youth also described facing racism and social
exclusion during their resettlement to North America. This youth described a situation where a police officer followed him, pulling him over twice in the same day:

> When I first come here, like, we all need vehicles to get to work and everything, and every time,
> especially, when I was in Alberta, they pull us over. I was even pulled over by the same office twice,
> in the same place – in my back alley, asking me the same question: "Is it your vehicle?" And I was
> like: "Didn't you just ask me that question two hours ago, when I was getting out?" ...
>
> MD: Same officer, same day?
>
> Youth: Same officer, same day.

The experiences described above were experienced not only individually, but
also as a collective hardship that often occurred when the youths were together
during everyday social gatherings. These communal experiences were described
with a deep sense of sadness, pain, and injustice:

> For example, we like to gather on the weekends. The neighbours see us every weekend and
> they're like: "Who are these people?" "Are they criminals?" And when we get together, a lot of
> people think a lot of bad things are going to come of it: drama, fighting, violence. The police
> get involved. So you've got to keep your ears open.
>
> It's happened a lot …. The neighbours don't seem to like [us being together]. They think that
> something that's not supposed to be going on, is going on. And that's just how we are. We like
> to gather in a group, have fun, talk, joke …. We try to [make sure we're not too loud] … but
> okay, somebody says [something] funny, we're laughing really hard, and it's like "Oh, okay,
> quiet down guys."
>
> We got pulled over [while driving] because they thought we had a gun, because someone 20
> blocks away at a gas station said: "Those people who left, one of them had a gun." And it wasn't
> even that we got pulled over it. It was a police takedown – one wrong move and you're shot.
> There was a helicopter and five police cars. Finally, it turns out that the people at the gas station,
> the people with the gun were not even black people. But the police see five black people in a car,
> and they gun you down. That's the thing they have in their minds about Black people …. If you
> are new to this society and you do not know what to do, you could make the wrong move and
> get shot. I didn't know what was going on. I could have jumped out of the car to see what was

"We Become One Family" 25

happening and been shot. The police were like "don't move and put your hands up." I knew a little bit of English. If I had not, I would not have understood and I would have been shot.

When Lost Boys and Girls moved to Canada, their wartime and flight challenges transformed into new forms of hardships, including the stigma of being both refugees and Black people living in North America. Their motivation to lean on one another was likely sustained in their new circumstances, perhaps even reinforced – thus highlighting the relevance of examining their experiences under the light of the kinship hypothesis.

Mutual Support and Collective Mindsets in Canada: Capacity and Resilience
Many hardships and profound experiences of racism, discrimination, and exclusion marked the young people's journeys resettling in Canada. They responded by being together to provide one another with support, which they identified during the focus group as fundamental to their well-being. The youth spoke of their closeness, and sense of belonging to each other as a group, despite being from diverse tribes, that are often divided in Sudan:

Most of us here are really close. We grew up together. We visit each other. So it's sort of like that. So we all support each other, as Sudanese.

Coming from Sudan, it is divided by tribe, very small groups. But the good thing with us – we all speak different languages, and we're from different tribes. But we all come back together. We are all Sudanese. We all know each other. We hang out, do things together, come downtown. Sometimes, we come over, we play cards – things like that ... have some fun.

The youth actively built community and formed networks of support in their post-war lives. Demonstrating their resourcefulness, the youth provided concrete examples of the importance of this collective support and the ways in which they ensured it:

Over here, the culture is different right? We laugh, we take care of the other, we offer financial support. Yeah, these guys support me.

Similar to their paths prior to their arrival to Canada, Lost Boys and Girls further built and deepened bonds with one another. They also described the care that they provided one another. Thus, in line with two core ideas underlying the kinship hypothesis, Lost Boys and Girls forged close relationships marked by mutual support.

Financial Challenges and Willingness to Sacrifice
This section explores the socio-economic hardships that the youth faced once resettled and the strategic ways in which they addressed these hardships as a community. For the youth who resettled to Canada, they reported surviving financially by relying upon one another and made decisions for the best of the collective. Similar to the strategies that the youth had incorporated during flight, these youth explained how the older youth worked and sacrificed in order to support the younger youth:

I don't know how we survived [upon resettlement to Canada]. We made decisions according to age, who is young and who was older. The three older ones had to go to work, so that the two younger ones could go to school.

This youth further illustrates collective support:

But it still comes back to the family, right? So, my sister, she is trying to manage the bills – it was hard for her. So, I had to come up with my brother to help her. The three of us put our heads together, and it was easy.

Chronically underemployed and unable to access formal support, the youth strategically pooled their resources not only to ensure their daily survival but also to seek a better future:

It's like our culture back home. We have, if somebody in a family works, and has good income, they take care of everybody else. That's how we carry on. So if today, if we're short on something, the other guys will make it work. And the next day it will be something else. It seems to work since we were suffering, and it still works. So, it's a good thing.

In addition to providing mutual support to one another, Lost Boys and Girls clearly showed a willingness to sacrifice financially to protect one another. These sacrifices ensured that the youngest among them could go to school and helped them push through dire financial times. Their behavior clearly illustrates the willingness to sacrifice – the third idea underlying the kinship hypothesis.

Ties with the Family Left Behind
Most participants were not only supporting themselves, they were also supporting other family members still living in Kenya, Sudan, and Ethiopia. The reality of remittance, and the stress associated with it, was significant:

I support my brother, my brother-in-law, and his wife in Sudan which means I have to work hard. I go to school full time, and I have a full-time job. I sleep 2 ½ hours a night. I'm doing that to finish my schooling and keep the job. Otherwise, I couldn't pay my rent and my families rent back home, no way.

Yeah, yeah, yeah to help them out with little stuff. I always want to, yeah this is, I feel that I have to contribute to, somehow, to give them more opportunities, school. And even when I was in grade 12, I was thinking that I should take the next year off. It's expensive, but I have to help them – I didn't have an income. It might take me long, I didn't have a good enough amount to pay tuition, and to give to my dad. So yeah, I supported them. I still do.

It is not easy .... My brother, I've been putting him through school. So, I have to pay for them, and my scholarship, I have to use my scholarship and send it all back. You know, you kind of feel like they don't have anything. I'm the only one who provides for them.

Youth participants stated that they would not be comfortable enjoying the standard of living that Canada could provide to them while knowing that their families, still displaced by war and violence, were suffering:

You can never feel at ease when your people are struggling. You can go to the bank and borrow some money to buy a nice house, but I imagine where my brothers and sisters are living and it doesn't feel right.

In Canada, you are free, but not entirely free. It's like 50–50 because of the family you are missing what you wish you could do for the people left behind.

In addition to the depth of the bonds between Lost Boys and Lost Girls, their mutual support, and their willingness to sacrifice for one another, which the kinship hypothesis predicted was likely to happen, they also provided support to the families that they left behind. While these findings describe a situation that the kinship hypothesis did not attempt to make predictions, it nonetheless sheds light on the impact of relationships for Lost Boys and Girls and puts in perspective the sacrifices that they were willing to make for one another, and especially their families still living in war and exile.

DISCUSSION: AGENCY, RESOURCEFULNESS, AND RESISTANCE

Many researchers have highlighted the importance of family and social support when facing migration stressors (Blanchet-Cohen & Denov, 2015; Salas-Wright & Schwartz, 2019). The relational ties between unaccompanied minors – who are unable to rely on parents or guardians to support them – can be vital but have not been studied in an in-depth way. Interviews and a focus group with Lost Boys and Girls of Sudan revealed that, having fled and left parents and siblings behind, many held broad definitions regarding the meaning of "family" (Perry, 2011), which was interwoven with the way they forged relationships with each other. Leaning on each other and weaving interdependent ties with one another became a powerful strategy to regain some agency and respond to their plight with resilience. Specifically, Lost Boys and Girls highlighted the profound role played by their relationships with one another as they faced immensely challenging circumstances while fleeing Sudan and building new lives. In doing so, their actions mirrored the core ideas behind the kinship hypothesis. For example, by protecting each other as they fled Sudan on foot, sometimes carrying each other, or defending each other against dangers, they displayed a desire to forge bonds when facing terrible hardships, developed deep forms of mutual support, and greatly sacrificed for one another. This willingness to sacrifice was sustained in North America, where they often lived together, pooled their money, and where older youth would sometimes work and make sure the younger ones could get an education. These relational ties were instrumental for them to survive, adjust to life in Canada, and cope with the racial stigma that characterized their new lives in North America. As such, the qualitative interviews powerfully demonstrate that highly interdependent and irreplaceable ties can represent a pathway to regain agency and become resilient for displaced youth, thus providing support for the hardship hypothesis. In doing so, the present research also extends research on the hardship hypothesis, which was focused on less rare and intense forms of hardships (e.g., dire economic circumstances; see Debrosse & Lefrançois, 2024).

The youth demonstrated powerful forms of agency, capacity, and resilience throughout their complex journeys, whether in Sudan, during their migration processes, and again upon resettling to North America. For example, under the repressive conditions of war, during the uncertainty and precarity of migration and resettlement, it took a significant amount of skill, vigilance, courage, creativity, and strength to avoid risk and remain as secure as possible. The youth narratives have uncovered the fact that despite the horrors of war, youth find creative ways to bring about change by themselves and for themselves. They shared social and economic resources, created family structures where there was none, and built community and networks of support throughout their long and treacherous journeys when they themselves were rejected, and dispossessed. The hardships endured in their quest for security shed light on their strengths and struggles with agency, resilience, resourcefulness, and risk.

Strategies of resistance by children and youth affected by armed conflict have been documented across multiple contexts (Denov & Gervais, 2007; Lenz, 2017). Forms of resistance were also visible in our sample, particularly the ways in which young people found ways to resist and oppose structural and interpersonal violence, and where remaining and keeping each other alive en route, can, in and of itself, be seen as an act of resistance. Of particular interest here is courageous capacity of youth to defend and protect themselves and each other in the most vulnerable of circumstances, often amid state breakdown and in the absence of formalized support. Once resettled, and compelled to deal with racism and social exclusion, the creation of strong support networks can be considered both acts of resistance and survival strategies. Moreover, more subtle forms of resistance in the form of solidarity and cohesion were instrumental to their psychological and social well-being and helped youth to withstand the effects of oppression and marginalization.

IMPLICATIONS FOR YOUTH REFUGEE SUPPORT AND RELATIONSHIPS

Supportive networks and relationships can protect the mental health of young refugees and asylum seekers in North America (Bennouna et al., 2019; Rodriguez & Dobler, 2021). The present findings reaffirm the key role of war-affected unaccompanied young people's relationships with one another, and possible mechanisms that shed light on the ways through which these relationships can come to take an irreplaceable quality. Yet, while the present study and others have noted that the relationships forged by unaccompanied youth were essential to their ability to cope, organizations and government bodies that aim to support unaccompanied youth often do not also consider their relational needs (De Graeve & Bex, 2017).

Furthermore, while unaccompanied youth face devastating circumstances when fleeing war and armed conflict, many other challenges mark their paths. In addition to the hardships they face during flight, they often resettle to countries where they may be stigmatized and not fully welcomed. In that sense, experiences of hardships and stigma reported by the present sample reflect the realities of many unaccompanied youth. The stories shared here reaffirm the importance of addressing stigmatizing experiences that many displaced communities are confronted with when resettling, whether it takes the form of racial oppression or xenophobia.

The myriad examples of the youth's problem-solving capacities in devastating and high-stake circumstances – whether during war or in its aftermath – underscore both their capacity and resilience. Ingenuity and creativity became vital to individual and collective survival and security. The creative ways that the youth coped, managed, and adapted to their constantly changing environments, call into question the stereotypical portrayal of youth as mere passive victims of war and migration. Indeed, child victims of conflict are often depicted as innocent, dependent, and in need of protection, ultimately lacking agency (Berents, 2020). The narratives reveal how youth actively engaged in efforts to minimize their victimization and ensure their individual and collective security. Young people's intrinsic capacity as agents of change, community building, and reconciliation has important implications for current post-conflict policies and programs that are being developed for children. As has been highlighted by Denov (2010), if young people are able to demonstrate both individual and collective agency during and following war, then it is imperative that current strategies of intervention and assistance adopt approaches that aim to redress youth marginalization by tapping into children and youth's agency and resilience.

IMPLICATIONS FOR YOUTH RELATIONSHIPS BEYOND THE KINSHIP HYPOTHESIS

While the kinship hypothesis was helpful in exploring the stories of Lost Boys and Girls, the present findings also pointed to other meaningful relationship dynamics, such as relationship with family members left behind. Many unaccompanied minors believe that parents and other family members who could not accompany them would protect them if they could and want to care for them in return. The present findings echo previous research in demonstrating a strong attachment and commitment to family members left behind. For instance, Lost Boys and Girls sent them resources when their survival was no longer on the line despite not being well-established or financially secure. Yet, they are also deeply isolated from them (Seidel et al., 2022). Future research could examine further the significance and influence of families left behind for unaccompanied youth. For instance, what are the connections between these experiences and unaccompanied youth's other relational needs? In this context, what is the meaning they ascribe to relationships with people present along their journey, such as people going through similar hardships, but also to people who altruistically supported them?

While previous research has pointed to the support unaccompanied youth receive, the meaning they give to the support they provide also deserves further examination. Many unaccompanied young people needed support from others, and this support was sometimes available, and sometimes not. In this context, becoming providers of support themselves could deeply shape their identities: it may be associated with purpose, perhaps even helping them push through particularly difficult challenges to sustain their support. It could also be adding pressure. This central aspect of mutual support and support provision has not been fully explored in the literature. Yet, it reveals critical avenues of research to deepen how the experiences of those who are displaced are understood.

CONCLUSION

In this chapter, we aimed to project the voices and narratives of a group of war-affected young people to share their lived experiences of war, migration, and resettlement. Their narratives reveal their immense capacity as decision-makers, risk assessors, actors, and strategizers. Their lived realities challenge assumptions that war-affected children are merely marginalized and vulnerable populations, with little ability for agency and resistance during and following armed conflict. However, like other scholars, we do not want to romanticize the harsh conditions that Lost Boys and Girls endured or overemphasize the resilience they showed when overcoming the myriad challenges (Denov & Fennig, 2024; Singh, 2020). While lessons can be drawn from how they fostered and nurtured social relationships, unaccompanied youth require more comprehensive support than what they can offer each other. For example, the media sometimes frames refugees and asylum-seekers as less legitimate immigrants than others, perceptions which are often mirrored in the Canadian population (Lawlor & Paquet, 2022; Lawlor & Tolley, 2017). In that sense, the stories shared here reaffirm both the importance of relationships through hardships, but also the importance of addressing stigmatizing experiences that many displaced communities are confronted with when resettling, including when it takes the form of racial oppression or xenophobia.

In terms of practice, our findings expand our understanding of the relational experiences of unaccompanied youth and could be relevant to understanding how other unaccompanied youth experience and survive migration and resettlement together. While many supports needed require significant investments with international, national, institutional, and local resources rather than relying on their capacity to support each other, there is much to learn from the pathways unaccompanied youth take that can provide them with protection and how they can be nurtured. Given the vast and growing numbers of unaccompanied children and young people currently fleeing war violence, persecution, and upheaval, alongside a lack of available formal resources to support these children and youth, understanding the role of the collective in providing support and assistance to other children and youth is vital.

AUTHORS' NOTES, FUNDING DETAILS, AND DISCLOSURE STATEMENT

This work was supported by funding to the first author through the International Development Research Centre, the Canadian International Development Agency (Government of Canada), McGill University, the Canada Council for the Arts (Killam Program), the Canada Research Chair program and by funding from a William Dawson Scholar Award conferred by McGill University to the second author. The authors report that there are no competing interests to declare.

REFERENCES

Balietti, S., Getoor, L., Goldstein, D. G., & Watts, D. J. (2021). Reducing opinion polarization: Effects of exposure to similar people with differing political views. *Proceedings of the National Academy of Sciences, 118*, e2112552118.

Bassoff, L., & DeLuca, L. (2014). *Lost girl found*. Groundwood Books Ltd.

Bates, L., Johnson, D. J., & Rana, M. (2013). Pathways of success experiences among the "Lost Boys" of Sudan: A case study approach. In C. Fernando & M. Ferrari (Eds.), *Handbook of resilience in children of war* (pp. 179–191). Springer.

Behrendt, M., Lietaert, I., & Derluyn, I. (2022). Continuity and social support: A longitudinal study of unaccompanied refugee minors' care networks. *Journal of Immigrant & Refugee Studies, 20*, 398–412.

Bennouna, C., Ocampo, M. G., Cohen, F., Basir, M., Allaf, C., Wessells, M., & Stark, L. (2019). Ecologies of care: Mental health and psychosocial support for war-affected youth in the US. *Conflict & Health, 13*, 1–13.

Berents, H. (2020). Politics, policy-making and the presence of images of suffering children. *International Affairs, 96*, 593–608.

Blanchet-Cohen, N., & Denov, M. (2015). War-affected children's approach to resettlement: Implications for child and family services. *Annals of Anthropological Practice, 39*, 120–133.

Breder, K., & Bockting, W. (2023). Social networks of LGBT older adults: An integrative review. *Psychology of Sexual Orientation and Gender Diversity, 10*, 473–489.

Byrne, D. (1997). An overview (and underview) of research and theory within the attraction paradigm. *Journal of Social & Personal Relationships, 14*, 417–431.

Campbell, D. T. (1958). Common fate, similarity, and other indices of the status of aggregates of persons as social entities. *Behavioral Science, 3*, 14–25.

Chanoff, D. (2005). Education is my mother and my father: How the Lost Boys of Sudan escaped the destruction of their ancient culture and landed in the 21st century. *The American Scholar, 74*, 35–45.

Chaudoir, S. R., & Fisher, J. D. (2010). The disclosure processes model: Understanding disclosure decision making and postdisclosure outcomes among people living with a concealable stigmatized identity. *Psychological Bulletin, 136*, 236–256.

Committee on the Rights of the Child. (2005). *General comment no. 6 – treatment of unaccompanied and separated children outside their country of origin*. CRC/GC/2005/6, 1 September 2005.

De Graeve, K., & Bex, C. (2017). Caringscapes and belonging: An intersectional analysis of care relationships of unaccompanied minors in Belgium. *Children's Geographies, 15*, 80–92.

Debrosse, R. (2023). *Chosen family: Introducing the kinship model of hardships & interdependence. Manuscript submitted for publication*. School of Social Work, McGill University.

Debrosse, R., & Lefrançois, H. (2024). Loyalty, loyalty, loyalty: A systematic review on social support and hardships. *Manuscript submitted for publication*. School of Social Work, McGill University.

Debrosse, R., Thai, S., & Brieva, T. (2022). When skinfolk are kinfolk: Higher perceived support and acceptance characterize close same-race relationships for people of color. *Journal of Social Issues, 79*, 21–49.

Denov. (2010). *Child soldiers: Sierra Leone's Revolutionary United Front*. Cambridge University Press.

Denov, M., & Bryan, C. (2012). Tactical maneuvering and calculated risks: Independent child migrants and the complex terrain of flight. *New Directions for Child & Adolescent Development, 2012*, 13–27.

Denov, M., & Fennig, M. (2024). *Research handbook on children and armed conflict*. Edward Elgar Publishing.

Denov, M., & Gervais, C. (2007). Negotiating (in) security: Agency, resistance, and resourcefulness among girls formerly associated with Sierra Leone's Revolutionary United Front. *Signs: Journal of Women in Culture & Society, 32*, 885–910.

El Jack, A. (2010). "Education is my mother and father": The "invisible" women of Sudan. *Refuge, 27*, 19–29.

French, K. A., Dumani, S., Allen, T. D., & Shockley, K. M. (2018). A meta-analysis of work–family conflict and social support. *Psychological Bulletin, 144*, 284–314.

Geertz, C. (1973). *The interpretation of cultures: selected essays*. Basic Books.

Gehlbach, H., Brinkworth, M. E., King, A. M., Hsu, L. M., McIntyre, J., & Rogers, T. (2016). Creating birds of similar feathers: Leveraging similarity to improve teacher–student relationships and academic achievement. *Journal of Educational Psychology, 108*, 342–352.

Geltman, P. L., Grant-Knight, W., Ellis, H., & Landgraf, J. M. (2008). The "lost boys" of Sudan: Use of health services and functional health outcomes of unaccompanied refugee minors resettled in the US. *Journal of Immigrant & Minority Health, 10*, 389–396.

Grabska, K. (2010). Lost boys, invisible girls: Stories of Sudanese marriages across borders. *Gender, Place & Culture, 17*, 479–497.

Harris, A. (2010). I ain't no girl: Representation and reconstruction of the "Found Girls" of Sudan. *Race/Ethnicity: Multidisciplinary Global Contexts, 4*, 41–63.

Higgins, E. T., Rossignac-Milon, M., & Echterhoff, G. (2021). Shared reality: From sharing-is-believing to merging minds. *Current Directions in Psychological Science, 30*, 103–110.

Hooker, E. D., & Algoe, S. B. (2022). Integrating research on social class and social relationships. *Social & Personality Psychology Compass, 16*, e12698.

Iraklis, G. (2021). Family bonds in the midst of adversity: Insights into refugee children's coping ways. *Clinical Child Psychology & Psychiatry, 26*, 222–230.

Jacob, G., Faber, S. C., Faber, N., Bartlett, A., Ouimet, A. J., & Williams, M. T. (2023). A systematic review of Black People coping with racism: Approaches, analysis, and empowerment. *Perspectives on Psychological Science, 18*, 392–415.

Kraus, M. W., Piff, P. K., Mendoza-Denton, R., Rheinschmidt, M. L., & Keltner, D. (2012). Social class, solipsism, and contextualism: How the rich are different from the poor. *Psychological Review, 119*, 546–572.

Lawlor, A., & Paquet, M. (2022). Deservingness in context: Perspectives toward refugees and asylum seekers in Canada. *Journal of Ethnic & Migration Studies, 48*, 3484–3504.

Lawlor, A., & Tolley, E. (2017). Deciding who's legitimate: News media framing of immigrants and refugees. *International Journal of Communication, 11*, 967–991.

Lenz, J. (2017). Armed with resilience: Tapping into the experience and survival skills of formerly abducted girl child soldiers in Northern Uganda. In M. Denov & B. Akesson (Eds.), *Children affected by armed conflict: Theory, method, and practice* (pp. 112–136). Columbia University Press.

Link, B. G., & Phelan, J. C. (2001). Conceptualizing stigma. *Annual Review of Sociology, 27*, 363–385.

Luster, T., Qin, D. B., Bates, L., Johnson, D. J., & Rana, M. (2008). The Lost Boys of Sudan: Ambiguous loss, search for family, and reestablishing relationships with family members. *Family Relations, 57*, 444–456.

Luster, T., Qin, D. B., Bates, L., Johnson, D. J., & Rana, M. (2009). The Lost Boys of Sudan: Coping with ambiguous loss and separation from parents. *American Journal of Orthopsychiatry, 79*, 203–211.

Luster, T., Saltarelli, A. J., Rana, M., Qin, D. B., Bates, L., Burdick, K., & Baird, D. (2009). The experiences of Sudanese unaccompanied minors in foster care. *Journal of Family Psychology, 23*, 386–395.

Mabeya, D. O. (2015). Capital matters: "Found" social capital of the Sudanese refugee lost boys living in Kansas City Area. *SAGE Open, 5*, 2158244015621955.

MacDonald, M. T. (2015). Emissaries of literacy: Representations of sponsorship and refugee experience in the stories of the Lost Boys of Sudan. *College English, 77*, 408–428.

Matsuyama, Y., Aida, J., Hase, A., Sato, Y., Koyama, S., Tsuboya, T., & Osaka, K. (2016). Do community and individual-level social relationships contribute to the mental health of disaster survivors? A multilevel prospective study after the Great East Japan Earthquake. *Social Science & Medicine, 151*, 187–195.

McKinnon, S. L. (2008). Unsettling resettlement: Problematizing "Lost Boys of Sudan" resettlement and identity. *Western Journal of Communication, 72*, 397–414.

McPherson, M., Smith-Lovin, L., & Cook, J. M. (2001). Birds of a feather: Homophily in social networks. *Annual Review of Sociology, 27*, 415–444.

Mills, J., Clark, M. S., Ford, T. E., & Johnson, M. (2004). Measurement of communal strength. *Personal Relationships, 11*, 213–230.

Morland, L., & Kelley, E. (2024). Children and parents separated at the U.S. border: A case of human rights violations in the Global North. In M. Denov & M. Fennig (Eds.), *Research handbook on children and armed conflict* (pp. 123–146). Edward Elgar Publishing.

Murray, S. L. (2005). Regulating the risks of closeness: A relationship-specific sense of felt security. *Current Directions in Psychological Science, 14*, 74–78.

Pachankis, J. E. (2007). The psychological implications of concealing a stigma: A cognitive-affective-behavioral model. *Psychological Bulletin, 133*, 328–345.

Perry, K. H. (2011). "Lost boys", cousins and aunties: Using Sudanese refugee relationships to complicate definitions of "family." In M. L. Dantas & P. C. Manyak (Eds.), *Home–school connections in a multicultural society* (pp. 35–56). Routledge.

Raithelhuber, E. (2021). 'If we want, they help us in any way': How 'unaccompanied refugee minors' experience mentoring relationships. *European Journal of Social Work, 24*, 251–266.

Rimé, B., & Páez, D. (2023). Why we gather: A new look, empirically documented, at Émile Durkheim's theory of collective assemblies and collective effervescence. *Perspectives on Psychological Science, 18*(6), 1306–1330.

Rodriguez, I. M., & Dobler, V. (2021). Survivors of hell: Resilience amongst unaccompanied minor refugees and implications for treatment – A narrative review. *Journal of Child & Adolescent Trauma, 14*, 559–569.

Rusbult, C. E., & Van Lange, P. A. (2003). Interdependence, interaction, and relationships. *Annual Review of Psychology, 54*, 351–375.

Salas-Wright, C. P., & Schwartz, S. J. (2019). The study and prevention of alcohol and other drug misuse among migrants: Toward a transnational theory of cultural stress. *International Journal of Mental Health & Addiction, 17*, 346–369.

Seidel, F. A., Hettich, N., & James, S. (2022). Transnational family life of displaced unaccompanied minors – A systematic review. *Children & Youth Services Review, 142*, 106649.

Sels, L., Ruan, Y., Kuppens, P., Ceulemans, E., & Reis, H. (2020). Actual and perceived emotional similarity in couples' daily lives. *Social Psychological & Personality Science, 11*, 266–275.

Sierau, S., Schneider, E., Nesterko, Y., & Glaesmer, H. (2019). Alone, but protected? Effects of social support on mental health of unaccompanied refugee minors. *European Child & Adolescent Psychiatry, 28*, 769–780.

Singh, A. L. (2020). Arendt in the refugee camp: The political agency of world-building. *Political Geography, 77*, 102149.

Walton, G. M., Cohen, G. L., Cwir, D., & Spencer, S. J. (2012). Mere belonging: The power of social connections. *Journal of Personality & Social Psychology, 102*, 513–532.

Zink, J. (2017). Lost Boys, Found church: Dinka refugees and religious change in Sudan's Second Civil War. *The Journal of Ecclesiastical History, 68*, 340–360.

CHAPTER 2

HUMANIZING AND AMPLIFYING VOICES OF DISPLACED CHILDREN: A NARRATIVE OF AN EIGHT-YEAR-OLD'S JOURNEY AND INTEGRATION

Roxanna M. Senyshyn

Abington College, Pennsylvania State University, USA

ABSTRACT

This chapter explores the impacts of war on children's education and psychological development, with a focus on the experiences of displaced Ukrainian children. Through the lens of Veronika, an eight-year-old Ukrainian student who came to the United States, it illustrates the challenges and resilience of children in adapting to new educational environments. The narrative explores the significance of supportive educational strategies that address the unique needs of displaced children, emphasizing the importance of individualized learning, compassion, and positive school culture as tenets for facilitating, language learning, integration, and healing. Drawing on the educational philosophy of Vasyl Sukhomlynsky (1976, 2016), a Ukrainian pedagogue and scholar, the chapter advocates for a holistic, child-centered approach that addresses the academic, emotional, and social dimensions of learning for children affected by war. It emphasizes the critical role of teachers in creating inclusive, nurturing environments that enable displaced children to thrive.

Children and Youth as 'Sites of Resistance' in Armed Conflict
Sociological Studies of Children and Youth, Volume 34, 35–54
Copyright © 2025 by Roxanna M. Senyshyn
Published under exclusive licence by Emerald Publishing Limited
ISSN: 1537-4661/doi:10.1108/S1537-466120240000034003

Keywords: Forcibly displaced children; educational integration; Sukhomlynsky's educational philosophy; trauma-informed teaching; holistic development compassionate education; English learner; English Language Development (ELD); cultural and linguistic support

INTRODUCTION: BRIEF INSIGHTS INTO WARS, DISPLACEMENT, AND EDUCATION

According to the Institute for Economics and Peace (2023), there has been a decline in the global peace experience over the last two decades. The ongoing armed conflicts in Syria, Myanmar, Afghanistan, Yemen, and Ethiopia, and the recent Russia–Ukraine and Israel–Hamas wars have resulted in the displacement of over 100 million people worldwide (UNHCR, 2023). Children are often significantly overrepresented among the forcibly displaced and face heightened vulnerability. One in six children lives in conflict or war zones and, as of the end of 2022, about 43.3 million children were displaced due to armed conflicts and violence, marking a severe global displacement crisis (UNICEF, 2023).

Understanding the impact of war and armed conflict on children and their development is crucial. However, as noted by Burgund Isakov et al. (2022), data on children's war-related experiences and their impact on their psychological development are limited. Hazer and Gredeback (2023) review psychological literature focusing on refugee children and youth (age 0–18), highlighting their susceptibility to stress from cognitive and neurological development disruptions. This stress can jeopardize their development and have enduring effects on their lives, as documented by Nelson and Gabard-Durnam (2020) and Samara et al. (2020) among others.

Recent studies that broadly examine effective educational adaptations in refugee contexts (e.g., Cochran, 2020; Salem, 2021) focus on Syrian refugee children and show emerging positive results of the effectiveness of different interventions on children's mental and emotional well-being (see review in Hazer & Gredeback, 2023). Research shows that school-based interventions activate various aspects of a child's natural environment (e.g., Vernberg et al., 1996). Traumas suffered by students from war and conflict zones need to be considered when teaching about topics that could trigger students to feel oppression or exclusion (Parker, 2021). Mental health and social and emotional burdens can make learning more challenging. Traumatized children appreciate speaking with other children who have the same or similar experiences and realize that they respond appropriately to the lived experiences (Vernberg & Vogel, 1993). Brummer (2020) advocates for a restorative justice in education (RJE) framework for supporting the inclusion of students who have been traumatized by war and resettle from war-torn places. Important aspects of RJE are addressing internalized trauma and utilizing equity-focused and trauma-sensitive approaches that encompass relationship building and creating a safe and welcoming community. The RJE framework (Brummer, 2020) also advocates for student agencies, emphasizing the active role newcomers should play in the classroom. For teachers to address students' traumatic experiences is often very challenging and they often lack training and support to accomplish such a purpose. However, studies show that it is beneficial when teachers take time to get to know their students and help them process traumatic experiences through relational connections and validation of their experiences. Studies show that such an approach strengthens the teacher-newcomer relationship and the relationship with the class community deepens (e.g., Gonzalez, 2015; Parker-Shandal, 2023).

RUSSIAN FEDERATION'S WAR AGAINST UKRAINE AND UKRAINIAN DISPLACED CHILDREN

The literature on refugee and forcibly displaced children in various contexts can be helpful when applying it to those who were displaced due to Russia's large-scale invasion of Ukraine on February 24, 2022. However, Ukrainian displaced children and youth may encompass a distinct history of displacement and a unique set of needs as well as bring a unique set of assets to understand how war, displacement, and trauma affect their development and education.

It is important to note that Ukrainian children from southern and eastern parts of Ukraine have experienced prolonged exposure to military aggression, particularly since 2014 when the Russian Federation invaded and occupied the Autonomous Republic of Crimea and large parts of Donetsk and Luhansk oblasts (or regions) in the eastern part of Ukraine. Many children had to cope with multiple displacements and trauma for many years and their connections with family or caregivers and teachers are the most critical for their psychological well-being (Bogdanov et al., 2021).

The large-scale invasion in February 2022, led to the displacement of 4.3 million Ukrainian children, "more than half of the country's estimated 7.5 million child population. This includes more than 1.8 million children who have crossed into neighboring countries as refugees and 2.5 million who are now internally displaced inside Ukraine" (UNICEF, 2022). "The war has caused one of the fastest large-scale displacements of children since World War II," said UNICEF Executive Director Catherine Russell. "This is a grim milestone that could have lasting consequences for generations to come. Children's safety, well-being, and access to essential services are all under threat from non-stop violence" (UNICEF, 2022). Some families and children returned to Ukraine after the initial shock wave of fleeing the country and after Ukraine liberated and reclaimed more than 50% of the territory that Russian Federation initially occupied. Still, many displaced Ukrainian students have continued to study online in Ukrainian schools, while being internally displaced or after finding refuge in other countries.

It has been estimated that more than 270,000 Ukrainian citizens arrived in the United States in 2022 and 2023 (NBC Universal News Group, 2023), and many were granted temporary protection. It is a relatively small number in comparison with European countries that accepted millions and close to half a million Ukrainian school children (Eurostat, 2024). Newcomer students with refugee or forcibly displayed status in the United States have legal access to resources and protection. However, the United States has not granted refugee status to Ukrainians arriving since the February 2022 invasion and they are considered displaced. Supporting the inclusion of displaced students has been addressed in every state, including the state of Pennsylvania where the author of this chapter resides. The welcoming process for displaced students ensures that they are supported in their socio-emotional transitions and their adaptation to new linguistic and cultural landscapes. Teachers and schools may not always be ready to meet the needs of displaced Ukrainian students, even when they have experience with refugee students joining their classrooms. Teachers are often met with the challenges of differentiating the instruction, and most importantly addressing the needs of newcomers who have experienced the trauma of war. When dealing with such trauma, teachers often feel unprepared. Often challenges are amplified by a lack of support from various parts of the educational system (school or district) and sometimes inadequate communication about the needs of these students and lack of professional development opportunities. Identifying the unique needs of displaced Ukrainian students involves taking time to understand their lived experiences.

CASE STUDY OF A DISPLACED CHILD'S EDUCATION AND ADAPTATION

In this chapter, the focus is on understanding the educational experiences of Veronika, an eight-year-old displaced Ukrainian student who enrolled in a second-grade class at a public elementary school in the United States. This school is located in a suburban district just outside a major city in Pennsylvania, known for its sizable Ukrainian community, where Veronika lived with her aunt's family. By centering on the experiences of a specific displaced learner, the goal is to personalize the broader issues. Such an approach not only *humanizes the statistics provided above about the displaced Ukrainian children* but also highlights the importance of student-centered educational interventions in addressing the unique needs of displaced children.

Therefore, this case study employs an ethnographic qualitative approach that focuses on narrating Veronika's journey. This approach allows for a deep, nuanced understanding of her experiences and the impact of displacement on her educational and psychological development. In addition, it utilizes a parent-as-researcher methodology and is inspired by Hackett's 2017 framework of involving actual parents; in this case, the researcher assumes a guardian role (as Veronika's aunt) to closely observe and document Veronika's adjustment and learning in naturalistic settings over 12 weeks, from the time Veronika arrived in the United States (March 2022) and until the end of the school year (June 2022). Observations were made not only in educational settings but also in personal interactions and daily living, providing a comprehensive view of the child's integration process. This included detailed documentation of school experiences, emotional responses, and adaptation strategies, particularly as viewed through Veronika's English Language

Humanizing and Amplifying Voices of Displaced Children 39

Development (ELD) teacher. An important part of the documentation was artwork and selected notes from Veronika's journaling (Notebook) to visually document and enhance the understanding of Veronika's experiences and interactions within her educational and social environment. They are included as images in this narrative to complement the observational data and school-to-family communication, helping to capture moments and contexts that are significant to Veronika's adaptation and learning processes to create a holistic view of the case. Overall, such methodological stance provides for a more comprehensive understanding of a child's journey and learning, allowing for an ongoing observation of a child's learning in a natural and authentic settings (Adler & Adler, 1997).

THE JOURNEY STARTS: FROM THE WAR-TORN COUNTRY TO A NEW CLASSROOM

It was February 24, 2022, when Veronika and her parents woke up to the sounds of explosions and phone calls from relatives and friends telling them that the Russian Federation started a large-scale invasion of Ukraine. Veronica's hometown of Lviv (in western Ukraine close to the Polish border) was under attack in the early hours of that day. Later that day and in the days and months following the invasion, Lviv was also a gateway to neighboring countries for those seeking safety outside of the country's borders. There would be no school, no play with friends, and no after-school activities that day, that week, and the following week. Her parents sent her to safety, unable to leave themselves. Veronika traveled with her grandmother to Poland first, where she attended school in Krakow for three weeks. In her Notebook (see Fig. 2.1) Veronika describes the first day of that journey and how that day felt. "It was the worst day!" she concludes her entry about that day, including a drawing of herself.

She also celebrated her eighth birthday in Krakow, Poland, and she recounted that she enjoyed exploring that new town with her grandmother. Veronika needed a US visa to enter the country, and once that permission was secured, they traveled to the United States. Veronika's art expresses powerfully the reason she had to flee her home country (see Fig. 2.2a). She proudly shared that drawing with her aunt and her family.

Fig. 2.2a captures Veronika's initial portrayal of Putin as a devilish figure amidst the onset of the Russian invasion of Ukraine. Two months later, Fig. 2b reflects an intensified expression of Veronika's ongoing distress. Her annotations, a mixture of English and Ukrainian, reveal an honest engagement with the ongoing war and aggression against her home country. Words like "liar," "chitter," and "loser" illustrate her growing confidence in using English and her need to articulate the injustices and cope with her stress through art. The Ukrainian annotations offer even harsher condemnation. The terms "гамно" (hamno) and "гамнюк" (hamniuk) directed at Putin carry the heavy insults of "shit" and "shitty person" or "scumbag" in English. Topping the Fig. 2.2b are the words "увага! увага! неправдивий президент" (uvaha! uvaha! nepravdyvyi prezident!) that call out, declaring "attention! attention! not a true president!" in English.

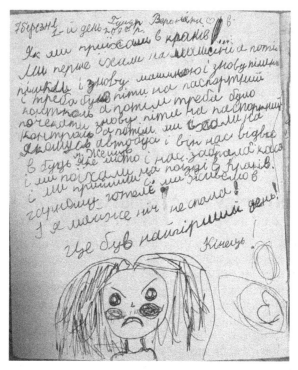

Fig. 2.1. Border Crossing and First Day in Poland: "It Was the Worst Day!"

Veronika came to the United States on March 26 (Saturday) and started school on March 29 (Tuesday). In Ukraine, before the invasion, she attended a small private school where she received instruction in English (45 minutes) as a world language twice a week in both first grade and second grade. Veronika knew the English alphabet, a few basic phrases in English, and many words. She could read short frequently used words in a picture book, such as "The Very Hungry Caterpillar," but she could not always comprehend everything she read.

Most importantly, she had a strong motivation to come to the United States and attend school. However, she worried about her parents who were remaining in Ukraine. She had the opportunity to speak with them via virtual platforms when the connection was possible.

Upon her arrival, there were tears mixed with hope. The sight of a Paddington-like bear on Veronika's sweatshirt brought an emotional depth, echoing a story her aunt shared with her college students just the day before. This tale, portraying a bear characterized by clumsiness yet filled with joy and hope, also subtly introduced the concept of war trauma. Originating as a refugee's story, Paddington's narrative resonated deeply with the unfolding events as Russia's war against Ukraine was escalating.

Michael Bond, the author of Paddington Bear, was inspired by the sight of Jewish refugee children walking through London's Reading Station as they arrived

Humanizing and Amplifying Voices of Displaced Children   41

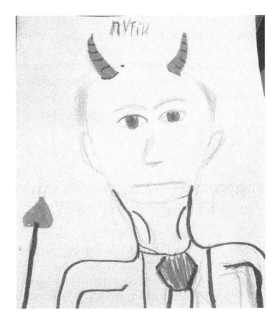

Fig. 2.2a.   Veronika's Explanation for the Reason for Fleeing Ukraine (Original).

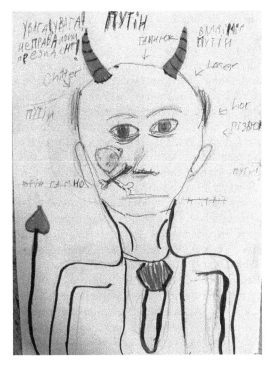

Fig. 2.2b.   Veronika's Explanation for the Reason for Fleeing Ukraine (with Annotations).

in Britain, escaping the Nazi horrors of Europe during World War II. Paddington Bear, with his blue overcoat, bright red hat, and a simple hand-written tag reading "Please look after this bear. Thank you," mirrors the appearance of many displaced children around the world. In a similar context, these elements resonated with the situation of Ukrainian children who were fleeing their country to escape the horrors of Russian military aggression, often doing it on their own. (e.g., NPR News, 2022).

Therefore, Veronika's experiences transformed into a rich source of inspiration for inquiry and reflection.

CONCEPTUALIZING AND FRAMING VERONIKA'S JOURNEY

Theoretical Framework

Veronika's journey of learning English and acculturation is examined through the framework that is based on the work of Vasyl Sukhomlynsky (1918–1970) who is one of the most influential Ukrainian educational thinkers of the post-World War II period. Sukhomlynsky served as a teacher and principal in a small Poltava region town in Ukraine during its time as a Soviet Union republic. Through his writing (30 books and 500 articles written in both Ukrainian and Russian) about his experiences as a teacher and a school principal, he became the most prominent educator in the Soviet Union of the 1950s and 1960s. One of his most influential publications, *My Heart I Give to Children*, has been published in more than 30 languages (Cockerill, 2009).

Sukhomlynsky's educational scholarship and practice resonate deeply in the turbulent context of today's war-torn Ukraine and are applicable to other contexts where displaced Ukrainian students seek refuge and temporary protective status. Sukhomlynsky's work is known for his devoted advocacy of humanistic and child-cantered education (Cockerill, 2009) and his contributions to educational practices can be represented through five tenets (based on Sukhomlynsky, 1976, 2016). These tenets are briefly discussed below and then followed by the narrative of Veronika's journey through the lenses of the five tenets.

First, Sukhomlynsky's most enduring contribution lies in his passionate support for *child-centered learning*. He advocated for and created in his own practice a learning environment where each child's unique needs, interests, and talents were the focal point. In the ongoing war on Ukraine, Sukhomlynsky's vision gains special significance because his ideas were developed and implemented in the aftermath of World War II when Ukraine was healing from the devastation of atrocities committed by Nazi Germany. Traumatized children, bearing the scars of conflict and war, require personalized support and understanding. By prioritizing each child's distinctive needs, educators can create a nurturing environment that helps students cope with trauma while continuing their educational journey.

The second tenet is creating a *positive school culture*. Sukhomlynsky emphasized in his own practice and his writings the critical role of fostering a positive school culture, wherein students felt valued and respected. He suggested

Humanizing and Amplifying Voices of Displaced Children 43

that a welcoming and inclusive school environment was contributing to effective learning. Amidst the post-war period or during conflict or crisis, schools often serve as sanctuaries for children facing instability and danger in their communities. Establishing a positive school environment is vital, ensuring that students encounter security and encouragement even amidst adversity.

The third tenet is *compassion and empathy*. Sukhomlynsky passionately promoted compassion and empathy as exemplary qualities of an effective teacher. He believed that educators should foster emotional connections with their students, understanding their feelings on a profound level. In times of stress and turmoil, children navigate a spectrum of emotions, from fear and anxiety to sadness (or even grief). Educators who embody compassion and empathy serve as sources of emotional support, guiding students through the web of their feelings and fostering trust that leads to the healing process.

The fourth tenet is *holistic development*. Sukhomlynsky ardently advocated for the holistic development of students, encompassing not only academic growth but also their physical, emotional, and moral growth. The trauma inflicted by war fills various facets of a child's life. Sukhomlynsky's holistic approach stresses the need to address all dimensions of a child's well-being. Schools in conflict-affected areas and teachers working with students affected by trauma must extend their approaches to encompass students' emotional and psychological needs alongside their academic progress.

Finally, the fifth tenet focuses on *respect for nature and the environment*. Sukhomlynsky instilled an appreciation for nature and the environment within his students, fostering a sense of responsibility and ecological awareness. Amidst the challenges of war and destruction, teaching lessons on environmental responsibility can offer a sense of hope and purpose. Educating children about preserving the environment empowers them to make positive contributions to their communities, even in the face of adversity.

VERONIKA'S JOURNEY: STRESS, ADAPTATION, AND GROWTH IN A SUPPORTIVE LEARNING ENVIRONMENT

This section discusses educational practices that supported Veronika's integration. They reflect compassionate, individualized, and inclusive educational support, emphasizing the importance of understanding and meeting the distinctive needs of a student.

Child-Cantered Learning

Veronika's experiences highlight the importance of educational practices that prioritize the needs and perspectives of children. Her transition into the US education system, despite the language barrier and cultural differences, stresses the need for approaches that are tailored to the unique circumstances of each child, especially those coming from a war-torn country.

Veronika had a strong desire to be in the United States and experience a US school; she expressed that desire on a few occasions to her host family (her aunt's family). Veronika's aunt made arrangements to introduce Veronika to her new school before the first day. During that initial visit, Veronika had an opportunity to visit the school with her aunt and meet her ELD teacher, the school principal, and another ELD teacher who popped into the ELD classroom to greet her. Touring the school with the principal and her aunt helped introduce Veronika to the building and important places, such as the cafeteria, library, playground, and other spaces. In the follow-up email (see the message below) sent by Veronika's ELD teacher after this introductory visit, the teacher conveyed a warm welcome to Veronika and her guardian. However, despite strong motivation and the preliminary school visit, Veronika wrote in her Notebook that "the first day was very stressful" in her new school. She wrote that she went to school-by-school bus, and her ELD teacher met her when she arrived at school, and all the students in her ELD class met Veronika with student-made welcome posters (see Fig. 2.3).

After the initial visit to the school, the ELD teacher followed up with the following message:

Hello!

This is A. B., Veronika's ESOL – Reading and Writing teacher. It was so nice meeting you and Veronika today. I am very much looking forward to being Veronika's teacher.

If you ever need to contact me about anything at all, please feel free to do so.

Veronika's second-grade classmates are so excited to meet her.☺

Just so you know, I will meet Veronika when she gets off the bus tomorrow morning. I will make sure that she gets to where she needs to be and I will try to make her feel as comfortable as possible.

Have a nice evening,

A. B.

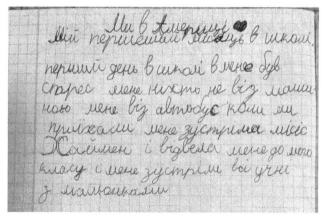

Fig. 2.3. About the First Day: "… It Was Stressful … All Students Welcomed Me with Pictures."

Humanizing and Amplifying Voices of Displaced Children 45

This communication expresses enthusiasm about teaching Veronika. In addition, the teacher offers an open line of communication for any needs or concerns and shares that Veronika's second-grade classmates are excited to meet her. The intention is to establish a positive and supportive relationship with Veronika and her host family, ensuring that she is entering a welcoming and inclusive educational environment.

It is also important to note that during the initial visit, the ELD teacher greeted Veronika by saying "Hello" in Ukrainian (Pryveet!) and showed that she keeps an English-to-Ukrainian dictionary in her class for translanguaging support. The teacher's use of translanguaging was intentional and had an immediate positive impact on Veronika, resulting in a warm smile. This practice shows that the teacher embraces translanguaging as a classroom norm (Daniel et al., 2019). Such a welcoming approach also resonates with the tenets of RJE (Brummer, 2020) by emphasizing intentional relationship building. For students arriving from conflict and war zones, building healthy relationships means understanding the needs that students bring to the classroom, including the need to validate their home language.

Positive School Culture

A welcoming and inclusive school culture is vital for the integration of newcomer students and students arriving from conflict and war zones. Veronika's story illustrates how a positive and supportive environment can encourage engagement and participation, helping a newcomer feel valued and accepted. In her Notebook, Veronika wrote that on her first day in the US school students were very welcoming and met her with friendly and welcoming drawings (see Figs. 2.4 and 2.5).

The ELD teacher followed up with Veronika's host family to inform them about the first day in school, and here is that message:

> Hello!
>
> I just wanted to let you know that Veronika had a great day in my class today. She and her friend Yulia seemed to communicate well and they were both happy to have a new friend. The children in our class were so excited to meet Veronika, and I hope she felt welcomed today.
>
> She was reading a Ukrainian book, The Mitten in Ukrainian and Yulia loved listening to her read.
>
> I am looking forward to getting to know Veronika more at school.
>
> I hope she enjoyed her first day at school.☺
>
> Thank you!
>
> A. B.

The teacher's communication highlights the creation of a positive classroom climate for Veronika on her first day, emphasizing the welcoming environment and social support facilitated through friendships and inclusive activities. The use of Veronika's first language, Ukrainian, played a significant role in her first-day integration. Veronika was paired up with another English learner who was more proficient in English but also a Ukrainian-speaking student. Allowing Veronika

Fig. 2.4. Peers' Welcoming Veronika on the First Day of School.

Fig. 2.5. Peers' Welcoming Veronika on the First Day of School.

to read a Ukrainian book, "The Mitten," not only made her feel valued and respected for her linguistic resources but also served as a bridge for mutual learning between the students. This approach stresses the importance of leveraging students' native/home languages as resources to enhance their sense of belonging and engagement in the classroom. Through these actions, the ELD teacher fostered a supportive and inclusive atmosphere that facilitated Veronika's smooth transition into the new educational setting, promoting positive interactions and cultural and identity connections among students. Such practices echo culturally

Humanizing and Amplifying Voices of Displaced Children 47

sustaining pedagogies (Alim et al., 2020). Following her positive initial experience, Veronika looked forward to attending school every day.

Compassion and Empathy

The interactions between Veronika and her educators, particularly her ELD teacher as previously discussed and to be addressed in the following section on *holistic development*, demonstrate the critical role of compassion and empathy in supporting newcomer students. Teachers who show understanding and sensitivity to the experiences of learners like Veronika can significantly ease their adaptation process and foster a sense of belonging and inclusion.

Living with her host/aunt's family and having the opportunity to speak with her parents in Ukraine over video calls, Veronika knew that her parents were "safe" despite several attacks on her hometown during the time Veronika was in the United States. When hearing adults speaking about the war against Ukraine, she pretended like she was not listening, but it was clear that she wanted to know how these adults felt about the evolving situation, and she was seeking assurances that her parents and other relatives who were remaining in Ukraine were safe.

There were times at school when Veronika worried about her mother and father and her friends who stayed in Ukraine. She never shared with the host family that she often cried at school throughout the first two weeks. It was the ELD teacher who reached out to inquire about Veronika's parents and possible reasons for such emotional distress in school. The ELD teacher thought it was due to Veronika's inability to speak with her parents and to be in touch with them was causing crying. However, as it became apparent, Veronika's crying in school was mostly because she often could not comprehend instruction and understand lessons in the general education classroom that were about complex topics such as a social studies lesson about township public services. She also cried in school, as shared with her aunt, because she was missing her friends from her school in Ukraine.

Veronika loved to give hugs to her new teachers and her classmates. It was a way to relieve stress, show her emotional state, and show her love for those who were kind and helpful, as she explained. However, the ELD teacher said that Veronika's hugs were so tight that some of her peers started complaining about such "tight" proximity. This had to be addressed; and in that case, collaborative efforts between the ELD teacher and Veronika's aunt resulted in newly gained awareness of personal space and "softer" hugs. As the ELD teacher stated in one of her emails, "[Veronika] has been using more and more English words in the classroom, which I have been trying to encourage by giving her hugs and praising her." The power of non-verbal communication is very symbolic and shows the teacher's compassion.

Holistic Development

The holistic development of students, encompassing academic, social, emotional, and physical growth, is essential for their overall well-being. Veronika's journey stresses the importance of educational practices that support the comprehensive development of children, ensuring they thrive in all aspects of their lives.

In Veronika's case, a thoughtful introduction of vocabulary and language scaffolding, including translanguaging and bilingual assessments, acknowledge the importance of developing both academic and language skills. Veronika's cognitive and social development is encouraged, allowing her to maintain her identity while learning English.

The following communication was sent to Veronika's aunt during the fourth week of Veronika's journey. It stresses her increased adjustment to classroom routines, emotional well-being, and participation in activities. It emphasizes the role of emotional support, positive reinforcement from the teacher, and peer encouragement in fostering Veronika's language development and confidence. The following ELD teacher's message underlines the importance of creating a supportive learning environment for English learners, celebrating their progress and the collaborative efforts supporting their newcomer journey:

> Hello!
>
> I just wanted to tell you that Veronika has been having a very very good week in my class this week. She seems much more adjusted to our routine and classroom. She has not gotten overly upset or cried at all this so far this week. She has been more willing to participate in classroom activities and even read a book with our whole class today. This was the first time I've gotten to hear her read, and it was wonderful to hear her voice! She has been using more and more English words in the classroom, which I have been trying to encourage by giving her hugs and praising her. She is choosing to read English books on her own in my classroom, which I was so excited about.
>
> I had another Ukrainian speaking student tell Veronika today that I am so happy and proud of the work she did today. ☺
>
> Thank you for your continued support,
>
> Mrs. B

It takes newcomers a different amount of time to integrate into a new educational setting, considering both the background and needs of the students as well as the environment and the support provided. In Veronika's case, week four of her schooling was *a major adjustment milestone that shifted her journey from stress to adaptation mode.*

While this narrative primarily focuses on the ELD teacher's role in supporting Veronika's integration, it's essential to recognize the strategies employed by her general education teacher to scaffold instruction and leverage Veronika's strength in mathematics. Veronika arrived with a solid background in mathematics, which she considered her superpower, though her understanding of English posed challenges in comprehending math problems and instructions. Notably, before the large-scale invasion in her home country, Veronika had begun learning multiplication and solving more complex addition and subtraction tasks. Upon her arrival in the United States, she found the math curriculum at the second-grade level to be very accessible (relatively simple) as it focused on basic addition and subtraction. To facilitate Veronika's success, her homeroom teacher incorporated translanguaging strategies, acknowledging that math is also a language-rich activity. This approach included translating key vocabulary for each chapter and using Google Translate to convert math unit tests into Ukrainian (the curriculum used by school was available only in Spanish as it is the most commonly spoken language by English learners in

Humanizing and Amplifying Voices of Displaced Children 49

the United States). It is important to note that Veronika completed her last math assessment in English (during week nine of her US school journey) without needing the Ukrainian translation of the test. She achieved a perfect score, which was a source of much pride for her. She also began to write some entries in her Notebook in English around that time (see Fig. 2.6) of her journey.

In the following weeks, the adaptation process was gaining strength, as is evident in the message sent by the ELD teacher during week eight of Veronica's journey. It provides a positive update on her integration into the classroom and notes a significant improvement in her willingness to engage with tasks:

> I just wanted to give you a quick update on Veronika's week. I have seen a huge change in Veronika this week! She is much more willing to complete work with Mr. S. and I. She is completing work without much/any resistance. She has not become upset during learning time once this week. She is definitely making a big adjustment with her behavior, and I have been so happy to see this! I have tried to encourage these wonderful behaviors as much as possible. She seems to be having a really happy week! Veronika has even been helping me with jobs around my classroom without me asking her.
>
> I am so glad you and I spoke last Friday, as I think this may have had a big impact on her behavior at school.
>
> Thank you so much for speaking with Veronika and all of your support!
>
> Mrs. B

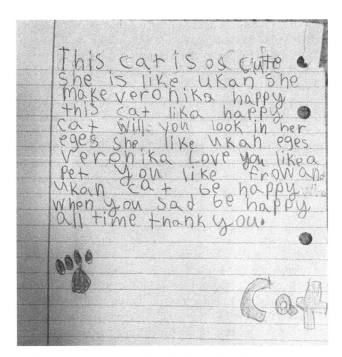

Fig. 2.6. Describing a Poster: "This Cat Is So Cute. She Is Like Ukraine. She Makes Veronika Happy."

Veronika showed more openness to completing work with teachers, demonstrating less resistance and not becoming upset during learning activities. This change indicates a substantial adjustment in her behavior and her educational growth, which was met with encouragement from the ELD teacher. Furthermore, Veronika took the initiative to assist with classroom duties without being asked, contributing positively to the classroom environment. The teacher attributes part of this positive change to a conversation they had with the aunt, suggesting that this interaction may have played a role in influencing Veronika's behavior at school. The teacher expresses gratitude for the host family's support and for speaking with Veronika, highlighting the collaborative effort between home and school in supporting Veronika's adjustment and integration. This aligns with the literature advocating for parental/guardian engagement (Housel, 2020). Additionally, Veronika's transition to an active classroom participant reflects restorative justice education principles (Brummer, 2020) in action. Restorative approaches encourage students to be responsible, active participants rather than passive followers of teacher directives. Moreover, communication from Veronika's ELD teacher is reflective of findings of studies that prove that engaging children within the classroom environment with a well-known set of rules and routines, conveys a message of normalcy (e.g., Wolmer et al., 2003).

Respect for Nature and Environment

While this aspect might not have been directly addressed in Veronika's journey in her US school, fostering an appreciation for the natural world and environmental stewardship can be an integral part of a holistic education as argued by Sukhomlynsky (1976, 2016). Such values can help displaced children like Veronika develop a sense of connection and responsibility toward their surroundings, promoting well-being and sustainability.

Over her 12-week experience in the second-grade classroom, Veronika frequently turned to drawing nature scenes during her free time or when she felt disconnected from lessons during the school day due to comprehension barriers. Her enthusiasm was evident when discussing any outdoor activity offered by her school, including time spent in the outdoor classroom, nature walks by the creek, and playground time (green space in school with part of the playground grassy and surrounded by trees and shrubs) and interactions during recess. These experiences underline the importance of integrating nature-based activities within educational settings to nurture environmental connection and awareness.

One of Veronika's fondest memories was a class trip to the Insectarium, reflecting her desire to engage with nature. At her host family home, she happily created art inspired by the flora, fauna, and scenic landscapes she encountered, further emphasizing her interest in the natural world. During the last week of the school year, when the class discussed summer plans, Veronika drew a picture depicting a camping trip with her parents to the Carpathian Mountains in Ukraine. This choice expresses a longing for her family and highlights her desire for peace and the solace that can be found in natural settings (see Fig. 2.7).

Fig. 2.7. Dreaming of Time with Family in the Carpathian Mountains of Ukraine.

The five tenets (Sukhomlynsky, 1976, 2016) provided a holistic framework for examining Veronika's experiences of going through stress, adaptation, and growth in her journey and the broader implications for educational practices with newcomer refugee or forcibly displaced children.

It is important to note that this case study has two possible limitations. First, considering the close familial relationship between the researcher and the participant, there may be inherent biases in how observations were interpreted and how Veronika's experiences were represented. The emotional involvement could affect the neutrality typically expected in research. However, some researchers argue that complete neutrality may not be possible and challenge traditional ideals of personal non-involvement in qualitative research (e.g., Skovlund et al., 2023). In addition, as this narrative focused on a single individual within a specific context (a displaced Ukrainian child in the United States supported by her host family), the findings may not be broadly applicable to other displaced children with different backgrounds or in different settings. The unique personal and environmental factors influencing Veronika's experience might limit the extension of conclusions to other contexts and identities.

CONCLUSION

As stated at the beginning of this chapter, conflicts, and wars have disrupted the educational journeys of millions of children worldwide, penetrating the classrooms with those who seek refuge and renewal in new cultural and linguistic contexts. Effective strategies that support learning and inclusion and promote mental health and well-being are crucial as these children integrate into new environments. Such strategies include focusing on individual student experiences, employing translanguaging in teaching, and prioritizing relationship-building through restorative justice pedagogies (Brummer, 2020).

This narrative case study gave voice to individual student experiences, emphasizing the importance of humanizing and amplifying the experiences and voices of displaced children beyond mere statistics. Veronika's journey of learning English and learning in English upon arriving in the United States from Ukraine testifies to her resilience. Having fled her war-torn native country with her grandmother, they first found refuge in Poland and then the United States. Despite Veronika's limited prior exposure to English in her home country, the transition presented unique opportunities and challenges. Her ELD teacher played a vital role in this transition, providing not just language instruction and supporting content learning but also emotional support and mentorship. From their first meeting, the teacher expressed enthusiasm about teaching Veronika, highlighting her rather smooth initial integration into the classroom and the excitement among her peers to meet her. Over time, Veronika made significant progress, increasingly engaging in classroom activities, choosing to read books in English, and using English more frequently and confidently – shift her ELD teacher encouraged with praise and support.

Overall, Veronika's journey highlights the critical role of educators in supporting newcomer students, emphasizing the need for patience, encouragement, and an inclusive and supportive learning environment for children resettled from war zones. This task can be challenging for educators, who may require additional resources and professional development to effectively support the inclusive and sustainable learning and emotional well-being of newly arrived students.

Finally, examining Veronika's journey – from stress to adaptation and growth – through Sukhomlynsky's (1976, 2016) tenets of humanistic and student-centered approaches point out the timeless relevance of his work in contemporary educational settings. This analysis also provides a symbolic connection to Veronika's experiences, reflecting the profound contemporary impact of his educational philosophy that was cultivated in the post-World War II environment in Ukraine. Furthermore, applying Sukhomlynsky's framework to analyze Veronika's adaptation to a new educational environment after being displaced by the war in Ukraine provides a holistic, child-centered approach. This framework helps draw meaningful conclusions about the essential support structures needed for displaced children like Veronika.

REFERENCES

Adler, P. A., & Adler, P. (1997). Parent-as-researcher: The politics of researching in the personal life. In R. Hertz (Ed.), *Reflexivity & Voice* (pp. 21–44). Sage.

Alim, H. S., Paris, D., & Wong, C. P. (2020). Culturally sustaining pedagogy: A critical framework for centering communities. In N. S. Nasir, C. D. Lee, R. Pea, & M. McKinney de Royston (Eds.), *Handbook of the cultural foundations of learning* (pp. 261–276). Routledge.

Humanizing and Amplifying Voices of Displaced Children

Bogdanov, S., Girnyk, A., Chernobrovkina, V., Chernobrovkin, V., Vinogradov, O., Garbar, K., Kovalevskaya, Y., Basenko, O., Ivanyuk, I., Hook, K., & Wessells, M. (2021). Developing a culturally relevant measure of resilience for war-affected adolescents in Eastern Ukraine. *Journal on Education in Emergencies, 7*(2), 311.

Brummer, J. (2020). *Building a trauma-informed restorative school: Skills and approaches for improving culture and behavior*. Jessica Kingsley.

Burgund Isakov, A., Husremović, D., Krasić, B., Marković, V., Milic, N., Ristić, T., Trkulja, A, & Žegarac, N. (2022). *Wherever we go, someone does us Harm: Violence against refugee and migrant children arriving in Europe through the Balkans*. Save the Children International, Save the Children North West Balkans. https://resourcecentre.savethechildren.net

Cochran, J. (2020). Jordan's solution to the refugee crisis: Idealistic and pragmatic education. *British Journal of Middle East Studies, 47*(2), 153–171. https://doi.org/10.1080/13530194.2018.1491290

Cockerill, A. (2009). *Each one must shine: The educational legacy of V. A. Sukhomlinsky*. American University Studies.

Daniel, S. M., Jiminez, R. T., Pray, L., Pacheco, M. B. (2019). Scaffolding to make translanguaging a classroom norm. *TESOL Journal, 10*(1), 1–14.

Eurostat. (2024). *Temporary protection for persons fleeing Ukraine – monthly statistics – Statistics Explained*. https://ec.europa.eu/eurostat/statistics-explained/index.php?title=Temporary_protection_for_persons_fleeing_Ukraine_-_monthly_statistics.

Gonzalez, T. (2015). Reorienting restorative justice: Initiating a new dialogue of rights consciousness, community empowerment and politicization. *Cardozo Journal of Conflict Resolution, 16*, 457–477.

Hackett, A. (2017). Parents as researchers: Collaborative ethnography with parents. *Qualitative Research, 17*(5), 481–497. https://doi.org/10.1177/1468794116672913

Hazer, L., & Gredeback, G. (2023). The effects of war, displacement, and trauma on child development. *Humanities and Social Sciences Communications, 10*, 909. https://www.nature.com/articles/s41599-023-02438-8.pdf

Housel, D. A. (2020). Supporting the engagement and participation of multicultural, multilingual immigrant families in public education in the United States: Some practical strategies. *School Community Journal, 30*(2), 185–209.

Institute for Economics and Peace. (2023). https://www.economicsandpeace.org/

NBC Universal News Group (2023, February 24). *U.S. has admitted 271,000 Ukrainian refugees since Russian invasion, far above Biden's goal of 100,000*. NBCNews.com. https://www.nbcnews.com/politics/immigration/us-admits-271000-ukrainian-refugees-russia-invasion-biden-rcna72177

Nelson, C. A., & Gabard-Durnam, L. J. (2020). Early adversity and critical periods: Neurodevelopmental consequences of violating the expectable environment. Trend Neuroscience, *43*(3), 3. https://doi.org/10.1016/j.tins.2020.01.002

NPR News. (2022, March 11). *A Ukrainian boy travels 620 miles to safety with a phone number written on his hand*. https://www.npr.org/2022/03/11/1086001579/11-year-old-ukrainian-boy

Parker, C. A. (2021). Refugee children in Canadian schools: The role of teachers in supporting integration and inclusion. In G. Melnyk & C. A. Parker (Eds.), *Finding refuge in Canada: Narratives of dislocation*. Athabasca University Press.

Parker-Shandal, C. A. (2023). *Restorative justice in the classroom: Liberating students' voices through relational pedagogy*. Springer Nature.

Salem, H. (2021). Realities of School 'integration': Insights from Syrian refugee students in Jordan's double-shift schools. *Journal of Refugee Studies, 34*(4), 4188–4206.

Samara M., Hammuda, S., Vostanis, P., El-Khodary, B., & Al-Dewik, N. (2020). Children's prolonged exposure to the toxic stress of war trauma in the Middle East. *British Medical Journal, 371*, 3155. https://doi.org/10.1136/bmj.m3155

Skovlund, H., Lerche Mørck, L., & Celosse-Andersen, M. (2023). The art of not being neutral in qualitative research. *Qualitative Research in Psychology, 20*(3), 363–381. https://doi.org/10.1080/14780887.2023.2223529

Sukhomlynsky, V. (1976). *To teach how to learn*. Soviet School.

Sukhomlynsky, V. (2016). *My heart I give to children*. EJR Language Service Pty Ltd.

UNHCR. (2023). *Global report 2023. The UN Refugee Agency Global Focus.* https://www.unhcr.org/us/global-trends

UNICEF. (2022, March 30). *More than half of Ukraine's children displaced after one month of war.* https://www.unicef.org/cuba/en/node/1761

UNICEF. (2023). *Child displacement and refugees.* UNICEF DATA. https://data.unicef.org/topic/child-migration-and-displacement/displacement/

Vernberg, E. M., La Greca, A. M., Silverman, W. K., & Prinstein, M. J. (1996). Prediction of posttraumatic stress symptoms in children after Hurricane Andrew. *Journal of Abnormal Psychology, 195*, 237–248.

Vernberg, E. M., & Vogel, J. M. (1993). Part 2: Interventions with children after disasters. *Journal of Clinical Child Psychology, 22*, 485–498.

Wolmer, L., Laor, N., & Yazgan, Y. (2003). School reactivation programs after disaster: Could teachers serve as clinical mediators? *Child and Adolescent Psychiatric Clinics of North America, 12*, 363–381.

CHAPTER 3

HOW MEMORIES AND NARRATIVES INFLUENCE YOUTH'S PERCEPTIONS OF CONFLICT AND THE "OUT-GROUP"

Natia Chankvetadze

Carter School for Peace and Conflict Resolution, George Mason University, USA

ABSTRACT

In societies divided by armed conflict, young people often develop conflicting memories and interpretations of the violent past. Relying on interview and focus group discussion records from a study conducted in Georgia proper and its breakaway region of South Ossetia/Tskhinvali in April–June 2021, this chapter examines what Georgian and Ossetian youth remember about the conflict in South Ossetia, and how their memories influence their views on the other group and the future of the conflict. By analyzing the stories Georgian and Ossetian young people tell about the root causes of the conflict and its dynamic, I argue that youth in conflict-divided societies develop contradictory memories of the conflict that mirror prevailing public and political narratives on each side of the conflict divide. These conflicting memories – and the lack of interaction between the two societies – foster negative perceptions of the out-group on

---

Children and Youth as 'Sites of Resistance' in Armed Conflict
Sociological Studies of Children and Youth, Volume 34, 55–71
Copyright © 2025 by Natia Chankvetadze
Published under exclusive licence by Emerald Publishing Limited
ISSN: 1537-4661/doi:10.1108/S1537-466120240000034004

each side, which in turn affect how the youth assess the war-related trauma experienced by each side.

Keywords: Memory; narrative; conflict-divided society; conflict-affected youth; Georgian–Ossetian context; South Caucasus

INTRODUCTION

In societies affected by armed conflicts, people often look to future generations for hope – the youth supposedly free from the painful past and keener to engage in conflict resolution efforts. The same perception prevails in Georgia, the country that has experienced three armed conflicts since the breakup of the Soviet Union in 1991. In this chapter, I explore the conflict in Georgia's breakaway region of Tskhinvali/South Ossetia (hereinafter referred to as "South Ossetia") and the Georgian and Ossetian youth's understandings and perceptions of the conflict. What young people on both sides of the conflict know and remember about the conflict and how their conflict-related experiences shape their perceptions of the "out-group" and their perspectives on the conflict's future. Examining their memories and perceptions of the conflict provides valuable insight into the potential of young people to contribute to efforts to resolve the conflict, as well as the challenges they may face.

This chapter builds from a 2021 study conducted in Georgia proper and South Ossetia. It analyzes the testimony of 50 Georgian and Ossetian young people (aged 18–30) who participated in interviews and focus-group discussions (FGDs) in April–June 2021. Although a report[1] based on the original study was published in 2021, this chapter revisits the underlying data and offers a new perspective on the topic. It presents three main findings from a review of the interview transcripts: (1) Based on the stories young people tell about the root causes of the conflict and its dynamics, I argue that youth in conflict-divided societies have developed conflicting memories and understandings of the conflict, which usually mirror prevailing public and political narratives; (2) These conflicting memories – and the lack of direct exchanges and interaction between the Georgian and Ossetian societies – facilitate both (i) unfavorable (negative) perceptions of the out-group and (ii) perceptions of the out-group as a homogenous society; (3) Differences in the conflict-affected youth's experiences impact how the young people view (i) the other side's war-related trauma and (ii) the future of the conflict.

The chapter repeatedly uses the terms "in-group" and "out-group." "in-group" refers to the society that the interviewee considers their own. Georgians consider Georgian society their in-group; Ossetians consider Ossetian society their in-group. "out-group" refers to the society that the interviewee considers the "opposing" side of the conflict. Ossetians consider Georgian society their out-group; Georgians consider Ossetian society their out-group.

The chapter is organized as follows. The first section provides context for the research with background on the conflict under review. The second section introduces key concepts. The third section reviews research methods, data, and limitations. The fourth section identifies three main thematic findings. The fifth section discusses those findings.

CONFLICT BACKGROUND

The country of Georgia is located at the eastern edge of the Black Sea. It borders Russia at its north and northeast, Azerbaijan at its southeast, and Turkey and Armenia at its south. Georgia has a population of approximately 3.7 million and an area of 69,700 square kilometers.[2]

Over the last three decades, Georgia has experienced three armed conflicts: two secessionist wars in the regions of Abkhazia and South Ossetia in 1991–1993, and a war with Russia in 2008. The armed conflicts in Abkhazia and South Ossetia arose shortly after Georgia regained its independence from the Soviet Union in 1991 and a civil war erupted in its capital – Tbilisi. Over the years, Georgia's conflicts have been variously described as "ethnic" conflicts (Cotter, 1999); "separatist" conflicts (Lynch, 2002); "geopolitical" conflicts (Tuathail (Gerard Toal), 2008); and "frozen" conflicts (Kapitonenko, 2009; MacFarlane, 2009). In 2016, the Organization for Security and Cooperation in Europe (OSCE) introduced the concept of "protracted conflict syndrome" to describe how residents of countries subject to prolonged conflicts experience diminishing hope for conflict resolution, and how the political leaders in such countries lose faith in negotiations and focus on merely preserving the status quo (Remler et al., 2016). The conflicts in Georgia, especially those in Abkhazia and South Ossetia, can also be described as "protracted" conflicts.

South Ossetia is considered a breakaway region of Georgia and also referred to as a territory occupied by Russia. Throughout the Soviet Union era, South Ossetia was an *Autonomous Oblast* (i.e., an autonomous district) within the Georgian Soviet Socialist Republic (1922–1991). As a result of the first armed conflict in 1991–1992, Georgia lost de facto control of the region. Over the ensuing years, Georgian and South Ossetian leaders (in some instances alongside the Russian Federation, North Ossetian leaders, and/or OSCE representatives) signed a number of protocols, declarations, agreements, proposals, and other agreements aiming to resolve or settle the conflict.

The Georgian–South Ossetian relationship experienced another breaking point with the Russo-Georgian War of 2008 (also known as the "August War"). Although that war took place primarily in South Ossetia, the Russian military also crossed an Administrative Boundary Line (ABL) and militarily assaulted several locations in Georgia proper (Asmus, 2010). The August War displaced thousands of Georgians and Ossetians. According to the Georgian Ministry of Justice, as of early September 2008, there were more than 125,000 internally displaced persons (IDPs) in Georgia. According to the UNHCR, 36,000 people crossed the border with Russia (Georgian Young Lawyers' Association et al., 2009).

The Russo-Georgian War of 2008 disrupted and profoundly altered the Georgian–Ossetian conflict: Russia officially became a party to the conflict; direct communication channels between Georgia proper and South Ossetia were suspended; and South Ossetia gradually became isolated from the outside world and fully dependent on Russia. South Ossetia's dependence on Russia increased markedly starting in 2015 when the region's de facto leadership signed with Russia an "Alliance and Integration" agreement (Alborova, 2021, p. 24). Since then, Russia has built three full-fledged military bases in the region, and as of 2019, 19 militarized border guard bases (Amnesty International, 2018). Beyond military bases, South Ossetia is also heavily dependent on Russian funding (Kanashvili, 2021, pp. 45–46). The region's dependence on Russia has led to increased surveillance and questioning of civil society organizations. This started in 2011 and accelerated in 2014 after the region's *de facto* parliament passed a law on "foreign agents" (Alborova, 2021). While the title of the law was later changed to "foreign partners," its essence has remained unchanged: to impose legal and logistical restrictions on the region's non-profit sector and eventually prevent it from operating at all. Currently, the International Committee of Red Cross is the only international organization allowed to operate in the region and only in a limited capacity.

The Georgian–South Ossetian relationship today is characterized by a pattern of low-intensity violence. After the Russo-Georgian War, Russian military personnel installed barbed wires for over 80 km along the line of separation between South Ossetia and Georgia proper (Crisis Group, 2022). Around 60,000 people who lived at the border found their houses and yards split between two sides. Anyone who tries to cross the line risks being detained and subjected to a fine or even a prison term (Crisis Group, 2022). This process – referred to as illegal "borderization" – has negatively affected members of both Georgian and Ossetian communities who have lost free access to their farmlands (Amnesty International, 2018).

This is the current context of the conflict in South Ossetia and Georgian–Ossetian relations. Even though there no longer is institutionalized civil society in South Ossetia, and organizations that are still registered on the paper are extremely limited in their function, individuals in the region still communicate informally with Georgians through international research and non-profit organizations. However, those informal dialogues involve only small numbers of individuals. The public in each society remains largely isolated from the other. As a result, younger generations in each society are learning about the other mainly from their families, communities, media (including social media), or other institutions and they are hearing stories that do not always reflect the unbiased, deep, and critical analysis of conflict history.

KEY CONCEPTS: MEMORY AND NARRATION OF CONFLICT HISTORY

Memory and narration play a significant role in shaping people's understanding and perceptions of conflict history and of the "in-group" and "out-group." As such, the field of peace and conflict studies has long focused on understanding the politics or semiotics of memory and narration of history in conflict-affected regions.

In the context of armed conflicts, "collective memory" is a critical concept. According to Olick & Robbins' historical chronology, "memory has been a major preoccupation for social thinkers since the Greeks" (Olick & Robbins, 1998, p. 106), but the first use of the term "collective memory" is associated with Hugo von Hofmannsthal, who, in 1902, referred to "the dammed-up force of our mysterious ancestors within us" and "piled up layers of accumulated collective memory" (cited in Olick & Robbins, 1998, p. 106). The term refers to a widely shared form of knowledge about the past – knowledge that is socially constructed rather than personally experienced (Paez & Liu, 2010; Schuman & Scott, 1989). Collective memory building is a powerful process. It often aims to strengthen positive in-group perceptions and provides people with clear guidance on their group's norms and values (Paez & Liu, 2010, p. 106). However, because it also has a strong symbolic meaning, it can be instrumentalized to legitimize or delegitimize particular political agendas and actions (Liu & Hilton, 2005). Collective memory is an important concept in the Georgian–Ossetian context: Georgian and Ossetian societies alike have constructed memories of the conflict that dominates social and political discourse to the present day.

The concepts of "communicative memory" and "cultural memory" help explain how people construct memories around specific events. Communicative memory usually refers to the oral transmission of vivid "first-hand" information about an event (Assmann, 2008, pp. 110–111). This type of memory can be passed on across generations. Cultural memory is more institutionalized. It is established through sites of commemoration, public education (history), and other means (Assmann, 2008). Both concepts are useful for understanding memory formation in relation to the conflict in South Ossetia.

Another helpful concept is the "memory project." Toria defines a "memory project" in Georgia's context as "a planned, state-sponsored construction of the past and creation of coherent national narrative for strengthening the sense of unity in a society" (Toria, 2015, p. 52). Memory projects in the Georgian–Ossetian as well as Georgian–Abkhazian contexts often facilitate historical narratives that revolve around the idea of primordiality (Toria, 2015, p. 54). In short, Georgians, Abkhazians, and Ossetians all claim to be the indigenous people of those regions.

Young people in Georgia proper and South Ossetia usually exhibit all the above-mentioned forms of memory formation. Their narratives about the histories of the conflicts and "in" versus "out" groups originate in collective, communicative, and cultural memories. History textbooks in particular have played an essential role in establishing and reinforcing collective and cultural memories in both societies. A recent study by Barkaia of seven Georgian and two Abkhazian accredited history textbooks concluded that the Georgian textbooks were more fragmented and episodic than the Abkhazian ones (Barkaia, 2019). For example, the Abkhazian textbooks dedicated entire chapters to conflict-related events, whereas the Georgian textbooks contained only a handful of pages. The Georgian textbooks were also more concerned with political history, whereas the Abkhazian textbooks paid attention to political and military events and even discussed the effects of the war on civilians (Barkaia, 2019). Although the study did not cover Ossetian textbooks,[3] it illustrates differences in how conflict-divided societies delve into and present histories of conflicts in public education, resulting in the construction of contradictory collective and cultural memories. Those differing memories in turn influence the narratives the societies build around conflicts and how they define "in" and "out" groups.

Conflict narration tends to be complex for two main reasons: (1) there are multiple competing narratives at play and (2) different levels of actors – local, regional, and international – produce and reproduce those narratives (Cobb, 2013). Narratives of individuals who experienced the Russo-Georgian War in 2008 contain the following elements: (1) personal suffering, loss of loved ones, and fear for the future; (2) stories about *others* (for Georgians, *others* are typically Russians and Ossetians; for Ossetians, *others* are typically Georgians; sometimes, the *others* do not have a particular ethnicity and instead are people who threatened, murdered, and robbed villagers); (3) stories that contain remorse; and (4) stories of neighbors who, despite their ethnic difference, helped one another, protecting one another's properties and sometimes even saved one another's lives (Chankvetadze, 2021, p. 79). In the Georgian–South Ossetian context, narratives of conflict-affected people do not prevail in the public and political realms. On the contrary, their narratives might become co-opted into the mainstream narratives regarding conflict and out-group.

Young people in Georgian and Ossetian societies harbor different memories of the conflicts and present different narratives regarding conflict history. The goal of this chapter is to examine young Georgians and young Ossetians' knowledge (memories and narration) of conflict history and perceptions of the out-group.

METHOD AND DATA

This section explains the primary data gathering and analysis methods employed. This chapter primarily revisits the interview and focus group testimony of 50 Georgians and Ossetians aged 18–30 in April–June 2021. Interviews and focus groups were conducted in Georgia-controlled territory; semi-structured interviews were conducted in the South Ossetia. In total, 22 semi-structured interviews and four focus group discussions were recorded.

In Georgia-controlled territory, the research involved young people from Tbilisi (Georgian capital), Kutaisi and Gori (Georgian cities with significant numbers of IDPs), Tserovani (IDP settlement), and four villages along the ABL with South Ossetia. Semi-structured interviews were conducted in Tskhinvali (South Ossetia's largest city) and Akhalgori (an ethnically mixed district in South Ossetia). The young people had various backgrounds. From South Ossetia, all participants were conflict-affected. From Georgia proper, respondents consisted of three groups: internally displaced youth (IDP), youth from ethnically mixed families, and youth who did not experience the war first-hand. While the research mainly involved students from universities, non-students were also welcome to participate. Participants were identified through the researchers' networks and using the "snowball" sampling method. Table A1 presents the anonymized list of conducted interviews and FGDs.

The interviews and focus groups were conducted by a group of Georgian and Ossetian researchers during April–June 2021 under the project Rebuilding

Memories and Perceptions of the Conflict-Affected Youth 61

Memory for the Future implemented by Indigo. The interview questions covered topics including the participants' knowledge of conflict history and the "other" side; where they get their information; their views on the out-group; whether they know people from the other side and how they interact with them; and their thoughts on the future of the conflict. Each interview lasted approximately one hour, whereas each focus group lasted approximately two hours. All interviews and focus groups were recorded and transcribed by research team members. To ensure confidentiality, all personally identifiable information was removed from the transcripts, which still retained basic information such as the date and location of the interview/focus group and the gender(s) of the participant(s).

The transcripts were analyzed using qualitative data analysis software (MaxQDA) and the logic of thematic analysis. All transcripts were initially coded with an open-coding approach. The participants' answers were not checked for factual accuracy because this project aimed to study their memories and narration of conflict history. However, differences between the Georgian and Ossetian interviewees' answers and between how participants with different backgrounds addressed the same questions were areas of focus. Themes emerged as the result of careful re-reading and coding of all transcripts.

I was mindful of my positionality in analyzing this data. I am an insider researcher and practitioner with years of experience working in the non-governmental sector in Georgia proper. While my Georgian background enhanced my ability to understand the context of the interviews and contextualize the research findings, it may have created unintentional biases. For example, with respect to terminology, this chapter refers to the city "Tskhinvali," but for Ossetian people, the city is written and pronounced "Tskhinval." As another example, this chapter refers to the name "Akhalgori," yet in the aftermath of the Russo-Georgian War of 2008 the Ossetian people revitalized the district's Soviet Union era name: "Leningor."

There are certain limitations to this research. First, the study engaged a greater proportion of young Georgians than young Ossetians: 43 Georgians versus 7 Ossetians. There are several explanations for this imbalance: (1) South Ossetia is a closed region with ongoing surveillance of any non-governmental activity, therefore fewer people are motivated or willing to engage in this type of research project or similar activities; (2) the project's lead researcher from the region unexpectedly passed away, and the organization had to recruit replacements on short notice; (3) the data-gathering process took place in a limited time frame. Second, relatedly, it is difficult to generalize the research findings insofar as they reflect the experiences and testimonies of a limited number of participants.

ANALYSIS

Memory and Understanding of Conflict History

The primary goal of the research is to examine young Georgians and Ossetians' memories and understanding about the conflict and assess to what extent those memories and understanding align with prevailing public and political narratives in their societies.

As a threshold issue, the Georgian and Ossetian youth rely on different sources of information for their knowledge of the conflict and its history. Ossetian youth learn about the conflict primarily through formal education, whereas Georgian youth do not consider formal education a mainstream source of information. This difference may be reflective of current realities in each society. Ossetian (and Abkhazian) history textbooks arguably provide more information about conflict history than Georgian history textbooks do. Thus, Georgian youth mostly rely on communicative memory, stories they have heard or witnessed due to their connection to the conflict, whereas Ossetian youth rely more on cultural memory – stories that are institutionally fixed. Perhaps relatedly, Ossetian study participants are more confident about their knowledge of the conflict, whereas Georgian study participants express more confusion.

The memories and understanding of Georgian and Ossetian youth about conflict history are intertwined with the prevailing public and political narratives in their respective societies. To filter how youth memories are linked with public narratives about the conflicts, I analyzed responses to the question on the root causes of the conflict from both – Georgian and Ossetian respondents.

Responses of Georgian participants on the root causes of the conflict in South Ossetia or between Georgians and Ossetians are divided into two parts. The first part focuses on Russia and Russian politics, while the second part seeks to uncover the complexity of the Georgian–Ossetian relationship history.

Almost all Georgian study participants considered Russia a central cause in provoking or escalating conflict in the region. Russia was mentioned in all four FGDs and multiple individual interviews. For example, Georgian participants often mentioned that the "Georgian–Ossetian conflict was a conflict provoked by Russia and it unfolded just the way they wanted it to" (interview 14), or "Wherever this issue [of conflict] is discussed – at home or with friends – it is always the Georgian–Russian conflict, not the Georgian–Ossetian conflict (FGD 1)." The following quote reflects how Georgian youth view the Georgian–Ossetian conflict as a manufactured (or "provoked") conflict and how tensions appeared between Georgians and Ossetians:

> What I remember is that there was no name of 'South Ossetia' and it got created. There was no status for a region and it got created. Tensions appeared between these two ethnic groups [means Georgians and Ossetians], distance appeared among them. This term Georgian–Ossetian conflict got a familiar term, which was not a case before. (FGD 3)

Ossetian participants provided different explanations for the root causes of the conflict. The following quotes are illustrative: "frankly, we never really had good relations with the Georgians, we never really loved each other" (interview 18); "the Georgians wanted to break away from the Soviet Union, but we did not, that's why the conflict started in the 1990s" (Interview 17); "word has it in Tskhinvali that the conflict between us started in 1920, and I agree" (Interview 19). These statements indicate that according to the Ossetian youth: (1) the root causes of the conflict pre-date the Russo-Georgian War of 2008 and (2) the conflict is solely between Georgians and Ossetians. If the Ossetian participants mentioned Russia, they did so cautiously, without attributing the conflict to it.

Memories and Perceptions of the Conflict-Affected Youth 63

The Georgian and Ossetian youths' memory and understandings of the conflict history mirrored prevailing public and political narratives in their respective societies. In Georgia proper, the public and political narrative shifted after the Russo-Georgian War of 2008 to treat the Georgia-Russia conflict as a leading factor in explaining the conflicts in Georgia's breakaway regions. By contrast, the public and political narrative in South Ossetia blames Georgia for the region's conflict and ignores Russia's involvement in it.

The following section discusses how the participants' memories and lack of direct interaction with the other side affect their perceptions of the "out-group" and uncovers the participants' experiences of war-related trauma.

PERCEPTIONS OF THE OUT-GROUP
AND EXPERIENCE OF WAR-RELATED TRAUMA

The picture of how Georgian participants perceive Ossetians as a society and "out-group" is not uniform. Georgian youth who directly (i.e., personally) experienced the conflict provided different responses to the questions "who are Ossetians?" and "what do you know about Ossetians?" than Georgian youth who did not. For the latter group, the general theme is that they do not know Ossetians and thus perceive them as "unfamiliar people." A nationwide study conducted by the CRRC[4] conducted in July–August 2021 corroborated this: 95% of survey respondents reported that they had not interacted with any Ossetian person in the past 10 years – neither online nor in person. For the former group, the testimony was mixed. Some recalled times of friendly and peaceful coexistence; others recalled antagonism and struggle. The following two quotes – from the same focus group – illustrate these contrasting memories and feelings: "I remember coming home and asking: are they [means Ossetians] bad? We spent our childhood together and now they are bad?" (FGD 3); "It was very hard for my family to learn that Ossetians from Tskhinvali, who drank wine made by my father in our house, looted our home" (FGD 3). The second quote further illustrates how, for some Georgians, the perception of Ossetians changed as a result of the consequences of the Russo-Georgian War of 2008.

Overall, however, the words used by the Georgian participants and the feelings they expressed in the course of talking about Ossetians suggested that they did not harbor aggressive or hateful emotions toward Ossetians as an out-group. Even in discussing charged war-related experiences, Georgians did not villainize Ossetians as a society. That said, the data does suggest that Georgians (intentionally or unintentionally) minimize the agency of Ossetians: Ossetians are often depicted as "manipulated" by Russian politics, "confused," vulnerable to Russian propaganda, and/or not having the "correct information" about Georgians.

Ossetian participants' perceptions of Georgians were more straightforward. A prevailing theme across the interviews was that "Georgians are nationalists." There is a perception that Georgians want the territory back. Ossetian participants did not question Georgians' agency, but they did question the knowledge and/or information Georgians have about Ossetians. For instance, one respondent said: "looking at social media comments from Georgians makes me think that Georgians' view of Ossetians is generic and inadequate" (Interview 18). Interestingly, Ossetian participants repeatedly mentioned that they believe that the Georgian youth are told bad things about Ossetians and that older generations of Georgians are turning the younger generations against Ossetians. This narrative is in tension with the testimony provided by the Georgian participants. As noted above, the Georgian participants generally either did not know about Ossetians or tended to dismiss their agency but did not display aggressive sentiments toward them or mention any transgenerational effect on their perceptions.

The Georgian and Ossetian participants share two ideas about their respective out-groups. First, they tend to portray the out-group as homogenous. This is an expected outcome, as conflict-affected societies tend to view out-groups as homogenous societies. Second, they occasionally (but not consistently) differentiated between so-called "ordinary" people and politicians or people in power. This differentiation helped them see and to some extent acknowledge the war-related trauma experienced by the out-group.

This research confirmed that war-induced trauma is prevalent in both societies. Although Georgian and Ossetian people experienced two armed conflicts since the fall of the Soviet Union, the study participants mostly spoke about trauma relating to the Russo-Georgian War of 2008, of which they have vivid memories.

There are three main takeaways regarding the Georgian participants' testimony about war trauma. First, conflict-affected and internally displaced Georgian youth are indeed traumatized by the war. They recall stories of war horror and ongoing fears: "even in my dreams, I always see leaving my home, but never going back to it" (Interview 7). The following quote conveys the depth of the trauma:

> I sleep next to a bookshelf and, like everyone else, thinking of something before falling asleep. My usual thoughts are what books I would take if we had to leave in case something sudden happens? I cannot get rid of this thought of uncertainty. (FGD 4)

Second, the Georgian participants repeatedly acknowledged the trauma experienced by the "out-group." They consider Ossetians equally traumatized people. The previously mentioned 2021 nationwide survey conducted by the CRRC corroborates this: 64% of surveyed youth consider people of Abkhazia and South Ossetia victims of conflicts, like Georgians. That said, the Georgian participants occasionally stressed that the "[Ossetians] stayed in their houses," potentially implying that they consider displaced Georgians more traumatized insofar as they also lost their homes.

Third, the Georgian participants repeatedly stated that it is essential for the societies to talk about each other's traumas, indicating that they believe such conversations will help them heal.

There were also three main takeaways regarding the Ossetian participants' testimony about war trauma. First, the Ossetian youth consider themselves – and the entire Ossetian society – heavily traumatized by the war: "I was only seven years old, but I remember so clearly running from our house. I know we could have been killed at any second. I cannot forget this moment of fear" (Interview 16).

Second, the Ossetian participants acknowledge that Georgian people (specifically IDPs) are traumatized by the war, but unlike the Georgian participants, describe the Ossetians' trauma as greater. One interviewee stressed how "the tanks swarmed the streets of Tskhinvali [main city in South Ossetia], not in Tbilisi [capital of Georgia]" (Interview 18). This and other similar statements from the interview transcripts confirm that the Ossetians perceive their war-related trauma as greater than that experienced by the other side.

Third, also unlike Georgians, the Ossetian participants did not consider talking about war-related trauma to be necessarily helpful. Their observations along these lines were somewhat in tension with the fact that Ossetian society maintains its memories about the conflict. Arguably, the participants were not suggesting to avoid or forget about the trauma, but rather expressing reluctance to engage in conversations about the trauma with Georgians. That said, some focus group participants in Tserovani (an IDP settlement in Georgia proper) mentioned that certain displaced families avoid talking about war and displacement and affirmatively "choose" to forget certain experiences to avoid having to confront past trauma.

All Georgian and Ossetian participants' accounts of war-related trauma shared one additional feature. The FGD and interview transcripts reveal that neither Georgian nor Ossetian youth have knowledge or awareness of the war-related tragic events for the out-group. This can probably be attributed to the selectivity of cultural or communicative memories in Georgian and Ossetian public and political realms.

EXPERIENCES AND VIEWS OF YOUTH FROM DIFFERENT BACKGROUNDS

This section describes the specific experiences of youth of three different backgrounds highlighting: (1) IDP (mostly Georgians who live in IDP settlements or private houses); (2) youth from mixed ethnic backgrounds (ethnic Georgians and ethnic Ossetians who have family members from the "other" ethnic group); and (3) youth with no firsthand experience of conflict (mostly Georgian study participants who were not directly influenced by the Russo-Georgian War of 2008 or displacement).

Youth with a background of internal displacement. One of the first things IDP youth talk about is the difference between being referred to as an internally displaced person or "IDP" versus as a "refugee." In Georgia, in the 1990s, internally displaced people were often labeled as "refugees." The term "refugee" had a negative connotation, as it was typically used to describe groups of displaced people who forcefully take locals' jobs or accommodations. Additionally, the term "refugee" suggested that the displaced people were strangers or outsiders and did not belong to local communities. Although the use of the term "refugee" was more prevalent in the 1990s and early 2000s, young IDPs of the Russo-Georgian War of 2008 remember the term being used in connection with that conflict.

Young IDPs contrasted how displaced people fared in the 1990s versus during and in the aftermath of the 2008 war: the IDPs of the 2008 war were quickly resettled (despite complaints about the accommodations) and mostly welcomed, unlike the IDPs of 1990s conflicts. A partial explanation lies in the Georgian state's greater institutional capacity in 2008.

Unsurprisingly, the stories young IDPs share are emotionally laden. They reveal layers of experienced trauma, uncertainty, fear, and instability: "Displacement affected me so badly, it left so many complexes that I am still struggling to get over them" (FGD 4); "It is hard to realize that on top of everything, people around you are unaware of your pain and unable to take it to their hearts" (FGD 3). Displaced youth emphasize the feeling of not being at "home." Most of them associate "home" with the place they were born and lived in before the war. Fear of forgetting the "home" is a recurrent theme. To resist this fear, respondents say that they try to remember all the details about their houses and keep their memories alive by routinely replaying them in their heads.

Youth from mixed ethnic backgrounds. Arguably, these youth are the most acutely affected by the war – especially those who left half of their families on the other side of the conflict. They often speak about the identity crisis they have experienced; those who ended up in the controlled territory of Georgia have more Georgian identity and vice versa. Ethnically mixed families often reside closer to ABLs and thus are also affected by "borderization," kidnapping, and fear of losing farmlands or family houses. They are also continuously affected by checkpoint closures and other disruptions of movement across the conflict divide.

Youth who did not experience the conflict directly. Young Georgians not directly affected by the war acknowledge that they do not fully understand the trauma and pain those directly affected by the conflict have experienced, and their war-related trauma is attenuated, if any. They also show mixed sentiments toward Ossetians as a society. They tend to perceive Ossetians as (1) strangers and unfamiliar people; (2) brothers and sisters (romanticization); or (3) manipulated or confused people (questioning their agency).

Table 3.1 summarizes the above-discussed points:

Table 3.1 shows that youth of different backgrounds have different memories of the conflict and perception of the "out-group." Also, their war-related trauma diverges.

Table 3.1. Youth Across Different Backgrounds and Their Perceptions.

Group	Memory	Perception of Out-Group	Trauma
IDP	Personal memories	Usually neutral. War of 2008 changed some people's perceptions	Trauma of war and displacement
Mixed ethnic background	Personal memories	Usually positive	Trauma of war, sometimes displacement, and identity crisis
No direct experience	Communicative memory	Usually mixed	Attenuated if any

Memories and Perceptions of the Conflict-Affected Youth 67

Additionally, Georgian and Ossetian youth also express divergent views on conflict resolution. For Georgian participants, South Ossetia being part of Georgia is the most favorable outcome and South Ossetia being part of Russia is the least appealing scenario outcome. For Ossetian participants, South Ossetia being part of Russia seems to be the most favorable development, and South Ossetia being part of Georgia is the least appealing. These opposite perspectives about the future signal that youth participating in dialogue or trust-building efforts will have contrasting underlying motivations.

Georgian and Ossetian participants also expressed contrasting views on dialogue and normalizing relations with the out-group. Georgians were more enthusiastic about participating in dialogue and trust-building efforts. The 2021 nation-wide survey confirms that a majority (66%) of Georgian young people are ready to participate in reconciliation efforts. That said, certain Georgian participants in this study acknowledged problems that are preventing youth from engaging in dialogue initiatives. The Ossetian youth, by contrast, do not see themselves as agents capable of making a difference in the conflict; thus, they do not feel the urge to participate in dialogue and trust-building initiatives. However, they do consider having a normalized relationship with Georgia proper an important goal. They spoke about how difficult it is to live in a region isolated from the outside world, with limited resources and opportunities. They view normalizing the region's relationship with Georgia proper as a potential way to improve their plight. A clear and consistent message from the Georgian and Ossetian participants alike was strong support for peaceful conflict resolution.

DISCUSSION

In conflict-divided societies, youth memories regarding the conflict history and the out-group are mostly conflicting. Public education and history textbooks usually reinforce the conflict. However, despite how differently public education is organized in conflict-divided societies, youth memory of the conflict and its history tend to align with and mirror prevailing public (and political) narratives about the conflict, its root causes, and prospects for resolution.

The Georgian–South Ossetian context exhibits all these dynamics. Although Georgian public education and history textbooks provide less information about the conflict in South Ossetia than Ossetian ones, memories and understanding about the conflict from youth in Georgia proper and South Ossetia alike mirror broader societal meta-narratives. That said, young people who have received less formal education tend to be more critical and open to questioning their knowledge and assumptions about the conflict and its history.

Conflicting memories and limited interactions facilitate negative views of the out-group (the other side of the conflict). For example, Georgian youth perceive Ossetian society as unfamiliar and strange people who are easily manipulated and confused, whereas Ossetian youth perceive Georgian society as nationalistic and lacking an accurate understanding of the Ossetians. These perceptions affect how the youth view the war-induced trauma of the other side: Although they tend to acknowledge that the other side has experienced trauma from the conflict, they believe that their own society's trauma is greater. Such perceptions of "out-group" trauma appear not to be based on factual information, as neither Ossetian nor Georgian youth know about the out-group's war-related tragic events. This can probably be attributed to the selectivity of cultural or communicative memories in Georgian and Ossetian public and political realms.

The testimonies of Georgian and Ossetian youth point to four essential topics for youth participation in dialogue and trust-building. First, get to know the other side. Both Georgian and Ossetian youth need firsthand information about the out-group. As direct contact is the only option to get firsthand information, various means of indirect contact should also be explored: informal educational initiatives, social media, and other online platforms could all play a role. Second, knowing firsthand information about each other will help develop empathy toward the out-group and their experiences of the conflict. As explained above, youth isolated from each other tend to consider their in-group more traumatized or affected by the conflict, even though war and displacement traumatize both societies. Third, acknowledging the agency of the out-group is vital. For this, youth need to know each other and have empathy toward each other's in-group. Fourth, acknowledging the risk of bias in one's in-group is essential for youth to avoid blindly mirroring prevailing public and political narratives of their societies and develop more critical perspectives.

CONCLUSION

This chapter used interview and focus group discussion records from a 2021 study conducted in Georgia proper and its breakaway region of South Ossetia to examine what Georgian and Ossetian youth know (and remember) about the conflict in South Ossetia and how their memories influence their views on the other group and the future of the conflict.

The collected testimonies indicate that youth in these conflict-divided societies have developed conflicting memories and understandings of the conflict. These memories have resulted in negative perceptions of the out-group (the other side of the conflict), perceptions that one's own group was more traumatized by the war, and some levels of ignorance of the trauma of the out-group. Nevertheless, youth have the potential to question and challenge their knowledge and assumptions about the conflict and resist blindly reproducing meta-narratives from their respective groups.

NOTES

1. Report is available at: https://indigo.com.ge/en/articles/axalgazrdebis-arqma-konfliqtze.
2. Georgia Statistics Office – https://www.geostat.ge/en/modules/categories/41/population.
3. Barkaia attempted to study Ossetian history textbooks but the textbooks did not cover the contemporary period.
4. *Survey on Youth Civic and Political Engagement and Participation in Peacebuilding in Georgia* (2021), available at: https://caucasusbarometer.org/en/ch2021ge/codebook/.

Memories and Perceptions of the Conflict-Affected Youth 69

The survey aimed to study young people's attitudes toward and experience of engagement in social, economic, and political life and peace processes. *Population*: Young adult population (aged 18–29), excluding populations living in territories affected by military conflict (South Ossetia and Abkhazia). *Sample Design*: Stratified multistage cluster random sampling.

REFERENCES

Alborova, D. (2021). Mechanisms for resolving the Georgian–Ossetian conflict and new challenges for dialogue: Georgian–Ossetian context. In S. Allen, N. Kalandarishvili, & M. Tadevosyan (Eds.), *The value of dialogue in Georgian–South Ossetian context*. George Mason University.

Amnesty International. (2018). *Georgia: Behind barbed wire: Human rights toll of "borderization" in Georgia*. Amnesty International.

Asmus, R. D. (2010). *A little war that shook the world: Georgia, Russia, and the future of the West* (1st ed). Palgrave Macmillan.

Assmann, J. (2008). Communicative and cultural memory. In A. Erll, A. Nünning, & S. B. Young (Eds.), *Cultural memory studies: An international and interdisciplinary handbook*. Walter de Gruyter. https://doi.org/10.1515/9783110207262

Barkaia, M. (2019). *History divided by war: Conflicts and history education in Georgia*. Caucasian House.

Chankvetadze, N. (2021). The monopoly of victimhood: The role of trauma narratives in the Georgian–South Ossetian dialogue. In S. H. Allen, N. Kalandarishvili, & M. Tadevosyan (Eds.), *The value of dialogue in the Georgian–South Ossetian context*. George Mason University. https://mars.gmu.edu/items/bddebe1f-2f65-4564-ac4f-822e61648e17

Cobb, S. (2013). *Speaking of violence: The politics and poetics of narrative in conflict resolution*. Oxford University Press. https://doi.org/10.1093/acprof:oso/9780199826209.001.0001

Cotter, J. M. (1999). Cultural security dilemmas and ethnic conflict in Georgia. *Journal of Conflict Studies, 19*(1), 1–27.

Crisis Group. (2022). *Fenced in: Stabilising the Georgia-South Ossetia separation line*. International Crisis Group. https://www.crisisgroup.org/europe-central-asia/caucasus/georgia/fenced-stabilising-georgia-south-ossetia-separation-line

Georgian Young Lawyers' Association, Article 42 of the Constitution, Human Rights Center, 21st Century, & Center for Constitutional Rights (2009). აგვისტოს ნანგრევებში: არასამთავრობო ორგანიზაციათა ანგარიში 2008 წლის აგვისტოს ომის დროს ადამიანის უფლებათა და ჰუმანიტარული სამართლის ნორმათა დარღვევის გამო [*In the ruins of August War: Report of NGOs on human right abuses and violating humanitarian law during August war in 2008*].

Kanashvili, G. (2021). Why is dialogue a big "No" for Tskhinvali?: An economic-financial dimension of the question. In S. Allen, N. Kalandarishvili, & M. Tadevosyan (Eds.), *The value of dialogue in Georgian–South Ossetian context*. George Mason University.

Kapitonenko, M. (2009). Resolving post-Soviet 'Frozen Conflicts': Is regional integration helpful? *Caucasian Review of International Affairs, 3*(1), 37–44.

Liu, J. H., & Hilton, D. J. (2005). How the past weighs on the present: Social representations of history and their role in identity politics. *British Journal of Social Psychology, 44*(4), 537–556. https://doi.org/10.1348/014466605X27162

Lynch, D. (2002). Separatist states and post-Soviet conflicts. *International Affairs, 78*(4), 831848.

MacFarlane, N. S. (2009). Frozen conflicts in the Former Soviet Union – The case of Georgia/South Ossetia. In K.-H. Nassmacher (Ed.), *Osce yearbook 2008: Yearbook on the organization for security and co-operation in Europe (OSCE)*. Nomos Publishers.

Olick, J., & Robbins, J. (1998). Social memory studies: From "collective memory" to the historical sociology of mnemonic practices. *Annual Review of Sociology, 24*, 105–140.

Paez, D., & Liu, J. H.-F. (2010). Collective memory of conflicts. In D. Bar-Tal (Ed.), *Intergroup conflicts and their resolution: A social psychological perspective*. Psychology Press.

Remler, P., Dimitrov, A., Goda, S., Jüngling, K., Kemoklidze, N., Lebanidze, B., Manton, I., Rastoltsev, S., Relitz, S., Saner, R., Schmidt, H.-J., Tamminen, T., Tytarčuk, O. H., Togt, T. van der Wolff, S., & Zellner, W. (2016). *Protracted conflicts in the OSCE area: Innovative approaches for co-operation in the conflict zones.* Centre for OSCE Research at the Institute for Peace and Security Policy (IFSH) at the University of Hamburg.

Schuman, H., & Scott, J. (1989). Generations and collective memories. *American Sociological Review, 54*(3), 359. https://doi.org/10.2307/2095611

Toria, M. (2015). Remembering homeland in exile: Recollections of IDPs from the Abkhazia Region of Georgia. *Journal on Ethnopolitics and Minority Issues in Europe, 14*(1), 48–70.

Tuathail (Gerard Toal), G. Ó. (2008). Russia's Kosovo: A critical geopolitics of the August 2008 War over South Ossetia. *Eurasian Geography and Economics, 49*(6), 670–705. https://doi.org/10.2747/1539-7216.49.6.670

APPENDIX

Table A3.1 Information about Research's Participants.

Georgian respondents	
Semi-structured interview 1	Male, 24 years old, Tbilisi
Semi-structured interview 2	Female, 20 years old, Zardiaantkari (village near the ABL in Gori)
Semi-structured interview 3	Female, 18 years old, Gori (displaced from Kurta Municipality)
Semi-structured interview 4	Female, 29 years old, Kere (village near the ABL in Gori)
Semi-structured interview 5	Female, 18 years old, Tserovani (IDP settlement in Georgia proper)
Semi-structured interview 6	Female, 20 years old, Gugutiantkari (village near the ABL in Gori)
Semi-structured interview 7	Female, 29 years old, Tbilisi (displaced from Akhalgori)
Semi-structured interview 8	Male, 25 years old, Tbilisi (displaced from Akhalgori)
Semi-structured interview 9	Female, 27 years old, Tbilisi
Semi-structured interview 10	Female 23 years old, Tbilisi
Semi-structured interview 11	Male, 23 years old, Tbilisi
Semi-structured interview 12	Female, 23 years old, Tbilisi
Semi-structured interview 13	Male, 25 years old, Kutaisi
Semi-structured interview 14	Female, 24 years old, Kutaisi
Semi-structured interview 15	Male, 23 years old, Zugdidi
FGD 1	4 females and 4 males, Tbilisi
FGD 2	2 females and 5 males, Tbilisi
FGD 3	8 females and 1 male, Tserovani (IDP settlement)
FGD 4	4 females, Gori (mixed)

Ossetian respondents	
Semi-structured interview 16	Female, 20 years old, Tskhinvali
Semi-structured interview 17	Male, 21 years old, Tskhinvali
Semi-structured interview 18	Male, 26 years old, Tskhinvali
Semi-structured interview 19	Female, 21 years old, Tskhinvali
Semi-structured interview 20	Female, 29 years old, Tskhinvali
Semi-structured interview 21	Male, 22 years old, Akhalgori District
Semi-structured interview 22	Female, 26 years old, Akhalgori District

CHAPTER 4

THE PROBLEMS OF RURAL YOUTH: A CASE STUDY ON CONFLICT, JUSTICE, AND RESILIENCE IN SINDH, PAKISTAN

Abdullah Khoso

Centre for Public Policy and Governance, Forman Christian College University, Lahore, Pakistan

ABSTRACT

This chapter employs a single case study of Safeer (pseudonym) (25 years old) who has been part of the tribal conflict involving the Rind clan against another Rind clan and the Lashari tribe in the Dadu district of Sindh, Pakistan. It investigates how youth, in the name of tribal honor, actively resist rival tribes, serving as potential actors during conflicts. Safeer actively engaged in numerous tribal conflicts during broad daylight. Not only due to tribal conflicts but also out of fear of the police, Safeer led a conscious and vigilant life from childhood to protect himself and his extended clan members, reflecting a shared sentiment among the youth of his clan. Safeer's case provides insight into the prevailing perception of youth across more than eight tribal districts in Sindh, excessively affected by conflict consequences yet actively resisting and challenging atrocities. He, like many others in his clan, felt compelled to seek revenge for the murder of an innocent clan member. Safeer's perspective also highlights the police's incompetence and the public's lack of trust in formal justice (especially courts), as a major cause leading young individuals into

---

Children and Youth as 'Sites of Resistance' in Armed Conflict
Sociological Studies of Children and Youth, Volume 34, 73–90
Copyright © 2025 by Abdullah Khoso
Published under exclusive licence by Emerald Publishing Limited
ISSN: 1537-4661/doi:10.1108/S1537-466120240000034005

tribal clashes. Safeer's case extends beyond an individual narrative, illustrating a broader political landscape in the vast geography of Sindh. It reflects the adversity and resilience of rural youth facing immense challenges, including declining agricultural activities due to reduced irrigation water, rising agricultural input prices, inflation, unemployment, and a shrinking small-scale industrial base in rural Sindh.

Keywords: Children; youth; Rural Sindh; tribal conflicts; tribal and feudal lords; justice; resilience

INTRODUCTION

Sindh is the second most populated province in Pakistan with 47,886,051 million people in 2017 (Khoso, 2023; of which, around 48% (23,021,876) live in rural areas (Pakistan Bureau of Statistics, 2017). According to Sindh's youth policy, a youth is a person between 15 and 29 years of age. Of the total Sindh population, around 26% are youth; of these, around 12% (5,890,890) of youth were living in rural areas of the province (Government of Sindh, 2018).

Among the 30 districts, 22 districts in Sindh witnessed around 1,566 tribal conflicts (also defined as "development in reverse" (Baliki et al., 2019)) reported between 2010 and 2014. These conflicts resulted in the death of 2,301 individuals, including 160 women and 45 children, with 3,697 sustaining injuries. In these conflicts, the youth of Sindh in rural areas are directly and indirectly impacted. However, research on the rural youth of Sindh (like youth in other parts of the world (Baliki et al., 2019), especially their problems stemming from tribal conflicts, and injustice, is rare except for a few scattered news reports on the problems of rural youth, which are also being used in this chapter to develop a complete picture of youth's conditions in tribal–rural areas of Sindh. Although, in Sindh's context, there are studies on youth in urban areas (Khoso & Chin, 2015; Khoso & Kousar, 2022; Khoso et al., 2018).

Children and youth in rural Sindh are not living a unique life in tribal conflicts but they share the same characteristics as many children and youth globally (Daiute et al., 2006; Kasi & Saha, 2021; Masten et al., 2023; Shah, 2020). For instance, research by Zakaria (2006) on the role of the youth in local conflicts across West Africa offers a better insight into the broader picture of the local conflicts that are perpetuated for larger political and economic interests. Baliki et al. (2019) revealed that in 2016 more than 350 million rural youth lived in conflict-affected regions, and they point to the wide broad range of economic and other indicators responsible for conflicts. Their research is a significant piece that offers insight into the rural youth's experience of and exposure to violence in continuous stages of life from childhood to adulthood, and how these stages relate to the broader political, economic, and social contexts. Shah (2020) shares the lived experiences of young children in the State of Jammu and Kashmir, who also construct meanings of armed conflicts in everyday life as their adults do. However, she asserts that the broader context also influences children's moral learning in specific combat-related societal challenges. This chapter uses a case study approach to investigate broader and wider contexts, which are responsible for creating conflicts, and injustice and making various other issues and impacting children and youth's lives.

RESEARCH APPROACH: CASE STUDY OF SAFEER

This chapter is based on a single case study of a young man (Safeer, age 25) from Dadu district in Sindh. The case study approach is commonly used in qualitative research because it is useful to decipher not only what an individual like Safeer goes through (detailed examination of his life) but also the broader contexts (Flyvbjerg, 2011) in which he and his tribe's young people and children live and practices similar lives as many other children and youth are living in different tribes across rural Sindh. This approach has also helped to detect (as Woodside (2010) has envisaged) the ground realities and broader contexts (Priya, 2021; Simons, 2014) of youth in tribal districts, which constitute a large portion of the province. This approach also helps us to see through a vivid picture of wrongs happening to youth in everyday tribal settings, which are self-perpetuated by the tribal and feudal lords for self-interests. His childhood starts seeing tribal conflicts within his village between his clan and another clan of his Rind tribe, and also with another Lashari tribe, and he sees the fire of tribal conflict spread across most of the districts of the province. Safeer's story offers the micro and macro contexts of youth in rural areas of Sindh and the ways they are encountering day-to-day challenges that have become a permanent feature of the tribal society.

Through a mutual acquaintance, the researcher encountered Safeer in a restaurant in Mehar town, located in the district of Dadu. Safeer had come to consult his lawyer regarding the potential of securing bail in a case where he was accused of murder. He asserted that he had been falsely implicated by a rival clan, highlighting the common practice of such nominations in Pakistan's criminal justice settings. The interview with the young man extended for approximately three hours, and subsequent follow-up interviews were conducted through mobile phone communication.

At the age of 15, Safeer was married; at the time of the interview, he had five children, including one son. For the past 15 years, he has been deeply involved in conflicts with the rival Rind clan and the Lashari tribe. In his extensive narrative, he shared that the conflict began around 15 years ago when members of another tribe allegedly, and without apparent reason, killed his 32-year-old cousin. The incident occurred at midnight while his cousin was sleeping in the guest room, accompanying a friend who was visiting from a nearby town. His cousin, a primary school teacher in the same village, fell victim to this tragic event, sparking clashes that resulted in casualties among members of both tribes over the subsequent three to four years. Safeer himself was implicated in a few cases where his clan members suffered casualties, but he refrained from confirming his involvement in those attacks on the rival tribe. He insisted on being falsely accused and, subsequently, became an absconder, living in various locations across Pakistan to avoid arrest and potential attacks from rival groups. Despite these challenges, he mentioned that with the support of his generous teachers, he managed to appear in the matriculation exam, albeit with uncertainty about passing the test.

Safeer claimed that he had managed to elude police arrests and ambushes set by rival clans, who were constantly on the lookout for him and often issued threats to him and his fellow clan members. Although he was not the sole child or young person in his clan, he expressed regret in revealing that most of his clan members had forsaken education, dropping out at the primary or higher secondary school level, and opting instead for a life focused on survival and livelihood. Safeer disclosed that he clandestinely visits his family to provide guidance and supervision to his minor children. While he no longer harbors an interest in tribal feuds, he explained that circumstances had forced him to adopt a lifestyle in hiding, aimed at defending and protecting his family and clan. His efforts also involved assisting clan members in bringing perpetrators to justice, an endeavor he hadn't witnessed in his local surroundings. Safeer clarified that he joined his clan members in seeking justice for his cousin's killing because they lacked trust in the formal justice system, including the police and judiciary. Furthermore, he asserted that if his tribe had refrained from taking matters into their own hands for vengeance, they would have led a cowardly life, and the innocent death of his cousin would not have been forgiven. He attributed the shortcomings in the criminal justice system, particularly the role of the police and judiciary, to the lack of relief provided to families affected by tribal feuds.

For their livelihoods, Safeer's younger brother cultivated a small piece of agricultural land, and occasionally, Safeer clandestinely worked in private companies in cities like Karachi and Hyderabad. These urban locations provided a level of anonymity, making it difficult for the police and rival groups to locate him. Safeer emphasized to the researcher that he opted not to join the *kacha* (a riverine belt on both sides of the Indus River, thick vegetation and forests provide the perfect sanctuary to criminals in rural areas) area to become involved in criminal activities like many other young boys. He distanced himself from such a lifestyle, expressing a disapproval of criminal activities. He also highlighted the predicament of many young people like him who, lacking education, become entangled not only in tribal conflicts but also in crimes such as robberies, theft, and murders.

In an attempt to resolve the matter, Safeer's elders sought negotiation and out-of-court settlements, but both the other tribe and his own clan were unwilling to cooperate. He noted that despite the reluctance of the young boys, the leaders persisted in continuing the fight. Safeer shared that after his cousin, the sole school teacher in the village, was killed, the school transformed into a donkey yard. For the next ten years, students ceased attending school, even though a new teacher was appointed. However, the new teacher lacked interest in education due to fear of a resurgence of tribal conflict. Safeer also mentioned that children from other tribes left the village, hiding alongside their adult family members while tending to livestock for their livelihood.

Safeer recounted an instance of a feud between the Chandio and Magsi groups over a piece of land, resulting in multiple deaths and numerous injuries in his hometown. These groups frequently engage in aerial firing, prompting teachers and students to seek refuge in a nearby mosque. In such circumstances, parents refrain from sending their children to school. For almost four years, the children from the group responsible for an individual's death did not attend the same school. This avoidance was due to the school's location in the victim's neighborhood, leading to a separation in the education of children from both sides.

Safeer additionally shared that the children of the group accountable for the murder faced consequences because most of their adult male members were either hiding in the *kacha* area, residing in major cities of Pakistan or were in jail. Consequently, the routine tasks related to livestock, agriculture, and other activities were performed by children under 12 years old who did not attend school. He highlighted that in areas where no adult men were present, only children, around 12 years old, carried guns for their safety and that of the women in their families.

Safeer's story offers insights into the harsh challenges faced by rural youth in Sindh. Through a case study approach, this chapter examines the macro-political contexts forming these circumstances. It investigates the various impacts on children and youth in rural Sindh, shedding light on the complex intersections of socio-political factors impacting their lives from childhood to adulthood. This analysis aims to disentangle the intricate connections between broader political landscapes and the specific experiences of the younger population and provides a comprehensive understanding of the challenges within this context.

THE POLITICAL LANDSCAPE FOR TRIBAL CONFLICTS

These tribal conflicts are rooted in the tribal nature of society and the concentration of various Baloch and Sindhi tribes and clans in the rural parts of the province, who live traditional norms surrounding the concepts of *ghairat* or honor and revenge (Laghari, 2016). Safeer also stated that his clan took revenge for the murder of his cousin to honor their clan. However, the real problem lies within the complex political landscape controlled by around 10 dozen feudal and tribal lords who control provincial and federal legislative assemblies and bureaucratic setup; and occupy massive arable land (Bengali, 2015; Hari Welfare Association, 2023). The vast majority of the members of the national and provincial assemblies from Sindh are tribal and feudal lords, and they control bureaucratic functions at the provincial level, including hiring and transfer of not only provincial bureaucrats but also, full influence in appointing teachers, approving funds for educational schemes, constructing, and operationalizing schools in most of the rural parts (Hari Welfare Association, 2023). In this landscape, almost, the entire rural Sindh, especially northern Sindh, is the power base for feudal and tribal leaders. They control political and economic resources and maneuver state institutions and their functions. Most of these lords have taken refuge in Sindh's political party (Pakistan Peoples' Party Parliamentarians – PPPP) which is again dominated by the feudal lords (Baxter, 1973; Hari Welfare Association, 2023; Hussain, 2018).

The current Chief Minister (CM) of Sindh is elected from Dadu district – the same district where Safeer and thousands of other children and youth are suffering tribal conflicts and lawlessness. The CM is the third time appointed for CM-ship by his party. The CM was born and educated in Karachi city (also Stanford educated) but got elected from his rural-native town in the Dadu district (The Express Tribune, 2016). However, he is crowded with Sindh's most influential feudal structure whose hegemony has brought a few educated members of the legislative assemblies to its knees (Hari Welfare Association, 2023).

In addition to the entire district administration including revenue and education departments (Business Recorder, 2005; Jamil, 2021), the police also work under the influence of these lords, with gangsters enjoying their full support, who regularly broad daylight harm (kill, kidnap, and injure) police officials with impunity and take refuge in the riverine (famous as *kacha* or *kacho*) areas along the Indus River flowing through most of the districts of Sindh, which are primarily no-go zones for the police (Business Recorder, 2023; Geo News, 2020).

In summer, the *kacha* area is often flooded; when water recedes, it leaves behind fertile land that feudal and tribal lords want. Thus, land in the *kacha* area is a prime source of conflict among several tribes and clans, causing unlawful occupations (Human Rights Commission of Pakistan, 2023). Also, this area is a haven for dacoits – the dense forests and rugged terrain provide cover for criminals to operate and evade capture (Khoso, 2023; Sindh Forest and Wildlife Department, n.d.). Law enforcement agencies including armed forces avoid entering *kacha* areas. The police avoid these districts due to safety concerns but are also not allowed by the tribal lords.

In 2022, dacoits killed five police officials in the Ghotki district; and, in 2023, dacoits kidnapped three police officials in the Kashmore district (The Nation, 2023; Tunio, 2022). They did these activities bravely in broad daylight. These tribal heads consistently lead their tribes and clans, encouraging conflicts between tribal members over issues such as theft, honor related to women, land disputes, and alterations in watercourse routes (Asian Human Rights Commission, 2009; Human Rights Commission of Pakistan, 2023; Khoso, 2023). Even the media reporter opines that these lords help to perpetuate poor law enforcement, illiteracy, unemployment, and honor killings so that their hegemony continues to be sustained (Hasan, 2020a). Similar circumstances are found in Sindh's rural areas where feuds are perpetuated by the feudal lords to remain relevant in tribal society (Kalhoro, 2021). The rural districts are also a prime route for smuggling Iranian oil and collecting illegal revenues (MM News, 2023). Safeer agreed that feudal and tribal lords had control over everything in rural settings but if the state and its apparatuses wanted to ensure the writ of the state or writ of the law, these lords were weaker. He inferred that the state authorities did not have the intention to ensure the rule of law; thus, lower cader police officials were easily killed by the dacoits.

In 2023, the clashes among 30 tribes and clans in only Kashmore district have resulted in scores of murders daily, which have severely hampered economic and social development in rural districts with restricted mobility, property damage, loss of livelihoods, and closure of numerous schools (Human Rights Commission of Pakistan, 2023). Tribal disputes can begin over something minor, such as cattle theft, disputed boundaries, or watercourse changes. Even when a wild animal wanders into a farm, it is slaughtered, which then sparks a fight. However, the main elements that continue to exist include feudal lords (who seek to maintain their position of authority), a lack of state-enforced laws, police protection of the powerful, illiteracy, unemployment, and honor killings (Hasan, 2020b). Tribal leaders often seek help from dacoits to carry out attacks and assassinations to settle their tribal course. The stronger tribal heads work best during elections. Most tribal leaders and high-ranking police officials have financial arrangements with criminal gangs in their jurisdiction. They receive payoffs in exchange for protection and patronage (Gul & Bairner, 2020; Yusuf & Hasan 2015). Feudal and tribal lords' (also known as *sardars*, *pirs*, *mirs*, *shahs*, and *waderas*) fear is pervasive across the tribal areas. These elites instruct the tribal men to vote, and tribal men instruct their women to vote (Bengali, 2015).

Personal insecurity of feudal and tribal lords is intensified by inter-tribal conflicts. Feudal and tribal lords wield armed gangs, similar to tribal militias involved in the forced occupation of state land, ransom kidnappings, theft of crops and livestock, and often targeting women and girls to dishonor opponents. These gangs also engage in reciprocal actions against rival tribes. These conflicts have disrupted daily life, while the state's writ is sternly undermined (Bengali, 2015). These have negatively impacted the education of children and youth and the duties of teachers, both of which are not sufficiently evaluated (Khoso, 2023).

EDUCATION FOR CHILDREN AND YOUTH UNDER THE SHADOWS OF TRIBAL CONFLICTS

Sindh's education system is an intricate macro-political economy. Its every facet is related to the distribution of economic resources by elites. This deep intricacy has badly impacted children's access to quality primary education. It is extremely crucial to address the issue of an estimated 6.6 million (in 2017) out-of-school children (from 5 to 16 years of age) mostly belonging to rural areas of Sindh (Hari Welfare Association, 2021). There are laws (for instance, the Sindh Right of Children to Free and Compulsory Education Act of 2013), however, the implementation is limited. In the rural tribal districts, the conditions are worse, primarily because of tribal conflicts (which are purely the outcome of macro-level policies) (Hari Welfare Association, 2023). In 2022, an average of 37% of children were out of school across eight tribal districts (Ghotki, Jacobabad, Kashmore, Khairpur Mirs, Larkana, Qambar Shahdadkot, Shikarpur, and Sukkur) in Sindh. Most out-of-school children are engaged in child labor and are also part of tribal conflicts, contributing to militancy and social crimes (Memon et al., 2022; Khoso, 2023).

Most importantly, these unending tribal conflicts have deprived millions of children of their childhood, and the fundamental rights enshrined in the United Nations Convention on the Rights of the Child including the right to survival (life), protection, and development (Khoso, 2023; United Nations, 1989). Safeer's childhood was not ruined but his youthhood was, and he remained in a vicious cycle of unending conflicts between his tribe and the Lashari tribe, and also with another clan of his tribe. However, he shared: "My children have suffered and are unable to attend school even within the village due to fear of being targeted by the rival groups." There is also a deep connection between out-of-school children or youth and conflicts (Faulkner et al., 2021); out-of-school youth have no other choice but to continue to associate with the unrest.

Tribal feuds and the feudal system are linked to each other and are also a prime cause of the deprivation of children and youth of their fundamental rights including the right to education. Generally, education is viewed as a prime means to empower youth (Gill et al., 2019) to challenge the tribal and feudal status quo (Bengali, 2015; Khan, 2021). The tribal leaders have formed their militias and are in regular warfare with each other. They forcefully occupy state (usually forest) land and lands belonging to rival tribes. Villagers in tribal areas are obliged to remain under the protection of the tribal leaders and suffer their oppression in return (Bengali, 2015). It implies that children and youth are no exception to these sufferings. Dacoits together with feudal and tribal lords played a role in ruining Sindh's rural areas' education system. Thus, rural areas of Sindh suffer from a lack of educational infrastructure including schools and trained male and female teachers – this limited infrastructure limits education opportunities for children and youth.

Generally, in rural areas of Sindh, most often schools exist only on paper; if these exist, there remains security as a prime concern for teachers and students; and school buildings are used for other purposes if these exist (Hari Welfare Association, 2021; Hussain, 2022). Education for Sindh's rural children population is entirely neglected as they form the vote bank of feudal and tribal lords – mostly part of the PPPP. Educating these tribal children could weaken the influence of these lords (Hari Welfare Association, 2021; Jamil, 2021; Riffat et al., 2016). Safeer informed: "My village's government primary school has turned into a donkey yard and also a defecation area because the teachers do not come. It is because of unending tribal tensions." He added: "I am not alone in my clan but most of my clan members had stopped education at the primary or higher secondary school level, but we opted instead for a life focused on survival and livelihood."

Many young teachers face intense and challenging conditions in schools in which they work, as well as in surrounding villages. Due to unending tribal conflicts between different tribes and clans, villagers have resorted to burning down schools and stealing furniture. This has led to teachers declining to attend school. Even after these feuds had reduced and grievances had been reconciled in some areas, teachers from outside the villages were always reluctant to return to teach. For instance, the feud between the Mahar and Jatoi tribes began in 1989 in Shikarpur and Ghotki districts and resulted in the loss of hundreds of lives on both sides. While it ended in 2009, the fear persists among both locals and teachers (Khoso, 2023; Said, 2021).

The Kakepota and Brohi feud has caused more than 30 fatalities and only concluded in 2021, with unsettled issues. Thus, most of the tribes' men were in hiding due to legal cases against them, compelling their children to engage in agricultural and livestock activities and none of them sent children to schools including education children. Also, due to tribal conflicts, children from one tribe attend school, while those from other tribes do not (Khoso, 2023). Like Safeer, tribal children often inherit the legacies of tribal feuds by joining their male adult family members in the *kacha* area as they grew older or ran to hide in populated cities like Karachi. In essence, tribal feuds, sustained by the feudal system in rural areas of the rural districts, have adversely impacted education and ruined children and youth's presence and future. These conflicts are intentionally sustained by feudal and tribal lords, causing substantial disturbances to education in these areas (Katpar, 2023; Khoso, 2023; Tangwani, 2022).

For most teachers including young teachers, it is scary to work in tribal areas, and, rarely, a committed teacher regularly comes to such areas, but if he comes, he has to face several hardships, including threats to his life. Recently, a determined primary school teacher (Allah Rakhiyo Nandwani) who defied the tribal bandit's rule by going to the no-go area in the Kandhkot-Kashomre district to educate children was gunned down by tribal bandits (Dawn, 2024). Overall, in Sindh, female teachers constitute only 32% of government schools' teaching workforce; and in rural areas, only 20% of the teaching workforce is female (Shah & Armstrong, 2019). Women teachers in these areas find it impossible to work, if they are appointed but never come to teach in tribal areas. The absence of teachers means compromising the education of children and youth in rural areas (especially girls' education) is compromised and tribal conflict has deprived them of the fundamental right to education to most children and youth in rural areas (Khoso, 2023). Safeer shared: "In my village, education is taken for granted, and girls' education is not possible… maximally, a girl attends primary school till 3rd grade, and after that, she stays back home to start learning family responsibilities."

During tribal feuds, it is of utmost difficulty for both sides' families to send children to schools because minor children cannot escape from the scene of the fight if it erupts. In the absence of male adult family members including youth who are often in hiding, women manage livestock and agriculture fields, which is their prime source (Katpar, 2023). The precarious conditions push young and old men to hide in *kacha* riverine areas (also considered no-go areas) in the same or adjacent districts, and sometimes, a few are caught by the police only when they travel to towns; or when the tribal head of another tribe supervises the police raids. In those families, whose adult male members are in hiding or in prison, their livelihood sources shrink; thus, most of these families' women and minor children are malnourished and carry out economic activities promoting child labor and exploitation of women's work (Khoso, 2023a).

Of the factors at the macro level, corruption in the education sector is also a mega reason for depriving children and youth of any level of education in tribal districts. In 2018, Transparency International Pakistan discovered that the education minister was involved in the purchase of 160,000 school desks, each costing PKR 29,500, while the actual market price of a desk was only PKR 5,000 (Javaid, 2022). Also, NGO representatives have time and again raised concerns about the existence of hundreds of ghost teachers and schools in the eight districts.

The media and NGO reports reveal around ten thousand ghost schools and thousands of ghost teachers in Sindh, particularly in rural areas of tribal districts. Ghost schools are officially on paper, but physically do not exist, and teachers do exist but do not serve function in reality; however, with the help of clerks in the education department continue to draw salaries (Hari Welfare Association, 2023). In 2021, it was disclosed on the Sindh legislative assembly's floor that the GoS had quietly decided to close 10,000 schools, which raised concerns about the initial reasons for their construction. In July 2020, the Sindh Education Minister disclosed that over 5,000 undesirable schools were built to appease politicians, and feudal and tribal lords by offering various benefits including jobs. The construction of these schools and teachers for these schools placed a substantial financial burden on public funds (Hari Welfare Association, 2021).

Under the nose of the provincial government (largely constituted by tribal leaders and feudal lords), the tribal conflicts are intentionally fabricated and perpetuated to sustain political, economic, and social control over the constituencies. Safeer also shared, "These conflicts are fully endorsed by the tribal leaders and *sardars* to maintain their statuesque and keep their *otaq* [in Sindh, it is a multipurpose guest house] alive." These all have an impact on rural children and youth, who continue to remain in the vicious cycle of violence and conflicts (as Zakaria (2006) witnessed in West Africa) like Safeer who is unable to restore his normal life. The absence of policies to intervene in tribal conflicts (and stop tribal norms tied to honor, land, and revenge), barricaded the educational development of children and youth of the areas (Pruitt, 2009).

LIMITED ECONOMIC OPPORTUNITIES FOR RURAL YOUTH

In addition to tribal conflicts' impact on the education of children and youth in rural areas, tribal conflicts have also kept rural areas of Sindh under serious social, economic, and political stress and constrained the growth and development of children and youth. Thus, the region is marred by terrible conditions of poverty, underdevelopment, and poor law and order. Poverty is also the outcome of a lack of employment opportunities created by the people controlling the region's political affairs. Safeer informed: "All development funds are used for their [tribal leaders and feudal lords] personal needs." The complex social, cultural, legal, and political environment that was the root cause of rural poverty was centered on the feudal connection between landowners, tenants, and landless laborers (Asian Development Bank, 2010).

Overall poverty rates in Sindh were estimated to be 37% in 2005, with 20% of urban residents and 53% of rural residents living in poverty (Asian Development Bank, 2010). In 2018–2019, poverty stood at 24% but in rural areas, poverty was observed much higher than urban poverty. The poverty level overall in Sindh has been higher because of inequality, poor education, and lack of job opportunities (Nadeem-ul-Haque et al., 2021). The family of a peasant sharecropping

Tribal Conflicts and Youth in Rural Sindh 83

or workers on farms hardly earned (Memon et al., 2019) around 10,000 rupees (around 65 USD in 2019) per month, whereas the average household off-farm income was around 5,000 and the average household livestock income was around 3,000. The facts of the lowest incomes indicate how widespread poverty is among peasants, who make up most of the rural population. The 2010 flood had washed away most of the villages in tribal districts, which provided an opportunity to rebuild organized and planned villages: "However, the feudal-tribal leadership opposed relocating the villages as they would lose control over their workforce, vote banks and most of their debts" (Ilyas, 2015, para. 2). Also, in rural Sindh, the pace of industrialization has fallen behind that of other provinces, which has resulted in excruciatingly slow improvement of agriculture and the miseries of sharecropper peasants have worsened as compared to the deprived urban dwellers (Bokhari, 2022).

Sindh has a very unequal distribution of land ownership. No government has ever had land reform on its agenda. A survey by Bengali (2015) reveals that over three-fourths of rural families are sharecropping peasants, working on the land belonging to big landlords.

> This share is greater in upper Sindh [extremely tribal districts]; where, for example, the share of tenant families in Shikarpur is 84pc. The tribal nature of the province is indicated by the fact that tribal and caste affiliations determine social relations, economic decisions, and political alliances. (Ilyas, 2015, para. 8)

Thus, a feudal elite dominates rural society and controls the major lands including the state lands (Malik, 2019; Panhwar, 2017). In rural Sindh, feudal families' landholdings have increased rather than reduced (Panhwar, 2017). Most rural households lacked access to agricultural land (Asian Development Bank, 2010).

Another factor is the lack of a small-scale industrial base in rural Sindh. Most of the large and small-scale industrial units are in between Hyderabad (after Karachi, Sindh's second-populated city) and Karachi, and a small number of industrial units are in other districts (Memon, 2017). In 2000–2001, 1,768 manufacturing units were in Sindh. Of these, 1,218 (69%) were in Karachi alone (Sindh Bureau of Statistics, 2009). In 2005–2006, there were 1,825 in Sindh. Of these, 66% were in Karachi (Pakistan Bureau of Statistics, 2013a). Recent district-wise data on manufacturing units are unavailable. However, the old data indicate a wide difference in manufacturing units in rural and urban areas. By 2013, a total of 6,893 industrial units (including manufacturing units) were reported in Sindh; of these, 82% (5,630) units were in Karachi and 1,263 units were in the rest of Sindh (Provincial Assembly of Sindh, 2014). According to the Pakistan Bureau of Statistics, in 2020–2021, a total of 54% of people (above 10 years) were employed in rural Sindh; and 46% in urban areas (Pakistan Bureau of Statistics, 2021); whereas in 2012–2013, 58% were employed in rural and 42% in urban areas (Pakistan Bureau of Statistics, 2013b). It indicates that besides a small industrial base, employment opportunities have decreased in rural areas as compared to urban areas. Whereas just 31% (around 14 million) of the population lives in Karachi and the remaining in other districts, which have a population of around 69% (Pakistan Bureau of Statistics, 2017).

Rural Sindh is directly dependent on agriculture as its major source of liveli-hood. Due to the lack of irrigation water and the degrading state of the land, people in rural areas were rapidly losing their ability to find employment in the agricultural sector. The prime cause of poverty and lack of employment oppor-tunities is the shortage of irrigation water due to the unending construction of dams and canals on the river Indus in other provinces (Talpur, 2017). Therefore, in rural Sindh, feudal elites get ample irrigation water but peasants with a few acres of land are often deprived of irrigation water. The government supports elites not only by creating informal mechanisms to provide them with irrigation water but also by providing energy panels and tractors at subsidized rates. Safeer shared:

> Like a landlord, a sharecropping peasant has to equally bear input expenses in the agriculture activities, but subsidies, loans, taxes waver, and flood or rain relief is only provided to landlords by the government, which also impacts a large portion of the rural population.

The agriculture sector has not improved, and peasants and workers are unable to get the same investment which they invest because of expensive agricultural input and low irrigation water (Hari Welfare Association, 2023). These are added by the drought, flawed water distribution systems, inadequate management of water resources, a lack of research, and poor market policies, the sources of live-lihood and employment were also severely threatened (Memon, 2008). Also, no significant investment is made in the infrastructure to promote rural industry by the government. Lack of opportunities is the prime factor, and the government has not created opportunities; this badly impacts rural youth (Pruitt, 2009).

A peasant or worker has to do extra work for the landlord if he does not do it, he is an outcast and punished in many other ways. Thus, a worker or peasant has to depend on financial markets controlled by landlords and rich people. Low wages in rural Sindh are also a factor in a poor economy. The labor force sur-vey reveals that in 2020–2021, the average wages in agriculture, fishing, hunting, and forestry were Rs. 13,173 (around 48 USD calculated on March 1, 2024) for Pakistan (Pakistan Labour Force Survey, 2021). In May 2020, an NGO HWA working for peasants' rights in Sindh claimed that unemployed youth in rural areas were compelled to work for 14–16 hours at restaurants, shops, and workshops for just Rs. 5,000 monthly (around 18 USD) but in Sindh, the minimum wage was Rs. 32,000 (around 115 USD) (The Express Tribune, 2020). Wages in rural areas are negligible, and there is a lack of resources and economic opportunities.

NOT TRUSTING THE FORMAL JUSTICE SYSTEM

Another discernible clue in Sagheer's story is the weak criminal justice system in Sindh, leading individuals, and groups to take the law into their own hands. It is because several critical issues surround the rule of law in Sindh, especially in rural areas, increasing challenges in accessing justice for the poor and power-less (Rohwerder, 2015), whereas crimes of the powerful often go unchecked and unpunished. In many cases, they buy justice, for instance, in November 2021, the sitting Member Provincial Assembly (MPA) of Sindh Awais Jokhio allegedly murdered young Nazim Jokhiyo in Thatta, and another sitting MPA Ganhwer Khan Isran had allegedly murdered a poor young woman Fahmeeda Sial in broad daylight in the Khairpur district. Both MPAs were members of Sindh's ruling PPPP and were rich feudal lords. The families of both victims have consistently accused the police of injustice and protecting the powerful (Khoso, 2023b). Not only in these two cases, but also generally, rural people (especially youth) struggle with the challenges of securing justice within a landscape tainted by corruption, inefficiency, feudalism, and lengthy procedures (Maniar, 2018). Within the criminal justice system, the role of the police is extremely significant and considered to be the gatekeeper of the justice system (Khoso, 2023).

In Sindh, it (the senior cadre) is viewed as a private army for the political and feudal elites. The ruling feudal lords and elites exerted influence in selecting heads of district police and also the Station House Office, ensuring control over their domains by suppressing dissent and opposition (Daraz, 2016). This collaboration with the police allowed them to exploit resources such as state land, forests, and other natural assets while engaging in criminal activities (Sehgal, 2019). In the recent National Corruption Perceptions Survey of 2023 by Transparency International Pakistan, the police are titled as the most corrupt department and the judiciary third most corrupt. Thus, young people like Safeer people do not trust the police and judiciary; either they resort to the informal justice system or take laws into their own hands (Ahmad, 2021). This entire political landscape completely negatively impacts children and youth in rural Sindh, who do not have education as well as employment opportunities to make their lives better. Thus, they end up becoming part of criminal activities including bandits (dacoits) tribal conflicts. Research (Memon et al., 2022) reveals that in rural areas various factors are responsible for children and youth's involvement in anti-social activities including murders and rapes. These factors include poverty, land disputes, and tribal rivalries.

CONCLUSIONS

This chapter used a case study of a young man Safeer caught in the unending trouble of tribal conflicts and violence around him at the micro level in his village; his story helped to examine similar trends, practices, and tribulations across the rural parts of the Sindh province of Pakistan. Generally, everyone is impacted by tribal conflicts, but here, the focus is on the children and youth. In this context, in the first place, it presents a complex stage of the political and socio-economic landscape controlled and hegemonized by feudal and tribal elites (known as *pirs*, *mirs*, *shahs*, khans, *sayeds*, *waderas*). It highlights the direct and indirect role of tribal elites in ruining the rural economy and education; thus, depriving children and youth of education, skills, and development; it highlights the way youth like Safeer have encountered multiple challenges for decades in rural settings, but policy corridors have not merely remained ignorant but part and parcel of violations of the fundamental rights of children and youth.

There are many conclusions to be drawn from Safeer's narrative and its deep and meaningful link with Sindh's rural children and youth's various emotional dimensions, and the complex macro level trap of challenges impacting youth in rural Sindh and provides a distressing narrative that captures ground realities (Woodside, 2010) and broader socio-political contexts (Priya, 2021; Simons, 2014). However, one ostensible conclusion is Sindh's rural youth know that the macro-political and economic contexts are the prime reasons for their deprivation and vulnerability, which is self-perpetuated by the tribal lords and tribal leaders. They know the broader context of conflicts and realize the impact of conflicts on their personal and family lives and also understand the broader social and political dimensions that drag them into this trap- and they are like children and youth in other rural areas of the world who also face challenges due to negligence by the state authorities (Boyd et al., 2007; Pruitt, 2009). However, at the micro level, the narrative underscores the profound impact of tribal feuds on the education system and children and youth, with schools transforming into unlikely casualties of long-standing conflicts. The cycle of violence not only disrupts the educational landscape but also entraps children in the consequences of adult actions, relegating them to tasks beyond their years.

Safeer's case and the contextual narrative around it also underline the grim facts of the criminal justice system. Safeer's evasion of arrests and the absence of trust in formal justice mechanisms (especially the police and judiciary) indicates the systemic flaws that add to a cycle of violence and revenge. However, as a result of the inadequacies in the criminal justice system, tribal feuds are perpetuated, leaving communities, particularly children and youth, caught in a persistent cycle of conflict and consequences. They live in violent environments and get badly impacted by these (Delaney, 2015); similarly, when children and youth do not have economic and educational opportunities; thus, become part of the violence (Al-Dawsari et al., 2011; Taher et al., 2022).

Safeer's narrative also underlines the tribal way of life surrounded by the concept of honor [or *ghariat*] and revenge; which is further manipulated by the political elites (Bakken, 2008; Bengali, 2015) to serve their vested interests; these elites control the entire legislative and bureaucratic structures in Sindh; and let rural children and youth to suffer through lack of infrastructure for education and other fundamental rights including the right to survival, protection, and development, but remain part of conflicts, underdevelopment, poverty, and marginality. However, the feudal elites cherish the first-world lifestyle, having multiple houses within the district and in provincial and federal capitals, and some even have abroad. Moreover, feudal and tribal elites' children study in elite English medium schools and/or in universities abroad (Bengali, 2015); for example, the current Chief Minister of Sindh is a graduate of Stanford.

This situation leads children and youth to take the law into their own hands (Morrow, 2013). Safeer's narrative indicates the immediate need for integrated and holistic interventions that address not only the immediate repercussions of conflicts but also the systemic broader context and issues lying within the power corridors that perpetuate this cycle, ensuring a more hopeful, secure, and just future for children and youth in rural Sindh. Sindh's middle class especially the business

Tribal Conflicts and Youth in Rural Sindh

community, teachers, academicians, and bar associations should come forward to get the children and youth of rural Sindh out of the clutches of unending and self-perpetuated tribal violence which they have been resisting for decades, which Sindh's ethnic political parties have not done over the last five decades (Khoso & Rovidad, 2023). However, there is also a dire need to conduct more comprehensive anthropological research with a bigger sample size in tribal districts to gauge the impact of feudal structure and tribal conflicts on children and youth and also on the overall development of the country.

REFERENCES

Ahmad, K. (2021). Trust of socially vulnerable groups on criminal justice system of Pakistan. *Journal of South Asian Studies, 9*(3), 175–185.

Al-Dawsari, N., Kolarova, D., & Pedersen, J. (2011). *Conflicts and tensions in tribal areas in Yemen.* Partners for Democratic Change International.

Asian Development Bank (2010). *Pakistan: Sindh rural development project.* https://www.adb.org/sites/default/files/project-document/63784/32024-01-pak-pcr.pdf

Asian Human Rights Commission. (2009). *PAKISTAN: Tribal conflicts in Ghotki district, Sindh province – Its causes and effects.* http://www.humanrights.asia/news/forwarded-news/AHRC-FAT-037-2009/

Bakken, B. R. (2008). The culture of revenge and the power of politics: A comparative attempt to explain the punitive. *Journal of Power, 1*(2), 169–187.

Baliki, G., Brück, T., Ferguson, N., & Stojetz, W. (2019). *IFAD research series 54: Rural youth in the context of fragility and conflict.* AgEcon Search. https://papers.ssrn.com/sol3/papers.cfm?abstract_id=3523806

Baxter, C. (1973). The People's Party vs. the Punjab "Feudalists". *Journal of Asian and African Studies, 3*(4), 166–189.

Bengali, K. (2015). *Profiles of land tenure system in Pakistan.* Pakistan Institute of Labour Education & Research.

Bokhari, J. (2022, April 11). *It is time for devolution.* https://www.dawn.com/news/1684350

Boyd, C., Francis, K., Aisbett, D., Newnham, K., Sewell, J., Dawes, G., & Nurse, S. (2007). Australian rural adolescents' experiences of accessing psychological help for a mental health problem. *Australian Journal of Rural Health, 15*(3), 196–200.

Business Recorder. (2005, December 19). *Feudalism main cause of backwardness in Sindh.* https://www.brecorder.com/news/3231888/feudalism-main-cause-of-backwardness-in-sindh-20051219367140

Business Recorder. (2023, July 28). *Curbing criminal gangs of Katcha Area.* https://www.brecorder.com/news/40255079

Daiute, C., Beykont, Z. F., Higson-Smith, C., & Nucci, L. (Eds.). (2006). *International perspectives on youth conflict and development.* Oxford University Press.

Daraz, U. (2016). *"This Crooked System": Police abuse and reform in Pakistan.* Human Rights Watch. https://www.hrw.org/report/2016/09/27/crooked-system/police-abuse-and-reform-pakistan

Dawn. (2024, March 19). *Bandits in Kandhkot–Kashmore kill teacher who defied their 'rule' by going to school in no-go area.* https://www.dawn.com/news/1822386

Delaney, A. X. (2015). Violent socialization and youth violence across different nations: International variations in familial and contextual factors. In S. R. Maxwell & S. L. Blair (Eds.), *Violence and crime in the family: Patterns, causes, and consequences* (pp. 129–151). Emerald Group Publishing Limited.

Faulkner, W. N., Nkwake, A., Wallace, N., & Bonifaz, A. (2021). Using social network analysis to explore community engagement for out-of-school youth (OSY) in the Mindanao region of the Philippines. *Quality Assurance in Education, 29*(1), 1–14.

Flyvbjerg, B. (2011). Case study. In N. K. Denzin & Y. S. Lincoln (Eds.), *The Sage handbook of qualitative research* (4th ed, pp. 301–316). Sage.

Geo News. (2020, February 16). *Geo special report: Understanding the infamous Kacha area of Sindh.* https://www.geo.tv/latest/272128-disputes-in-tribal-areas-kachcha

Gill, S. A., Aftab, R., Rehman, S. U., & Javaid, S. (2019). Youth empowerment and sustainable development: An evidence from Pakistan's Prime Minister's Youth Program. *Journal of Economic and Administrative Sciences, 35*(3), 202–219.

Government of Sindh. (2018). *Sindh Youth Policy 2018.* https://www.prb.org/wp-content/uploads/2020/06/Sindh-Youth-Policy-2018.pdf

Gul, S., & Bairner, A. (2020). Narratives of nationalist politics and sport in Sindh. In M. Vaczi, & A. Bairner (Eds.), *Sport and secessionism* (pp. 171–185). Routledge.

Hari Welfare Association. (2021). *The political economy of education in Sindh in 2020.* https://hariwelfare.org/wp-content/uploads/2021/06/The-Political-Economy-of-Education-in-Sindh-2020.pdf

Hari Welfare Association. (2023). *The state of Peasants' rights in Sindh in 2022.* https://hariwelfare.org/wp-content/uploads/2022/07/Hari-Welfare-Report-2022.pdf

Hasan, T. A. (2020a, February 16). *Geo special report: Understanding the infamous Kacha area of Sindh.* https://www.geo.tv/latest/272128-disputes-in-tribal-areas-kachcha.

Hasan, T. A. (2020b, February 16). *Geo special report: The never ending Teghani-Bijarani conflict in Sindh's Kashmore.* https://www.geo.tv/latest/272278-the-never-ending-teghani-bajrani-conflict-in-sindhs-kashmore

Human Rights Commission of Pakistan. (2023). *Northern Sindh: In search of solutions: An HRCP fact-finding report.* https://hrcp-web.org/hrcpweb/wp-content/uploads/2020/09/2023-Northern-Sindh-In-Search-of-Solutions-EN.pdf

Hussain, Z. (2018, July 16). *Sindh politics revolves around feudal lords.* https://www.nation.com.pk/16-Jul-2018/sindh-politics-revolves-around-feudal-lords

Hussain, S. S. (2022, December 9). *Ghost schools: Letter.* https://tribune.com.pk/letter/2254256/ghost-schools-1

Ilyas, S. (2015, March 30). *Landlords oppose village uplift to perpetuate feudal-tribal system: Study.* https://www.dawn.com/news/1172680

Jamil, K. M. (2021). *Development, disease, and democracy: Understanding the roots of poor social development in Sindh, Pakistan and outlining the possibilities for reform.* [Bachelor thesis, Harvard College]. https://dash.harvard.edu/bitstream/handle/1/37367826/Kamran%20Jamil%20Social%20Studies%20Senior%20Thesis_Final.pdf?sequence=1

Javaid, R. (2022, December 9). *Sindh education minister slams TI's 'agenda-based' report.* The News International. https://www.thenews.com.pk/latest/1018449-sindh-education-minister-slams-tis-agenda-based-report

Kalhoro, M. B. (2021, July 3). *Feudal lords keep people fighting to remain relevant in tribal society.* https://www.dawn.com/news/1632850/feudal-lords-keep-people-fighting-to-remain-relevant-in-tribal-society

Kasi, E., & Saha, A. (2021). Pushed to the margins: The crisis among tribal youth in India during COVID-19. *Critical Sociology, 47*(4–5), 641–655.

Katpar, Y. (2023, August 11). *Tribal conflicts in Sindh continue to have devastating effects on women, seminar told.* https://www.thenews.com.pk/print/1099032-tribal-conflicts-in-sindh-continue-to-have-devastating-effects-on-women-seminar-told

Khan, N. A. (2021). *Educational strategies for youth empowerment in conflict zones: Transforming, not transmitting, trauma.* Palgrave Macmillan.

Khoso, A. (2023a). Challenges for the government school teachers during COVID-19 and tribal conflicts/feuds in Shikarpur district, Sindh, Pakistan. *Education and Conflict Review, 4*, 30–36.

Khoso, A. (2023b). *Sindh's Human Rights Institutions and Paris principles: Do common grounds matter?* [Discussion Paper 2, Centre for Public Policy and Governance].

Khoso, A., & Chin, V. W. (2015). Recognizing invisible structural violence on juveniles: A case of Pakistan. *Mediterranean Journal of Social Sciences, 6*(4), 141.

Khoso, A., Khoso, P. A., & Khushk, G. M. (2018). Factors influencing Juveniles' perception of the police in Karachi, Pakistan. *Pertanika Journal of Social Sciences & Humanities, 26*(1), 59–74.

Khoso, A., & Kousar, U. (2022). Theoretical and practical challenges to stop recidivism among juveniles: Three case studies of male juveniles in Karachi, Pakistan. *Institutionalised Children Explorations and Beyond, 9*(1), 79–86.

Khoso, A., & Rovidad, M. (2023). Pakistan's ethnic parties' religious narratives and practices. *The Review of Faith & International Affairs*, *21*(3), 124–136.

Laghari, S. (2016). *Honour killing in Sindh: Men's and women's divergent accounts* [Doctoral dissertation]. University of York.

Malik, I. H. (2019). The politics of ethnic conflict in Sindh: Nation, Region and community in Pakistan. In S. Mitra, R. A. Lewis, R. C. Oberst, & R. A. Lewis (Eds.), *Subnational movements in South Asia* (pp. 68–103). Routledge.

Maniar, O. B. (2018). *The victim and the accused: An analysis of legal needs in the criminal justice system in Sindh.* Legal Aid Society. https://www.las.org.pk/wp-content/uploads/2019/12/The-Victim-and-Accused-An-Analysis-of-Legal-Needs-in-the-Criminal-Justice-System-in-Sindh.pdf

Masten, A. S., Tyrell, F. A., & Cicchetti, D. (2023). Resilience in development: Pathways to multisystem integration. *Development and Psychopathology*, *35*(5), 2103–2112.

Memon, N. (2008, May 5). *Unemployment in rural Sindh.* https://www.dawn.com/news/301270/unemployment-in-rural-sindh

Memon, N. (2017, July 9). *Tackling unemployment in rural Sindh.* https://www.thenews.com.pk/tns/detail/563621-tackling-unemployment-rural-sindh

Memon, H. A., Arain, M. A., Kalhoro, H. B., & Shaikh, S. A. (2022). Crimes and determinants of young criminals: A study of Interior Sindh, Pakistan. *Journal of Management Practices, Humanities and Social Sciences*, *6*(4), 71–77.

Memon, Q. U. A., Wagan, S. A., Chunyu, D., Shuangxi, X., & Jingdong, L. (2019). An analysis of poverty situation of landless peasants: Evidence from Sindh Pakistan. *Journal of Poverty*, *23*(4), 269–281.

MM News. (2023, October 24). *IG Sindh suspends 19 cops involved in smuggling of Iranian oil.* https://mmnews.tv/ig-sindh-suspends-19-cops-involved-in-smuggling-of-iranian-oil/

Morrow, V. (2013). Troubling transitions? Young people's experiences of growing up in poverty in rural Andhra Pradesh, India. *Journal of Youth Studies*, *16*(1), 86–100.

Nadeem-ul-Haque, Nazuk, A., Burgess, R., Rasul, I., Albasit, S. J., Ahsan, H., Iqbal, N., Khan, A. Q., Shoail, A., Afzal, H., & Zulfiqar, F. (2021). *The state of poverty in Pakistan.* Pakistan Institute of Development Economics. https://file.pide.org.pk/uploads/rr-050-the-state-of-poverty-in-pakistan-pide-report-2021-68-mb.pdf

Pakistan Bureau of Statistics. (2013a). *Census of manufacturing industries-2005 district-wise report.* https://www.pbs.gov.pk/sites/default/files/industry_mining_and_energy/publications/CMI_2005-06_district-wise.pdf

Pakistan Bureau of Statistics. (2013b). *Sindh.* https://www.pbs.gov.pk/sites/default/files/labour_force/publications/lfs_Annual_2012_13/t16-pak.pdf

Pakistan Bureau of Statistics. (2017). *Table - 4 area, population by sex, sex ratio, population density, urban proportion, household size and annual growth rate of Sindh.* https://www.pbs.gov.pk/sites/default/files/population/2017/sindh_district_wise.pdf

Pakistan Bureau of Statistics. (2021). *Sindh.* https://www.pbs.gov.pk/sites/default/files/labour_force/publications/lfs2020_21/tables/Table_15.pdf

Pakistan Labour Force Survey. (2021). *Key findings of labour force survey 2020–21.* https://www.pbs.gov.pk/sites/default/files/labour_force/publications/lfs2020_21/Key_Findings_of_Labour_Force_Survey_2020-21.pdf

Panhwar, N. A. (2017, June 3). *Tackling poverty in rural Sindh.* https://tribune.com.pk/story/1425879/tackling-poverty-rural-sindh

Priya, A. (2021). Case study methodology of qualitative research: Key attributes and navigating the conundrums in its application. *Sociological Bulletin*, *70*(1), 94–110.

Provincial Assembly of Sindh. (2014, June 7). *List of business.* http://www.pas.gov.pk/index.php/business/stn/en/31/771

Pruitt, L. R. (2009). The forgotten fifth: Rural youth and substance abuse. *Stanford Law and Policy Review*, *20*(2), 359–404.

Riffat, F., Chawla, M. I., & Tariq, A. (2016). A history of Sindh from a regional perspective: Sindh and making of Pakistan. *Journal of the Research Society of Pakistan*, *53*(1), 251–267.

Rohwerder, B. (2015). *Initiatives to strengthen rule of law in Sindh.* Governance, Social Development, Humanitarian and Conflict. https://assets.publishing.service.gov.uk/media/57a0896640f0b652dd0001e6/hdq1206.pdf

Said, E. (2021, November 10). *PPP Govt must act against those involved in Tribal Feuds in Sindh*. https://www.thefridaytimes.com/2021/11/10/ppp-govt-must-act-against-those-involved-in-tribal-feuds-in-sindh/

Sehgal, I. (2019, May 10). *Leave Sindh Police alone*. https://tribune.com.pk/story/1969536/leave-sindh-police-alone

Shah, S. A., & Armstrong, G. (2019, March 28). *Sindh and the state of gender equality in education*. https://tribune.com.pk/story/1938552/sindh-state-gender-equality-education

Shah, T. M. (2020). Children of Kashmir and the meaning of family in armed conflict. In S. Frankel, S. McNamee, & L. E. Bass (Eds.), *Bringing children back into the family: Relationality, connectedness and home* (pp. 213–216). Emerald Publishing Limited.

Simons, H. (2014). Case study research: In-depth understanding in context. In P. Leavy (Ed.), *The Oxford handbook of qualitative research* (pp. 455–470). Oxford University Press.

Sindh Bureau of Statistics. (2009). *Development statistics of Sindh 2009*. https://sbos.sindh.gov.pk/files/SBOS/Development%20Statistics/Development-Statistics-2009-.pdf

Sindh Forest and Wildlife Department. (n.d.). *Riverine Forest*. https://sindhforests.gov.pk/page-riverine-forests

Taher, A., Khan, Z., Alduais, A., & Muthanna, A. (2022). Intertribal conflict, educational development and education crisis in Yemen: A call for saving education. *Review of Education, 10*(3), 1–31.

Talpur, M. (2017, June 6). *In Sindh water is only for rich and powerful*. https://www.thethirdpole.net/en/uncategorized/in-sindh-water-is-only-for-rich-and-powerful/

Tangwani, N. K. B. (2022, March 27). *Never-ending menace of tribal clashes in upper Sindh!* https://www.dailyparliamenttimes.com/2022/03/27/never-ending-menace-of-tribal-clashes-in-upper-sindh/

The Express Tribune (2016, July 27). *Who is Murad Ali Shah?* https://tribune.com.pk/story/1150274/syed-murad-ali-shah

The Express Tribune (2020, May 2). *Rural workers paid a third of minimum wage*. https://tribune.com.pk/story/2211867/rural-workers-paid-third-minimum-wage

The Nation. (2023, July 9). *Several policemen abducted by bandits*. https://www.nation.com.pk/09-Jul-2023/several-policemen-abducted-by-bandits

Tunio, H. (2022, November 6). Five cops killed, two injured in attack on police camp in Ghotki. *Express Tribune*. https://tribune.com.pk/story/2384977/five-cops-killed-two-injured-in-attack-on-police-camp-in-ghotki

United Nations. (1989). *Convention on the rights of the child*. https://www.ohchr.org/EN/ProfessionalInterest/Pages/CRC.aspx

Woodside, A. G. (2010). *Case study research: Theory, methods and practice*. Emerald Group Publishing.

Yusuf, H. & Hasan S. S. (2015). *Conflict dynamics in Sindh*. United States Institute of Peace. https://www.usip.org/sites/default/files/PW104-Conflict-Dynamics-in-Sindh-Final.pdf

Zakaria, Y. (2006). *Youth, conflict, security, and development*. The Reality of Aid Network. http://www.realityofaid.org/roareport.php?table=roa2006&id=6

CHAPTER 5

THE CHILD QUILTERS OF WORLD WAR I: BRINGING HOPE AND COMFORT TO CASUALTIES AND SURVIVORS OF WAR

Aisha Manus

Independent Historian, USA

ABSTRACT

During World War I, more than 11,000,000 children, or over half of all school-children in America, joined their local Junior Red Cross and engaged in volunteer war work. What these children learned in school from their work with the Junior Red Cross, as well as those who did the same work outside of the organization, was an important part of the war work underway in the nation. While they may not have been working for wages, they were still an essential part of the war work economy. Across the nation, they made thousands of quilts, not just for the soldiers in the hospitals but also for the orphans of France, Belgium, and Armenia. Their colorful and warm quilts are the perfect example of youthful resistance against the pallid and cold realities of war. By focusing more on the journalism of the day, rather than the secondary sources related to the economics of the war, this chapter strives to tell their stories and return to the children the praise and admiration they got during the war for their dedication to their country that was, unfortunately, forgotten over time. By making these quilts, the children not only showed great patriotism and interest in the war, for they were responsible for providing comfort to the casualties of war and hope for the survivors of genocide, but they also served as valuable economic

---

Children and Youth as 'Sites of Resistance' in Armed Conflict
Sociological Studies of Children and Youth, Volume 34, 91–111
Copyright © 2025 by Aisha Manus
Published under exclusive licence by Emerald Publishing Limited
ISSN: 1537-4661/doi:10.1108/S1537-466120240000034006

AISHA MANUS

sources in the war economy. And as we all know, a good citizen contributes to the economy, and good citizens deserve recognition.

Keywords: Homefront studies; textiles; World War I; Junior Red Cross; quilt studies; economic history

INTRODUCTION

During World War I, more than 11,000,000 children, or over half of all schoolchildren in America, joined their local Junior Red Cross and engaged in volunteer war work (Our History, n.d.). President Wilson addressed the children of the United States on September 19, 1917, writing, "You will learn by doing kind things under the direction of your teachers, to be the future good citizens of this country which we all love" (Aldrich & Brow, 1918, p. 23). But what does it mean to be a good citizen in the United States? If you consider Thorstein Veblen's (1994) theory that, "the habits of thought which are so formed under the guidance of teachers and scholastic traditions have an economic value – a value as affecting the serviceability of the individual – no less than the similar economic value of the habits of thought formed without such guidance under the discipline of everyday life" (p. 363), what these children learned in school from their work with the Junior Red Cross was an important part of the war work underway in the nation. While they may not have been working for wages, they were still an essential part of the war work economy.

In a December 6, 1917 newspaper article found in *The Barnwell People-Sentinel*, entitled "What Can We Do?," the focus was not on "we" in general but rather on what children could do to help. The article stated, "The work of the Red Cross benefits the children in many ways so that they are helping themselves as well as others. They are much more keenly interested in the war than they otherwise would be, and their patriotism is stimulated by all that they do and learn" (p. 7). This was further reiterated that same month when *The Modern Priscilla* magazine declared that "organizations of the Junior Red Cross among public school children [having] been warmly approved by President Wilson, the work is developing rapidly throughout the country" (Angell, 1917, p. 2). And it was true. Children across the United States were joining their Junior Red Cross in droves, with some schools attaining 100 percent membership ("Much Work Done," 1918, p. 1).

Then in the summer of 1918, the American Red Cross headquarters stated that they would need an unlimited supply of heavily padded, 55 × 65 inch quilts, because they expected three million men to be on the front in the fall and it was up to the children to make them ("Junior Red Cross Notes," 1918, p. 1), as the task of making quilts for the Red Cross up until that point was overwhelmingly undertaken by the children of the Junior Red Cross compared to their adult counterparts. Even when a global pandemic fell upon them that fall, closing the schools and the Red Cross sewing rooms, the children still worked feverishly, for it was their duty to get the job done. Across the nation, they made thousands of quilts not just for the soldiers in the hospitals but also for the orphans of France, Belgium, and Armenia. Their colorful and warm quilts are the perfect example of

The Child Quilters of World War I   93

youthful resistance against the pallid and cold realities of war. By making these quilts, the children not only showed great patriotism and interest in the war, for they were responsible for providing comfort to the casualties of war and hope for the survivors of genocide, but they also served as valuable economic sources in the war economy. And as we all know, a good citizen contributes to the economy.

As there is nothing else published on the topic of child quilters of World War I, that I have found, the information for this chapter is predominantly derived from local newspapers whose reporting varied from small one-line blurbs to entire articles dedicated to their war work, with some of the best reporting written by the children themselves. By focusing more on the journalism of the day, rather than the secondary sources related to the economics of the war or on the volunteerism of adults of the era, this chapter strives to tell these children's stories of hard work, love, dedication, and sacrifice for their country through the eyes of those present. These children earned much praise and admiration during the war and it was those who were there with them who could tell their stories best.

JUNIOR RED CROSS QUILTS FOR SOLDIERS

In 1917, American author and poet Hermann Hagedorn released a book entitled *You Are the Hope of the World! An Appeal to the Girls and Boys of America*, in which Hagedorn called upon the nation's children to take responsibility for the future of both their own and the entire world, for "if, therefore, you live for the highest interests of America, you live at the same time for the highest of interests of the world" (p. 99). In an editorial in the *Oroville Daily Register* on February 16, 1918, the author echoed this call to action, telling the readers, "You are indeed the world's hope for democracy, for justice, for international friendship. How can we make you feel this, we older people working now to help our nation in our fight for these things? Well, one way is the Junior Red Cross" ("Join Junior Red Cross," 1918, p. 2).

One such child who found herself thinking about joining her Junior Red Cross and making quilts for soldiers was 10-year-old Bonnie Babb, a fifth grader at Marion Graded School in Kentucky. In October 1917, she wrote to her local newspaper to let them know what she planned to do to help win the war. She wrote:

> I can't go to the front and fight like soldiers, but there is something else I can do … I could help by joining the Red Cross and knit and sew for our dear boys who are going to fight for us and spend their dreadful nights in the trenches …. We can do without dressing our dolls so fine and save the scraps and make quilts for the soldiers … I can do all this and maybe more to fight this great war. (Babb, 1917, p. 2)

Children all across the country joined the newly formed Junior Red Crosses and got to work. However, the focus of this chapter will be on the work of the children within the states of Kentucky, North Carolina, South Carolina, Georgia, and Louisiana.

Kentucky Junior Red Cross

The Stephensport, Ky Junior Red Cross with its 105 members, under the direction of superintendent Mrs C.B. Waggoner, completed 17 quilts in the first six months of 1918 ("Active Red Cross," 1918, p. 1), while in Louisville, their Junior Red Cross, which was only first organized in February, had already completed eight quilts by May of that year. One of the quilts, knitted by fifth and sixth graders out of scraps of donated wool, was even displayed at the Tea Room for others to admire the work that was done. The ability of the children to accomplish so many quilts, in addition to all the other war work they did in such a short time, was due to the fact that the superintendent, O.L. Ried, along with the Board of Education, incorporated the war work into their curriculum by authorizing all the industrial work normally taught in school to be replaced by Red Cross work ("Junior Red Cross Does Good Work," 1918, p. 4). The Junior Red Cross Auxiliary of Caldwell High School in Richmond, KY also incorporated war work into their school curriculum and over the course of 1918 they made 54 quilts for soldiers and refugees. By replacing the normal handwork activities they normally did during school hours with war work instead ("Caldwell High School News," 1919, p. 1), they were able to make nine times the amount of quilts than the rest of Richmond Junior Red Cross had made from September 1917 through May 1919, which was seven ("Good Work of Junior Red Cross Appreciated," 1919, p. 1).

North Carolina Junior Red Cross

In North Carolina, the Junior Red Cross undertook an extraordinary amount of quilt work. In June 1918, the Red Cross put out an urgent call for quilts that were 65 × 90 inches and Mrs Lee Presley of Wesley Chapel, NC immediately donated a quilt. Hoping to keep this momentum, Mrs Randolph Redfearn, the chairman of the Junior Red Cross, which was established in February 1918 and had twenty-two auxiliaries, including five-colored auxiliaries, arranged for her girls to work each Monday afternoon in the Red Cross workroom to work on more quilts "Report of Junior," 1918, p. 8; ("Work of Junior," 1918, p. 4). Three weeks later they had already put together one quilt and had made squares for two more. The auxiliary in Union, NC, had made two quilts as well ("Junior Red Cross Notes," 1918a, p. 1). By the end of July, the Monroe Junior Red Cross had 18 quilts ready to be sent to Camp Wadsworth near Spartanburg, SC ("Junior Red Cross Notes," 1918b, p. 8).

The next week 68 men were sent from Union County to Camp Wadsworth to train, including Lieut. Frank Redfearn, the son of the Chairman of the Monroe Red Cross Chapter. Such a direct connection left the people of Monroe and Union County motivated to keep making quilts. While these women trusted "that none of our boys will ever be sick at Camp Wadsworth, still it is pleasant to think that our quilts may help to keep them warm should they ever find themselves in the base hospital ... we may be contributing to the comfort of our own boys in khaki" ("Junior Red Cross Notes," 1918c, p. 1). Come mid-September the Monroe Junior Red Cross had completed 25 quilts; however, with the addition of a new auxiliary out of Jackson Forest, which provided thirteen quilts, the total number of quilts rose to forty-one by the beginning of October ("Report for Junior Red Cross," 1918; p. 8; "Red Cross Auxiliaries," 1918, p. 8). With the girls working quickly, supplies began to run low, leaving Mrs Walter Crowell, the

The Child Quilters of World War I   95

Executive Secretary of the Junior Red Cross to ask, "You farmers, haven't you a pound or two that you can donate?" ("Junior Red Cross Notes," 1918d, p. 8).

Even though the Spanish Flu pandemic forced the girls to stop meeting in the workrooms and to work from home, the number of quilts did not suffer or decline. Over the next three months the Junior Red Cross of Monroe, NC, and all of its auxiliaries, made 41 additional quilts, with nearly half coming from the Walkerville, NC auxiliary ("Local and Personal," 1918, p. 5). In February of 1919, the Monroe chapter of the Red Cross received a substantial allotment from the Southern Division of the American Red Cross headquarters. Due to the Monroe chapter's previous shipments of items, showing their capability to meet the demands put upon them, headquarters classified their chapter as a Class A, which meant they consistently sent items that met all uniformity standards set by the American Red Cross. To meet the demands of the additional 48 quilts requested, the local paper urged "all patriotic ladies … to assist in the work in order that it may be ready in time" ("Local and Personal," 1919, p. 5). They no doubt accomplished their requested allotment, if their work in the second half of 1918 and Mrs Crowells declaration that they "must make 1919 a banner year in achievement" (Junior Red Cross Notes," 1919, p. 4), is an indicator of their production abilities; however, I was unable to locate any records of their work that year to confirm.

South Carolina Junior Red Cross

In South Carolina, the members of the Junior Red Cross were meeting regularly to get the work completed. In February 1918, working Tuesdays and Thursdays in the Red Cross room, The Junior Red Cross in Kingstree, SC was already hard at work on three quilts ("Red Cross Activities," 1918, p. 1). When Red Cross rooms were not available, they often gathered at the homes of others. In July 1918, the Fairfield, SC Junior Red Cross Auxiliary quilted a quilt for soldiers overseas at the home of Miss Ethyl Davies ("Fairfield Items," 1918, p. 7). That same month, the Lancaster, SC Junior Red Cross received a letter from the Southern Division of the Red Cross headquarters requesting that they send quilts "as soon as possible as they are most useful and much needed." Mrs Hugh, the director of work, asked that members of the community send in dark and light scraps of outing for the girls to work with which they immediately began constructing a quilt ("Mr Daniel," 1918, p. 1). Later in the fall, the Junior members of the Caston School Auxiliary pledged to make five more quilts because they were the only auxiliary to be organized at the time to take on work. This was surprising because, during the previous spring semester, there was 100 percent membership enrollment at 18 different schools in their county ("Much Work Done," 1918, p. 1).

Georgia Junior Red Cross

In Georgia, which has the honor of being the first state to establish a Junior Red Cross chapter in the United States (Lustrat, 1919, p. 3), at the Ira Street School in Atlanta, GA they had three classes that attained 100 percent participation in the Junior Red Cross at the beginning of 1918. The children of this auxiliary also began knitting squares for a quilt for nearby Fort McPherson during Christmas 1917 which they finished in early March. The quilt was briefly displayed at King Hardware store located on Peachtree, and according to Juanita Greer (1918a), a student at Ira Street, "We hope you saw it, for it is beautiful. Mrs John Hienz put it together for us" (p. 2). The quilt was finally presented to the hospital at the beginning of April when "the knitters of sixth and seventh grades carried our quilt to Fort McPherson, to Ward 'K'" (Greer, 1918b, p. 7). In North Georgia, another quilt was completed by the freshman members of Fassifern, GA Junior Red Cross during the fall 1918 semester as well (Graham, 1918, p. 1).

In Eastern Georgia during the summer of 1918, the seventh-grade class at Houghton in Augusta also made a knitted blanket that featured the United States flag, in which they cross-stitched the stars, that they sent to the Southern Division of the American Red Cross headquarters. After completing their quilt, the seventh-grade class encouraged the third and fourth-grade class at Houghton to donate the quilt the lower classmen had made and displayed in the window of Bailie-Edelblut's to the Red Cross as well ("Beautiful Quilt," 1918, p. 7).

Down in Southern Georgia during the Spring 1918 semester, the Junior Red Cross in Thomasville knitted 14 quilt squares, while students at Thomasville High School, Miss Merrill's School, and East Side School, knitted one quilt each ("Red Cross Report," 1918, p. 5). In nearby Americus, GA, their recently organized Junior Red Cross sent 12 quilts to the Americus Light Infantry, stationed at Fort Wheeler, in December 1917 inspiring the local papers to write, "The spirit displayed [*sic.*] by the children is a beautiful one and should be an inspiration to their elders" (Allen, 1917, p. 5). An inspiration to their elders it was not but to their peers, it may have been. In neighboring Leesburg, GA, a group of two dozen little girls who were members of the Junior Red Cross, formed their own little group that they called "Lee's Little Liberty Laborers" to supplement their time while school was out for the summer. As a group, they adopted a French orphan and in one of their letters to her in August 1918 they mentioned

> We love to work for the Red Cross .... We wish we could help in a better way to win the war and we are going to do more when school starts and we have our teacher to direct us. We are making quilts now for the soldiers. ("Lee County Children," 1918, p. 5)

While the solo efforts of Lee's Little Liberty Laborers were a most admirable action, the guidance of teachers to direct them often gave the children the boost they needed to accomplish more work. The Georgia branch of the National Congress of Mothers and Parent-Teacher associations, reported in March 1918 that the Virgil Powers school in Macon, GA had recently donated 14 quilts to Camp Wheeler that were made by the students. They also speculated that with the Junior Red Cross being actively inserted into the schools, these numbers would rise greatly as the children continued to be "engaged in patriotic work of one kind or another" ("Parent Teacher Activity," 1918, p. 3). One of the Georgia schools that also set aside time during the school day for war work was in Milledgeville. They set aside two periods each week to work, with one day for Red Cross educative work and the other for service work. For the service work, the fourth and fifth graders worked on a quilt to send to a soldier (Seventh Grade, 1918, p. 5).

Louisiana Junior Red Cross

In Louisiana, in the September 21, 1917 issue of *The Rice Belt Journal*, the weekly local paper for Jefferson Davis Parish's Landing in Welsh, LA, it was reported that Misses Ecker and Johnson, members of the Red Cross Entertainment committee, planned to make a quilt using the scraps from the Red Cross. Set to begin the next Saturday, these two women were going to organize the local school children, fifth grade and up, in the domestic science room at the local high school and have them work for three hours every Saturday afternoon starting at 1 pm. They planned to display the quilt at the State Fair in Shreveport several weeks away as part of the school exhibit ("Great Ball Game," p. 1). Two weeks later, in a section entitled "Notice to the Ladies" (1917, p. 1), the paper made mention of the quilt progress, stating "girls from several grades are busily engaged in making a quilt from the scraps left from the Red Cross garment.s"

In early November, a few days after the end of the State Fair in Shreveport, the paper reported that "the Red Cross quilt exhibited by the Welsh high school domestic science department attracted much attention and brought forth favorable comment, but those present were unable to state whether it drew a prize or not" ("Visitors to the State Fair," 1917, p. 1). A week later, the paper then reported that not only had they submitted one Red Cross scrap quilt but had displayed two of these quilts at the fair. They also reported they had completed a third and that they were now going to auction off all three quilts with the proceeds going to the Red Cross. Even though it was the children who were making the quilt, much praise was given to Misses Ecker and Johnson "for the excellent results of their efforts in this work" ("Red Cross Quilts to Be Auctioned," 1917, p. 4). The two quilts that were displayed at the fair were then auctioned off on the 11th of December and brought in a sum of $14 ("Red Cross Auto Will Go at Next Sale," 1917, p. 3) and also received first prize at the Parrish fair (Faught, 1918, p. 2). The students of the Fenton school in Welsh, LA were also hard at work. Led by Miss Gates, a teacher at the school, the 62 members turned in a four-foot by seven-foot knitted quilt in June 1918 ("Fenton Red Cross," 1918, p. 1).

THE IMPORTANCE OF JUNIOR RED CROSS WAR WORK

According to some, including the work of the Junior Red Cross in the classroom, was contradictory to the overall mission of the Junior Red Cross. In an article in the *Macon Daily Telegraph* in September 1918,

> the prime object of the Junior Red Cross is an emphasis on education. Contrary to the enlistment of a regular soldier, entrance into the Junior Auxiliary means that legitimate work and play are not to be itnerfered [*sic*] with by patriotic efforts. Second in importance is the spirit of service to humanity. Lastly, comes the duty of production. ("Junior Red Cross Red," 1918, p. 6).

However, the *Macon Daily Telegraph* had it wrong. The war was an active participant in these children's lives whether they wanted it to be or not. From nursery rhymes to paper dolls, storybooks to toy guns, it shaped their play to be patriotic in nature, and by enlisting in the Junior Auxiliary, and including war work into the education system it was not just teaching the children valuable skills that were both applicable and valuable to the real world at that time, but also gave the children the opportunity to fight in the only way that they could. For the third graders at Grant Park School, in Atlanta, GA who were putting together a quilt made from a variety of colored squares for their Junior Red Cross auxiliary in April 1918, they created a motto "If you can't fight, knit!" (Keeney, 1918a, p. 9).

The *Atlanta Journal* said it perfectly in their April 29, 1918 issue, when reporting Ashby Street School in Atlanta, GA, obtaining 100 percent membership in their Junior Red Cross chapter:

> Through the war savings society and other war activities the smaller children acquire that feeling of citizenship which comes from doing their bit in aiding their country. They also gain a habit of thrift that will be a benefit to themselves and to their country for years to come. The second grade children have been savings scraps of silk and cotton goods for quilts which they are for to make for the soldiers. They are also interested in knitting, and may be seen at recess working away with their big needles and many colors of wool.... In all of our work there has been a wonderful school spirit of loyalty, and the children feel that the opportunity to salute so great a flag each day is truly a privilege. ("Thrift and War Savings," 1918, p. 2)

A shining example of a child who felt this privilege was 14-year-old Muriel Perkins, "one of Atlanta's patriotic young girls, who has done fine war work." Featured in the August 18, 1918 issue of the *Atlanta Constitution*, along with her picture, Miss Perkins was a member of both the Junior Red Cross and a patriotic knitting club formed with eight other girls of the North Avenue Presbyterian school and had "made several quilts by herself, and has assisted in the making of others" and spent the summer of 1918 "busy devising ways and means by which she and her young associates can do the most work this fall and winter" ("A Young Patriot," p. 3).

That winter, following the end of the war, in an editorial entitled "What Can We Do?" found in the November 29, 1918 issue of the *Celina Democrat* out of Celina, OH, the president of Vassar College, Dr Henry MacCracken, had much to say about the work of the Junior Red Cross:

> "The Junior Red Cross today finds itself engaged in doing almost as many things as there are miles between the Atlantic and the Pacific, but always with one object – national service."
> "National Service" – What an ennobling idea to constantly cultivate in the minds of the young! For this one reason alone every parent should do more than encourage the activities of the Junior Red Cross. The idea of service takes patriotism for granted, and instills its best part all the time in the minds of children. But the work school children have done has been beneficial in other ways, and moreover the young people are intensely interested by it. Thoughtful and practical men complain that courses of study in the public schools are too detached from the everyday business of living. Here is where the work of the Junior Red Cross will help out. The sewing, knitting, cooking, rug-making, toy and furniture making are all as practical as brushing one's teeth. The children learn that their work must be up to the Red Cross standards, in order to be accepted, and they become painstaking. Their resourcefulness and ingenuity are stimulated and in their efforts to raise money have revealed their enterprise and thrift. Parents know that all these are the things that make for success and happiness. We know the patriotism may be taken for granted, that it lies in the hearts of nearly all Americans, but the war has seen it translated into service – to the great benefit of the children. Let us hope that the activities of the Junior Red Cross will be kept up after the war is over. (p. 6)

Dr MacCracken's hopes were realized, once the war was over, and the work for many of these children continued, such as in Newberry, SC ("Red Cross Notes," 1919, p. 7), and Madisonville, VA where many classes attained still 100 percent

The Child Quilters of World War I 99

membership during 1919 (Argyle, 1919c, p. 5). However, the mission of the Junior Red Cross moved from physical labor, like quilting for soldiers, toward education and helping war orphans in Europe. The work of these children with the Junior Red Cross during and after the war, though not paid, still served to give them a similar experience to their wage-earning counterparts. While the act of making quilts for soldiers was not something that was gendered among the children, as boys and girls alike worked tirelessly to meet the needs of the government, for girls, in particular, working was a part of the eventual path to marriage and domesticity because "wage earning was an essentially domestic obligation; their wages belonged to the family. Neither the emotional nor economic realities of working-class life prepared them to assume a role independent of this loyalty" (Tentler, 1979, p. 86).

By engaging in volunteer war work that remained within their gendered spheres, these Junior Red Cross members were practically training for their future roles as housewives. Betty Graeme, an associate editor for the suffrage journal *Woman Citizen*, lamented in the summer 1917 issue that next to all the women learning or practicing taking up arms to fight, sewing seemed "relegated to the limbo of forgotten arts." However, sarcastically she continued to say that a sewing machine was "a good thing to have in the family during wartime to place alongside of great-grandmama's spinning wheel and beneath Aunt Jemima's sampler. Just to show that you came from the right sort of stock, you know?" further reinforcing the notion that society still expected women to return to their gendered sphere upon the end of the war and marry appropriately (Jensen, 2008, p. 57).

According to a study by Claudia Goldin, the first female economics professor to receive tenure at Harvard, more than half of the female college graduates during the 1910s never had children because they had to choose between career or family (Crittenden, 2010, p. 33). The graduates of Vassar College before 1912 indicated that the main reason for attending Vassar was their desire for a career. Furthermore, during this time, women who were involved with the preparedness movement, and therefore more apt to engage in war-related work, were less college-educated than those who were part of the pacifism movement. However, Vassar graduates following World War I stated school popularity as their reason for attending. In 1923, a newspaper poll of Vassar women indicated that only 11 of the 152 women polled were seeking a career after graduation (Steinson, 1982, p. 71). Unlike previous generations, this change in the desires of female college graduates after the war may have been due to the fact that the girls who did work with the Junior Red Cross, and would have represented this generation of college graduates, may have been influenced by the praise they got for the domestic work they did during the war, such as Vassar College President MacCracken praise a few years prior, leading to their aspirations to be homemakers rather than wage workers.

NON-JUNIOR RED CROSS CHILDREN'S QUILTS FOR SOLDIERS

The Junior Red Cross were not the only children who were making quilts for soldiers. The school children of the metro Atlanta area were hard at work over the course of 1918 making quilts for the soldiers at the nearby military hospitals at Fort Mcpherson and Camp Gordon. Sometimes they met outside of school, like the fourth and fifth-grade students at W.F. Slaton School, who were knitting squares for quilts to be given to soldiers in May of 1918. They were even collecting dues to pay for the wool so that they could make as many quilts as possible for the soldiers (Clayton, 1918, p. 8).

At Tenth Street School, multiple grades were each working on quilts. The second and third graders worked on a quilt during May of 1918, with the third graders making as many as 50 squares in a week. For the second graders, the task of quilt making for the soldiers was more personal as one of their classmates, Faith Jordan, was the daughter of an officer who was stationed at Camp Gordon, GA, just outside of Atlanta (Smith, 1918a, p. 11). The quilt was finished by Mrs Fitzhugh Knox near the end of May and presented to one of the hospital units at Fort McPherson (Patterson, 1918, p. 4). After the quilt was presented the children of the second-grade class began work on a second quilt right away (Smith, 1918b, p. 3), inspiring the seventh-grade class to also begin work on a quilt. Though they had only been knitting for a short amount of time the seventh graders already had 50 squares by the beginning of June (Smith, 1918c, p. 3). By June 7th, the third-grade class had finished another quilt and the sixth-grade class had just finished the squares for theirs and was in the process of putting it together (Smith, 1918d, p. 11).

For the Junior class at Girls High, an all-girls public high school in Atlanta, GA, they sought to do "something different" than their upperclassmen who were sewing gun cases for the Red Cross. With the help of their teacher, Miss Nolan, they made "a nice, warm, comfortable, gay quilt" knitted from odd bits of wool into squares. But rather than donate it to the usual Patriots League or the school Social Service club so that it can be donated to no military unit in particular, they sent their quilt to the University of Chicago hospital unit, which happened to be at neighboring Fort McPherson at the time, in honor of their teacher who was a graduate of the University ("Girls' High Seniors," 1918, p. 6). The seventh-grade class of the Williams School (McKibben, 1918, p. 4) and the children of the second and fourth grades at Calhoun School were also working on quilts for the soldiers who had returned from France and were at the hospital at Fort McPherson (Thompson, 1918, p. 4). While over at the Fraser Street school, the seventh graders had knitted 22 squares in the early spring of 1918 for a quilt that would be sent to Camp Gordon (Miller, 1918, p. 7).

Interestingly, most of the reporting of the children's work in the metro Atlanta Georgia region was done so by children themselves. The *Atlanta Constitution* featured a weekly section that was written by the local schoolchildren about the newsworthy events at their local schools. If it weren't for the efforts of these child reporters much of the work done by these children might have been dismissed entirely or combined with the efforts of their mothers or teachers when the paper chose to feature the war work of women's civics groups. You can see this in the case of some of the quilts made by the school children of Covington, GA, who made a "number of interesting quilts of patchwork stuffed with feathers, for children's [*sic*.] beds" for the children of France. They were shipped in February of 1918 from the Southern Division of the Red Cross after they were donated there

The Child Quilters of World War I 101

by the Georgia division of the National League of Women's Service. Even though the children did the work, the assistant director of the Southern Division, W. R. Bush wrote a letter in which he praised the "good ladies responsible for this work" yet neglected to praise the children who were responsible for this contribution to the cause (Bush, 1918, p. 6).

Fortunately, other Civic groups who sent quilts on behalf of the children who made them were sure to mention their participation in the work. For example, the Patriotic League in Carrollton, GA made and sent two quilts to local hospitals in February of 1918. The first quilt, sent to the base hospital at Camp Wheeler, GA, was assembled by Mrs John Crider after squares were made by students of the Margaret Wilson Chapter based out of Maple Street school. The second quilt, which was sent to the base hospital at Fort Oglethorpe, was assembled by Mrs L.L. Bonner after squares were made by the High School Units of College Street School. These students completed these squares while still doing their regular schoolwork, leading the local paper to ask its residents to let these girls know "all the nice things said about the quilts and the patriotism that inspired the accomplishment of the task as well as the other things they have been doing for 'our boys at the front'" ("Patriotic League," 1918, p. 1). Then during a March 1918 rally for the Patriotic League in Macon, where 150 young women were present, as the songs were song and the entertainment sent laughter through the room, a quilt knitted by the students of the Whittle school was placed on exhibition for all the attendees to admire ("Patriotic League Rally," 1918, p. 6). Later that summer, the Gainesville, GA Chapter of the United Daughters of the Confederacy had their auxiliary group, the Children of the Confederacy, knitting a quilt for soldiers ("Children Confederacy," 1918, p. 1).

QUILTS BY THE CHILDREN OF THE
PRESBYTERIAN OF THE SOUTH CHURCH

One of the most active groups in the South, outside the Junior Red Cross, that used children to make quilts for soldiers was the Presbyterian of the South Church in Richmond, VA. In December 12, 1917, issue of the weekly newsletter for the church in the Children's sermon section, Helen Argyle, influenced by the recent call from the Red Cross to women stateside to make quilts for hospitals, put out a call to her children's readers to send in quilt squares so that they could have a quilt done by Christmas to send to the Red Cross. "I have one square nearly finished," she wrote, "and my sister has two; so, you see, our quilt is already begun. Who will make the next square?" She requested that all the squares "must measure six inches on each of the four sides ... knit or crochet, any wool, any needles, but all must be 6 inches square, or they won't fit together." Readers were directed to send her the squares and she would sew them all together. The quilt would be made of 80 squares put together in eight rows of ten squares, making the quilt 48 by 60 inches in size. Within one week five additional quilt squares, some made in two shades of green and another that was half red and half blue, had been made and sent in for the quilt. Because their newsletter, which was published out of Atlanta,

102 AISHA MANUS

GA circulated to readers across the South, this gave them an extensive reach to children from all. Soon quilt squares began to arrive en masse, like the six squares that came from a Sunday school in Wedgefield, SC just before Christmas (Argyle, 1917a, 1917b, 1917c, 1919b).

At the beginning of January 1918, they had a total of 46 squares and by mid-January the church had received 24 more squares, bringing the total to 70 squares. Some of these squares came from a pair of sisters, aged 11 and 7, in Harrisonburg, VA who learned to knit from their grandmother so they could send in squares. The older sister, Evelyn, knitted her own red, white, and blue square, while her sister, Sue, knitted the red cross that went on the gray square her grandma knitted. With the help of these squares, the first quilt was completed by the time the January 23, 1918 issue of the newsletter was sent out, allowing Helen Argyle to describe it, telling the readers, "Right in the middle I put an American flag, a French flag, a Red Cross, and one marked U.S." She also mentioned that she already had plenty of squares to begin work on a second quilt, as 91 squares had arrived that week and "will just keep right on working and making more quilts to help the Red Cross as long as you want to; and I know you want to do all you can." Children kept sending them in, like ten-year-old Ethel who, "got my grandmother's cedar kneedles [sic.] out and went to work," sending in four squares for the quilt (Argyle, 1918a, 1918b, 1918c, 1918d, 1918e).

By the February 6, 1918 newsletter another 257 squares had arrived, enabling Miss Argyle to finish three more quilts. On one of the quilts, she "made a big Red Cross flag of five red squares and four white ones and put it right in the middle." She also let the readers know that "some soldiers who saw one of our quilts said that they thought it was fine. They liked the flags and the Red Cross so much." By the February 20 issue, Miss Argyle had completed six total quilts and received 645 total squares. Just one week later she had received an additional 117 squares, bringing the total to 762 squares. By the end of the month, nine quilts had been completed and 877 squares had been sent in (Argyle, 1918f, 1918g, 1918h, 1918i).

In mid-March the Junior Missionary Society of Fairfield, VA sent in 47 squares, the largest number sent from any one group. These squares along with the others that had been sent so far brought the number to 1,100 squares and enough to make a total of ten quilts. By the end of March, Miss Argyle had completed 13 quilts from the 1,182 squares readers had sent in, and by the beginning of April readers of the Presbyterian of the South had sent in another 64 squares, making the total 1,246 squares. Squares that week came from children in Katrine, VA, Amelia, VA, and Chase City, VA (Argyle, 1918k, 1918l, 1918m).

At the beginning of May, 18 quilts had been completed and two more were started. This was in part due the donation of three quilts that were completed and sent by readers of the newsletter. One quilt came from the Philatheas of the First Church in Richmond, VA and two came from the Philthea class of Granite, VA. A few squares came from an 11-year-old girl in Gum Spring, VA who wrote in to let everyone know that she "made these squares with the knitting-needles my Great-Grandmother used to knit socks for the slaves before the war between the states." By July, readers had sent in 1,435 squares, and a group of girls in Staunton, VA had sent in an entire quilt, bringing the total number of quilts completed to 22. As it was summer, Miss Argyle made sure to tell her readers to not

The Child Quilters of World War I 103

stop the momentum because "we are not as busy as when we are in school and we can do good work now getting ready for the winter." And the momentum was not stopped (Argyle, 1918n, 1918o, 1918p).

Over the summer she received quilt squares from across the South. In Jonesboro, GA two eight-year-old twin boys each knitted squares and sent them in, prompting her to tell the boys, "It is good to be soldiers in our own places, and do our part, isn't it?" In addition, the Miriam Band from Staunton, VA sent an entire quilt, and the Philathea Class finished their third quilt. This brought the total number of quilts to 25. After seeing much success when the children were out of school over the summer, once again Miss Argyle encouraged her readers to knit in their free time, especially "now that so many schools are closed, and we are afraid to go about much for fear we will get influenza." By the beginning of December, a total of 1,653 squares were sent in. Throughout 1918, in total 35 quilts were finished from both the squares and full quilts sent. However, it is not possible to know how many were sent to the soldiers because as Miss Argyle wrote to her readers, "some went to the hospitals here, some to the hospitals 'over there', some to the Belgians, and I am saving two for our French children" (Argyle, 1918r, 1918s, 1918t, 1918v, 1919a).

The 35 quilts created by Miss Argyle and her readers are a great example of how quilting, as war work, is conducive to the work of children. Quilting is unobtrusive, it can be done anywhere with anyone or alone. It can be done in short bursts or for long periods. A sense of self can be maintained through quilting when the world is turned around. The nature of the work also allowed for children of all ages to participate, as evidenced by all the quilt squares sent in from children of various ages across her readership. These quilts taught the children that the smallest of actions, such as sending in a single quilt square, can lead to large results, and that their work mattered. That they mattered. Juliette Low, founder of the Girls Scouts, understood this well. According to her, "Needlework is good for all of us; it rests and calms the mind. You can think peacefully over all the worries of Europe whilst you are stitching. Sewing generally solves all the toughest problems, chiefly other peoples" (Low, 1917, p. 107).

QUILTS FOR ORPHANS

In the Second Inaugural Address of Abraham Lincoln, he asks the nation "to bind up the nation's wounds; to care for him who shall have borne the battle, and for his widow, and his orphan" (1865). This service to the orphans of war continued into World War I but this time it was the children of our allies as well. In the first few months of 1917, the Germans deported thousands of French citizens to Belgium. Then in July of 1917, the American Red Cross began the relief effort of repatriating them. One woman, Elizabeth Ashe, the chief of nursing service for the Children's Bureau, wrote to her friends in October 1917 upon receiving 680 repatriating French children:

It was the most tragic sight imaginable. Two-thirds of the children were taken from their parents and sent to France to be supported. These children were facing starvation and their mothers parted with them to save them. These children were tired and forlorn after a three days' trip,

but shouting at the tops of their voices, "Vive la France!" with joy in their faces at being again
in France.... These poor "repatries" seem to have such faith in the American that they trust us
implicitly. (Gavin, 1997, pp. 183–184)

It was letters like this that helped to inspire American children to support the
children of Europe with their quilting.

Quilts for Armenian Orphans

During World War I, Armenia suffered a devastating genocide at the hands of
the Ottoman-Turkish empire which was fighting on the same side as the Central
Powers, comprised Germany and Austria-Hungry. The horrors of this genocide
were shocking. Armenian babies were buried alive in the trenches with the bodies of their executed parents, mothers drowned their children in the Euphrates
River to prevent the Turks from taking them, and regions "where thousands of
bleached skeletons on each side of the way told the story of a waterless [*sic.*]
journey across the plains in August." More than 485,000 Armenians were forced
to flee their country by January 1916, and by May 1917 only 112,000 survived,
the rest having either starved to death or massacred. Without the help of the
American Committee for the Armenian and Syrian Relief in New York, the
numbers would have been greater ("How Turks Put Armenians to Death," 1915,
p. 11). Fleeing for their lives, the Armenian people had little to their names.
"One man told of how one blanket, or quilt, was made to serve three families,
by the device of sleeping in three shifts of eight hours each" (Religious Rambler,
1917, p. 10).

In the summer of 1920, Helen Argyle of the Presbyterian of the South Church
in Richmond, VA, who had previously sent quilts to Belgian and French orphans,
sent one quilt to Armenian orphans. The quilt was sent to Miss Argyle by the
Betsy Ross Knitting Club, and she suspected that it had been started by the children when she was looking for quilts and squares for soldiers through the Red
Cross a few years before. Not wanting the quilt to go to waste, she decided that
"the Armenian orphans need this one more than the French do, so I am going to
send it right along and it will be there in time for cold weather" (Argyle, 1920, p. 4).

The limited number of quilts made and sent to Armenia may have been due
in part to a news story that circulated in several newspapers throughout 1915
and 1916 about the Armenian genocide. In his descriptions of the war, author
Frederic Haskin described a time when those fleeing the country

had to climb into the high mountains and, being almost without clothes, the missionaries gave
certain of them quilts to protect them from the cold. One mother received a quilt but asked
whether, after she had passed the mountain, she should discard the cover or carry her babe, as
she had not enough strength to carry both. All along the rough babies are offered for sale for
pittances. ("Armenians and the War," 1915, p. 10)

Knowing that a mother may choose the quilt over her own child would be
quite the deterrent, especially for those who saw these children as worthy of their
donations only because "they are Christians and if allowed to live will serve
Christianity [which] commends them especially to Christian America" ("Others
Contribute to Near East Relief," 1922, p. 5).

The Child Quilters of World War I 105

Quilts for Belgian Orphans

In the March 21, 1918, issue of *The Union Times*, of Union, SC, there was an article about a quilting bee that took place at the home of Mrs W.M. Gregory in Tinker Creek, SC. After two quilts were made, the bee was followed "by a bountiful turkey dinner. Everyone was glad that Herbert Hoover was not around to see the loaded table. He would have eaten too much" ("Tinker," 1918, p. 3). This tongue-in-cheek humor of the time related to the fact that Herbert Hoover was the Director of the United States Food Administration. He held this position concurrently with his position as Chairman for Relief to Belgium. Formed on August 8, 1914, the mission was to provide relief to Belgium during and after its occupation by German troops ("The Babies of Belgium," 1915, p. 4). During its time it raised more than $20 million and sent hundreds, if not thousands, of quilts to the people of Belgium (Maxwell & Walker, 2008, p. 26).

In Richmond, VA the Presbyterian of the South Church began making quilts for orphans in March of 1918. This was due in large part to the generous number of quilt squares Miss Helen Argyle received while soliciting six-inch squares from her child readers to make Red Cross quilts. She decided to also make quilts for a "French baby out of some of the lovely white, light blue and pink squares that have come in" because "they just look like they were meant for a baby... [and] they must be needing warm covers too." She made a second baby quilt that month, however, both quilts were sent to Belgium instead of France (Argyle, 1918j, p. 6; 1918m, p. 6). Down in Donaldsonville, LA, the Junior Red Cross Auxiliary from St. James High School sent in three quilts by mid-April 1918. Under the direction of Miss Jeannie Simpson, a teacher at the school, "these patriotic workers" sent in an additional seven quilts two weeks later. The quilts were intended for "the little destitute Belgians" (Pujos, 1918, p. 3; Singer, 1918, p. 3). That summer the Children of the Confederacy auxiliary unit of the Margaret Gaston Chapter of the United Daughters of the Confederacy, of Chester, SC, had each of their 12 members make a quilt for a Belgian baby (Argyle, 1918r, p. 6). Come fall, in Canfield, OH, the students of the Turner Street school began making a quilt for the orphans of Belgium in September 1918 ("Turner Street," 1918, p. 1).

The work of these children making quilts for these Belgian orphans did not go unnoticed. During a visit to Washington, D.C. in June 1918, Queen Elizabeth of Belgium was photographed inspecting colorful quilts that were made by the children of Dennison Public School for the children in the orphanages in Belgium ("Here and There," 1918, p. 69).

Quilts for French Orphans

While there were many successful efforts to send quilts to Armenia and Belgium, the focal point of American humanitarian efforts remained largely in France after the war ended. As the bulk of the war was fought on French soil, many children during World War I in France found themselves orphans after losing one or both of their parents. For those in the United States, 53,513 American men were killed in action (Gavin, 1997, p. 63), resulting in about 6,000 orphans according to a conservative estimate from the War Department. For the men in France, who had been fighting since the beginning and averaged 2,000 deaths a day during the last five months of 1914 (Kuhlman, 2012, p. 54, 87), an estimated 1,385,300 men died in battle or went missing (Cruttwell, 1997, p. 631). However, because these men were considered war heroes, their orphan children, unlike typical child victims whose parents are often blamed for their status, benefited from their father's sacrifices in large part due to the public romanticization of war heroes. This influenced many Americans to step up and "adopt" the estimated 250,000 orphaned French children for 10 cents a day or $36.50 a year. As one Georgia newspaper so generously put it:

> The most beautiful of all the war work is that of which we hear the least. In it there are no uniforms; no crosses of honor; no citations for fidelity or courage; no public attest of "well done." It is the work of caring for the little children of France whose fathers have been killed in the battles, or who are held in enemy prison camps. It is an organized work, wit[h] officers[,] rules[,] and headquarters offices. ("Talking It Over," 1919, p. 2)

Because the adoption of French children was only a financial sponsorship, the relationship with these children was often one of only letters and occasional gifts. For some, these gifts were quilts made especially for them. In August 1918, the War Relief Association of Virginia sent a child-sized quilt to the *Comite Franco-American Pour Le Protection Des Enfants De La Frontero*. This patriotic-inspired quilt, which was made of 30 white squares, each with a different design, the groundwork in blue and outlined in red, was made by four girls. These four girls, Mary Eulalie Stearns, Elizabeth Thomas, Elizabeth Hardwicke, and Loulie Shore, fully lined and quilted it too. The quilt included pictures of birds, people, animals, and fruit "so that the child who looks at it will forget for a time any bad feelings of unhappy thoughts." They also took photographs of the quilt as they made it and included them with a little pamphlet entitled "A Love Story." Inside the pamphlet they wrote:

> When people love each other, the first thing they do is give a present – isn't it so? Sometimes the love is between people who have never seen each other, and that is the kind of love in this story. Four little girls – Mary and Loulie and the two Elizabeths – felt such a great love and sympathy for the sick and unhappy children in France that they determined to form themselves into a club and make something for their sad little sisters across the sea. ("Little Girls," 1918, p. 4)

They called themselves the After-Supper Porch Club and they met regularly throughout June and July, often sewing until 9 p.m., and each member brought one cent dues to the meeting to help pay for the quilt. If they missed a meeting they owed two cents. When they finished the quilt, they had a little ice cream party but felt "sorry that their little French friends couldn't have come with them." So, they vowed that "the red, white and blue in their hearts will not fade, and sometimes they will send something else they have made" ("Little Girls," 1918, p. 4).

In nearby Richmond, VA Miss Helen Argyle received a letter from one of her child readers in November 1918. The child suggested that they "go 'over the top' like we did with the soldier quilts and be able to help several children." Taking that into account, by January 1919 she had made more quilts and was "saving two for our French Children" (Argyle, 1918u, 1919a).

CONCLUSION

Bright and colorful quilts were a prized possession at the hospitals as the "gay knitted squares go to make up a cheery covering for invalid soldiers or refugees that is as bright as 'Jacob's coat of many colors'" ("Ship Military Relief Supplies," 1918, p. 8). Creating such colorful pieces was a task perfect for the youthful perspective of the child. When 15 fifth-grade boys, "between baseball games and boy scout drills," along with 19 girls in their grade, of the Breck school in Germantown, PA made a 110 square "all-wool quilt of many colors," for the local Naval hospital, the medical director, Sergeant Pickerel, "promptly detailed it to the use for the crippled boys in the surgical ward" ("Boys and Girls," 1918, p. 2). In the Margaret Will Hut at Camp Stuart, VA, a brightly colored quilt made by the sixth-grade class at the John W. Daniel School in Newport News, VA, served too as an item of comfort for convalescent soldiers and the relatives visiting them ("Quilt for Hut," 1918, p. 2).

With their quilts often ending up at their local military hospitals, these young children understood the importance of their bright and colorful quilts on the morale of the convalescent soldiers. Just ask Eunice Wheeler, a student at Georgia Avenue in Atlanta, GA. When writing about the second and third-grade students at her school who made a quilt for a soldier in May 1918, the quilt had "many bright colors in it and I know that the soldiers who sleep under it will think of the little girls who made it and hope to be able to thank them someday" (Wheeler, 1918, p. 4). Even young Eunice knew that the colorful quilts were a welcome distraction from the harsh realities of the war and the sufferings that they endured.

Miss Schuyler, the great-granddaughter of Alexander Hamilton and a surviving leader of the New York branch of the United States Sanitary Commission during the Civil War, also understood the value of children's participation in the war to end these sufferings. Addressing the pupils of the Louisa Lee Schuyler Public School in New York, on May 2, 1917, she proclaimed, "But I know all that the sufferings of war are not to be compared with the joy of sacrifices made for one's country. It is that which lifts us above the sufferings" (Aldrich & Brow, 1918, pp. 1, 3–4). And the children desperately sought to lessen the sufferings and burdens of the soldiers overseas and bring joy to them instead. Their "knitted squares which are made into quilts give evidence that the primary grades are a[t] work" ("Junior Red Cross Auxiliary," 1918, p. 2), like the second graders at Grant Park school in Atlanta, who were "knitting very fast for they have decided not to leave one soldier cold during the next winter" (Keeney, 1918b, p. 3). The children felt it was up to them, and them alone, to care for every last solider.

While this information in this chapter is far from complete, as most of the focus is on the children of the Southeast region of the United States, it was not only found there. In Oklahoma,

the superintendent of one of the boarding schools for girls of the five civilized tribes of Oklahoma declared the girls are deeply interested in all war work and respond readily... [where] they utilize the scraps from the hospital garments making quilt blocks ... [and] Commissioner Sells believes that the national spirit which President Wilson and other statesmen foresee as a result of the war will be splendidly exemplified by the Indian. ("Girls Deeply Interested," 1918, p. 7).

And on the west coast, in Orange County, CA,

> The school children realize that this is not a war of army against army entirely. They realize that the combined forces of all the people of the nation must be brought to bear to win for the freedom of the world from the misrule of the Hohenzoilerns. ("School Children Do Their Bit," 1918, p. 11)

Children all across the nation were active participants in this war work and they were expected to do their part just like the adult. As the *Bakersfield Morning Echo* so graciously put it in their March 15, 1918 issue,

> President Wilson showed his usual wisdom when he organized the Junior Red Cross. If you give men opportunity, opportunity will give you men, and following, if you give children work to do there will always be children to do it. ("Junior Red Cross," 1918, p. 3)

REFERENCES
PRIMARY SOURCES

Aldrich, R., & Brow, W. A. (1918). *Before the Red Cross: Personal reminiscences of relief work for soldiers in the north during the Civil War by two members of the United States Sanitary Commission; together with a brief historical account of the commission.* American Red Cross Library.

Angell, C. W. (December, 1917). *Wartime activities of significance to women: One thousand dollars for the Red Cross can be raised on a memorial quilt.* The Modern Priscilla.

Hagedorn, H. (1917). *You are the hope of the world! An appeal to the girls and boys of America.* The Macmillan Company.

Lincoln, A. (1865, March 4). *Abraham Lincoln papers: Series 3. General Correspondence 1837 to 1897: Abraham Lincoln, March 4, 1865 Second Inaugural Address; endorsed by Lincoln* [Manuscript/Mixed Material]. https://www.loc.gov/item/mal4361300/

Low, J. (1917). *Handbook for girl scouts: How girls can help their country.* Press of M.B. & D.S. Rich Co.

Our History. (n.d.). *A brief history of the American Red Cross.* https://www.redcross.org/content/dam/redcross/National/history-full-history.pdf

Georgia Newspapers (Chronological Order)

Allen, H. B. (1917, December 10). Junior Red Cross. *The Americus Times Recorder*, 5.

Bush, W. R. (1918, February 2). Garments for French children. *The Atlanta Journal*, 6.

(1918, February 7). Patriotic League doing good work. *The Carroll Free Press*, 1.

McKibben, L. L. (1918, March 2). Seventh grade of Williams making quilts for soldiers. *The Atlanta Journal*, 4.

Greer, J. (1918a, March 17). Ira Street School. *The Atlanta Constitution*, 2.

Greer, J. (1918, March 17). Parent–teacher activity. *The Atlanta Constitution*, 3.

Greer, J. (1918, March 17). Patriotic League rally. *The Macon News*, 6.

Greer, J. (1918, March 21). Red Cross report. *The Daily Times-Enterprise*, 5.

Greer, J. (1918, March 30). Girls' high seniors busy with graduation books. *The Atlanta Journal*, 6.

Miller, D. (1918, April 7). Fraser Street School. *The Atlanta Constitution*, 7.

Greer, J. (1918b, April 7). Ira Street School. *The Atlanta Constitution*, 7.

Keeney, K. E. (1918a, April 28). Grant Park. *The Atlanta Constitution*, p. 9.

(1918, April 29). Thrift and war savings work in the Atlanta public schools. *The Atlanta Journal*, 2.

Smith, S. (1918a, May 12). Tenth Street School. *The Atlanta Constitution*, 11.

Patterson, M. (1918, May 18). Tenth Second Grades Make Quilt for Soldiers. *The Atlanta Constitution*, 4.

Clayton, S. (1918, May 19). W.F. Slaton School. *The Atlanta Constitution*, 8.

Wheeler, E. (1918, May 25). School prize is won by Georgia Avenue. *The Atlanta Constitution*, 4.

The Child Quilters of World War I   109

Thompson, J. (1918, May 25). Returned American soldiers to be given quilts by Calhoun. *The Atlanta Constitution*, 4.
Smith, S. (1918b, May 26). Tenth Street School. *The Atlanta Constitution*, 3.
Keeney, K. E. (1918b, May 26). Grant Park School. *The Atlanta Constitution*, 3.
Smith, S. (1918c, June 2). Tenth Street School. *The Atlanta Constitution*, 3.
Smith, S. (1918d, June 9). Tenth Street School. *The Atlanta Constitution*, 11.
(1918, June 18), Beautiful quilt made by seventh grade Houghton girls. *The Augusta Herald*, 7.
(1918, July 14). Girls deeply interested. *The Atlanta Constitution*, 7.
(1918, July 24). Children Confederacy. *Gainesville News*, 1.
(1918, August 18). A young patriot. *The Atlanta Constitution*, 3.
(1918, August 21). Lee county children. *Americus Times-Recorder*, 5.
(1918, September 15). Junior Red Cross ready to begin work as schools open. *Macon Daily Telegraph*, 6.
Seventh Grade. (1918, November 6). Junior Red Cross doing splendid work. *The Milledgeville News*, 5.
(1919, March 15). Talking it over. *The True Citizen*, 2.
Lustrat, E. L. (1919, August 22). Woman's council of national defense makes unusual report. *The Weekly Banner*, 3.

Louisiana Newspapers (Chronological Order):

(1917, September 21). A great ball game Tuesday afternoon. *The Rice Belt Journal*, 1.
(1917, October 5). Notice to the ladies. *The Rice Belt Journal*, 1.
(1917, November 9). Visitors to the state fair are well pleased. *The Rice Belt Journal*, 1.
(1917, November 16). Red Cross quilts to be auctioned soon. *The Rice Belt Journal*, 4.
(1917, December 14.) Red Cross auto will go at next sale. *The Rice Belt Journal*, 3.
Faught, W. E. (1918, February 18). Red Cross department. *The Rice Belt Journal*, 2.
Pujos, E. C. (1918, April 20). Red Cross notes. *The Donaldsonville Chief*, 3.
Singer, F. (1918, May 4). Red Cross notes. *The Donaldsonville Chief*, 3.
(1918, June 21). Fenton Red Cross. *The Rice Belt Journal*, 1.

North Carolina Newspapers (Chronological Order)

The Religious Rambler. (1917, April 22). Turkey and Bulgaria not to break with America. *The Wilmington Dispatch*, 10.
(1917, October 15). How Turks put Armenians to death. *Hickory Daily Record*, 11.
(1918, June 7). Work of Junior Red Cross. *The Monroe Journal*, 4.
(1918a, June 28). Junior Red Cross notes. *The Monroe Journal*, 1.
(1918b, July 26). Junior Red Cross notes. *The Monroe Journal*, 8.
(1918c, August 9). Junior Red Cross notes. *The Monroe Journal*, 1.
(1918, September 20). Report for Junior Red Cross. *The Monroe Journal*, 8.
(1918, October 1). Red Cross auxiliaries. *The Monroe Journal*, 8.
(1918d, October 4). Junior Red Cross notes. *The Monroe Journal*, 8.
(1918, December 10). Local and personal. *The Monroe Journal*, 5.
Graham, E. B. (1918, December 26). Fassiefern news. *French Broad Hustler*, 1.
(1919, January 10). Junior Red Cross notes. *The Monroe Journal*, 4.
(1919, February 14). Local and personal. *The Monroe Journal*, 5.
(1922, March 3). Others contribute to Near East relief. *The Daily Times*, 5.

South Carolina Newspapers (Chronological Order):

(1917, December 6). What can we do? *The Barnwell People-Sentinel*, 7.
(1918, February 28). Red Cross activities in Williamsburg. *The County Record*, 1.
(1918, March 2). Junior Red Cross auxiliary. *The Watchman and Southron*, 2.
(1918, March 21). Tinker. *The Union Times*, 3.
(1918, July 31). Fairfield items. *Keowee Courier*, 7.

(1918, August 2). Mr Daniel talk to Red Cross folk. *The Lancaster New*, 1.
(1918, November 29). Much work done by the Red Cross. *The Lancaster News*, 1.
(1919, September 9). Red Cross notes. *The Herald and News*, 7.

Virginia Newspapers (Chronological Order):

Argyle, H. (1917a, December 12). Knitting for soldiers. *The Presbyterian of the South*, 5.
Argyle, H. (1917b, December 19). Our quilt. *The Presbyterian of the South*, 6.
Argyle, H. (1917c, December 26). Six squares for our quilt. *The Presbyterian of the South*, 5.
Argyle, H. (1918a, January 2). Questions about our quilt. *The Presbyterian of the South*, 5.
Argyle, H. (1918b, January 16). Our quilt grows. *The Presbyterian of the South*, 4.
Argyle, H. (1918c, January 16). Three splendid squares. *The Presbyterian of the South*, 6.
Argyle, H. (1918d, January 23). One quilt finished. *The Presbyterian of the South*, 5.
Argyle, H. (1918e, January 30). Want to work. *The Presbyterian of the South*, 4.
Argyle, H. (1918f, February 6). Four quilts. *The Presbyterian of the South*, 5,
Argyle, H. (1918g, February 20). Our quilts. *The Presbyterian of the South*, 4.
Argyle, H. (1918h, February 28). Quilt squares. *The Presbyterian of the South*, 5.
Argyle, H. (1918i, March 6). Our ninth quilt. *The Presbyterian of the South*, 4.
Argyle, H. (1918j, March 13). Red Cross quilts. *The Presbyterian of the South*, 6.
Argyle, H. (1918k, March 20). Hospital quilts. *The Presbyterian of the South*, 5.
Argyle, H. (1918l, March 27). Red Cross quilts. *The Presbyterian of the South*, 4.
Argyle, H. (1918m, April 3). Red Cross. *The Presbyterian of the South*, 6.
Argyle, H. (1918n, May 1). Red Cross work. *The Presbyterian of the South*, 4.
Argyle, H. (1918o, May 15). Historic needles. *The Presbyterian of the South*, 6.
Argyle, H. (1918p, July 10). Quilt squares. *The Presbyterian of the South*, 5.
(1918, July 21). Quilt for hut. *Daily Press*, 2.
Argyle, H. (1918q, July 24). Quilts for Belgian babies. *The Presbyterian of the South*.
Argyle, H. (1918r, August 7). Red Cross quilts. *The Presbyterian of the South*, 6.
Argyle, H. (1918s, August 21). Twin knitters. *The Presbyterian of the South*, 5.
(1918, August 22). Little girls send messages of cheer. *Richmond Times-Dispatch*, 4.
Argyle, H. (1918t, October 23). Quilt squares. *The Presbyterian of the South*, 5.
Argyle, H. (1918u, November 6). Over the top. *The Presbyterian of the South*, 5.
Argyle, H. (1918v, November 27). Quilt squares. *The Presbyterian of the South*, 6.
Argyle, H. (1919a, January 8). Will save candy pennies. *The Presbyterian of the South*, 4.
Argyle, H. (1919b, January 15). Thanksgiving dollar. *The Presbyterian of the South*, 6.
Argyle, H. (1919c, February 12). Our dollar. *The Presbyterian of the South*, 5.
Argyle, H. (1920, July 21). Betsy Ross knitting club. *The Presbyterian of the South*, p. 4.
(1921, April 17). Tell of Chinese aid. *Richmond Times*, 2.

Various States Newspapers (Chronological Order):

(1915, March 15). The babies of Belgium. *The Arizona Republican*, 4.
Haskin, F. (1915, October 1). Armenians and the war. *Evening Post*, p. 10.
Babb, B. (1917, October 4). What I can do to win this war. *Crittenden Record-Press*, 2.
(1918, February 16). Join the Junior Red Cross without delay. *Oroville Daily Register*, 2.
Bemus, H. (1918, February 28). School children do their bit to help win the Great War. *Santa Ana Daily Register*, 11.
(1918, March 15). Junior Red Cross. *Bakersfield Morning Echo*, 3.
(1918, May 3). Junior Red Cross does good work. *The Hartford Republican*, 4.
(1918, June 11). Ship military relief supplies. *The San Bernadino Country Sun*, 8.
(1918, June 12). Active Junior Red Cross. *The Breckenridge News*, 1.
(1918, June 30). Here and there. *Evening Star*, 69.
(1918, September 20). Boys and girls in knitting. *Fulton County Tribune*, 2.
(1918, September 27). Turner Street. *The Mahoning Dispatch*, 1.

The Child Quilters of World War I 111

(1918, November 29). What can we do? *The Celina Democrat*, 6.
(1919, February 12). Caldwell High School news. *Richmond Daily Register*, 1.
(1919, May 27). Good work of Junior Red Cross appreciated. *Richmond Daily Register*, 1.

SECONDARY SOURCES

Crittenden, A. (2010). *The price of motherhood: Why the most important job in the world is still the least valued*. Picador.

Cruttwell, C. R. M. F. (1997). *History of the Great War: 1914–1918*. Chicago Review Press.

Gavin, L. (1997). *American women in World War I: They also served*. University Press of Colorado.

Jensen, K. (2008). *Mobilizing Minerva: American women in the First World War*. University of Illinois Press.

Kuhlman, E. (2012). *Of little comfort: War widows, fallen soldiers, and the remaking of the nation after the Great War*. New York University Press.

Maxwell, D. G., & Walker, P. (2008). *Shaping the humanitarian world*. Taylor & Francis Group.

Steinson, B. J. (1982). *American women's activism in World War I*. Garland.

Tentler, L. W. (1979). *Wage–earning women: Industrial work and family life in the United States, 1900–1930*. Oxford University Press.

Veblen, T. (1994). *The theory of the leisure class*. Penguin Books.

CHAPTER 6

UNVEILING SUDAN'S YOUTH: HUMANITARIAN TALES AND THE UNFOLDING RIGHTS AGENDA IN SUDAN

Sonali Jha

Ohio University, USA

ABSTRACT

Sudan's challenges are deeply rooted in a complex web of societal, political, and health-related issues. The nation is currently experiencing a challenging period that is impacting various aspects of human life, including the healthcare system for the youth, who are significantly impacted by this crisis that has persisted for a decade. Sudan, located in northeastern Africa, is an Arab nation and a member of the Greater Horn of Africa, along with Ethiopia and South Sudan. Despite its strategic location near the Nile River – a hub for global oil trade and other merchandise – it does not possess any military equipment. Its history, unfortunately, is marked by prolonged social conflicts. These conflicts have significantly affected essential infrastructures, social services, and the overall well-being of the population. We examine the conflict through humanitarian and socio-economic factors affecting Sudan and its people. This chapter explores the role of global economic forces and international relations in Sudan's ability to address these challenges. Secondly, we explore the social structures, power dynamics, and interdependencies, examining how institutions and societal functions hinder comprehensive issue resolution through structural functionalism. Lastly, we will analyze the legal recognition and protection as

---

Children and Youth as 'Sites of Resistance' in Armed Conflict
Sociological Studies of Children and Youth, Volume 34, 113–131
Copyright © 2025 by Sonali Jha
Published under exclusive licence by Emerald Publishing Limited
ISSN: 1537-4661/doi:10.1108/S1537-466120240000034007

foundational elements for human rights and assess the acknowledgment of rights, its absence influences the endurance of multifaceted challenges like health care and educational system by the Right to have Rights.

Keywords: Sudan; social conflicts; children; power dynamics; human rights

INTRODUCTION

British colonial rule in Sudan resulted in the country's separation into North and South Sudan in 2011 (Kumsa, 2017). This split, like India's partition, emphasized religious and tribal divisions (Shah, 2023, 2024a). Civil conflicts erupted, characterized by bloodshed and a loss of faith in democracy (Breidlid, 2014; Rolandsen & Daly, 2016; Shah, 2013). In 1989, Omar Al Bashir took control in a military coup, intensifying tensions between the north and south of Sudan. The South desired independence, sparking rebellions, particularly in the Darfur region. Al Bashir's government exacerbated tribal tensions, reminiscent of the Taliban's radicalization strategy. External pressures, such as the Soviet–Afghan War, exacerbated the situation, with neighboring countries and extreme groups contributing to the chaos. Efforts to keep South Sudan united failed, and the country obtained independence in 2011. However, challenges remained, including economic hardship and human rights violations by the Rapid Support Force (RSF; previously known as the Janjaweed) (Breidlid, 2014; Collins, 2008; Nyadera, 2018).

New leaders have risen in Sudan, with Lal Barhan becoming president through military support in 2019. Barhan, along with his deputy Mohammed Hamdan Pour, worked together despite differences. Barhan ousted Omar Al Bashir with the backing of the army and tribal alliances, leading to the formation of the RSF. Conflict arose as Barhan sought control, causing clashes between the army and RSF. On April 15, 2023,[1] violence erupted in the capital, endangering civilians as both sides fired upon residential areas (Middleton & O'keefe, 2006; Sawant, 1998). The civil war has left no one safe. The desert may seem vast in Africa, but the reality is different, especially in the region known as the Greater Horn of Africa, which includes countries like Ethiopia, Somalia, South Sudan, Kenya, and Uganda. This area is crucial because of its water resources. However, conflicts have always been present, and external powers like the USA, China, and Russia, along with countries like Saudi Arabia, have interests here. The strategic location near the Red Sea and the Gulf of Aden is significant, as it's close to the Middle East and oil resources. Controlling this area means controlling a significant chunk of world trade with the potential for significant tax revenues (Bosworth et al., 2005; Shay, 2019). Recent events, such as the traffic chaos in the Suez Canal in 2021,[2] highlight the importance of this narrow strip for global trade.

Trade between India and Saudi Arabia also passes through this route, making it even more strategically important (Ehteshami & Murphy, 2013; Morton, 1989). Some countries aim to control oil supplies, which can lead to higher oil prices for ordinary people. Countries like Russia and China have significant interest in the region due to its vast reserves of natural resources and eventually looking to strategically invest in building ports and increase trade in the weapons industry making them powerful partners in global trade. Sudan's coastline on the Red Sea is attracting attention from the UAE and Russia which are looking to establish military bases there for strategic purposes (Ehteshami & Murphy, 2013; Ramani, 2021). In February 2023, the Sudanese army rejected Russia's attempt to build a base but eventually allowed it. Russia has promised weapons and advanced fighter jets to Sudan and has been exploiting Sudan's gold mines since 2017. China is also heavily involved in Sudan through its Belt and Road Initiative, investing in infrastructure projects, and dominating sectors like oil and healthcare (Ramani, 2021; Vertin, 2019). Egypt, which shares a border and the Nile River with Sudan, supports Sudan's army but is also wary of the UAE's influence, as they support Sudan's paramilitary forces. The UAE's long-term goal is to control ports and invest in farmland to ensure control of the food industry and trade routes. These interests often lead to conflict and negatively affect the lives of ordinary people, corrupting both domestic and foreign governments in Africa.

Today, Sudan still struggles with war because of religious and ethnic differences between the North and South. Building a unified nation is hard because people focus on their differences like language and religion (Johnson, 2014). Outsiders sometimes make things worse by getting involved for their benefit. To fix this, Sudan needs to depend on itself and avoid toxic nationalism. Practical solutions are better than dividing people. Africa can learn from other global southern countries' examples.

In this chapter, we look at how political unrest, economic crisis, and legality of Sudan have in making to recognize its effects on the humanitarian crisis. The chapter delves mostly into the past literature published before and to get current statistics, and the chapter relied partially on the international bodies' public data. It is a systematic literature review that first explores the political unrest history, examines the economic crisis, explores the legality formation, and lastly, concludes its effects on humanitarian crises especially women and children, and what measures have been taken to comprehend the issues.

HISTORICAL CONFLICT ASSESSMENT

The Political Unrest

Sudan is located immediately south of Egypt and has a coastline along the Red Sea. It shares its border with another country known as South Sudan. Originally, South Sudan was a part of Sudan, but on July 9, 2011, a referendum was held, leading to South Sudan gaining independence from Sudan. The reason behind this separation can be traced back to the constant civil war that has plagued both countries since 1980. This conflict primarily stems from differences in religious practices, ethnicity, economics, and politics (Abunafeesa, 1985; Collins, 2008).

The northern region of Sudan is predominantly inhabited by Arab Muslims, who have historically supported the Sudanese government. In contrast, the southern region of Sudan is home to the Sudan People's Liberation Movement/Army

(SPLM/A), a group mainly composed of Black African Christians and followers of traditional African religions. Over approximately 30 years, the war between the government and the SPLM/A persisted due to their inability to reach a common ground (Collins, 2008; Howell, 1978; Sawant, 1998). This prolonged conflict resulted in immense suffering, with an estimated 2 million lives lost and millions more displaced from their homes, seeking refuge elsewhere (Collins, 2008; Howell, 1978; Sawant, 1998).

In January 2005, the Sudan government and the SPLM/A signed a significant peace agreement. This agreement encompassed various aspects, including power sharing, wealth distribution, security, and governance. Consequently, on July 9, 2011, South Sudan emerged as an independent nation, marking the birth of Africa's 55th country. The USA played a crucial role as the mediator and architect of this comprehensive peace agreement between North and South Sudan, assisting South Sudan in achieving independence (Wassara, 2014). However, the current issue does not lie between Sudan and South Sudan. Instead, violence has erupted in the capital city of Khartoum and a few other adjacent areas, involving the two factions led by General Abdel Fattah al-Burhan and his Deputy General Mohammed Hamdan Dagalo (Howell, 1978).

On one side, we have General Abdel Fattah al-Burhan, the leader of the Sudanese army and the de facto ruler of Sudan, often referred to as the president. On the other side, General Mohammed Hamdan Dagalo holds a lower rank than al-Burhan and serves as the leader of the RSF, a paramilitary group in Sudan. A power struggle is currently unfolding in Sudan between General Abdel Fattah al-Burhan, the chief of the Sudanese army, and his second in command, General Mohammed Hamdan Dagalo (Natsios, 2008; Peace, 2019). This internal conflict between these two influential individuals has plunged Sudan into chaos as they compete for control and influence within the country. South Sudan gained independence in 2011. In Sudan, the presidency has traditionally been held by members of either civil society or the military. Sudan also has a Prime Minister, who is usually elected through democratic processes. Omar al-Bashir served as Sudan's president from 1999 until 2019. After seizing power, al-Bashir and a group of army officers abolished the position of Prime Minister, thereby overthrowing the democratically elected government of Prime Minister Sadiq al-Mahdi in 1989 (Gerenge, 2015; Natsios, 2008).

Since 1989, Omar al-Bashir has eliminated the role of Prime Minister in Sudan, consolidating authority completely in the presidency. He sought to administer Sudan without an external civil government, retaining control of the country. Sudan faced severe turbulence during his presidency from 1989 to 2019,[3] including the North-South Sudan civil war. In 2019, President Omar al-Bashir nominated Abdel Fattah al-Burhan as an inspector. However, just two months later, General al-Burhan and his partner and deputy, General Mohammed Hamdan Dagalo, engineered President al-Bashir's coup. Following this, General al-Burhan seized Sudan's presidency on April 11, 2019 (Makonye, 2023; Natsios, 2008; Peace, 2019).

Omar al-Bashir, mindful of the military's possible threat, began relying on Mohammed Hamdan Dagalo and the RSF to provide a counterbalance to the regular army. He hoped that by splitting power, a single armed group would not be

Unveiling Sudan's Youth 117

able to topple him. However, both General Abdel Fattah al-Burhan and Dagalo conspired to depose al-Bashir in April 2019.[4] This alliance resulted in a tight working relationship between them. With Dagalo's support, al-Burhan became Sudan's president in 2019. During his tenure, al-Burhan improved Sudan's relations with major states and regional players, especially the USA. Sudan's goal of building relations with democratic countries such as the USA and Israel needed the development of a democratic veneer. Recognizing that admitting to a military coup would impair diplomatic efforts, they formed the Transitional Sovereignty Council (TSC) in August 2019. This council, which included civil political organizations and military personalities, most notably General Abdel Fattah al-Burhan as chairman, was meant to offer a veneer of democratic governance (Makonye, 2023; Natsios, 2008; Peace, 2019).

General Burhan appointed Mohammed Hamdan Dagalo as deputy chairman of the TSC, bolstering Sudan's democratic image. The TSC was formed for two reasons: to present an appearance of democratic governance and to fulfill a political agreement reached between the military and opposition factions opposed to Omar al-Bashir's presidency. This decision was intended to please those who wanted to see leadership changes. Following its establishment, General Burhan, the TSC's chairman, engaged in diplomatic efforts, including a meeting with US Secretary of State Mike Pompeo in Khartoum in December 2019. President Trump invited General Abdel Fattah al-Burhan to the USA, reflecting efforts to strengthen bilateral ties between the USA and Sudan after years of tension. However, in October 2021, General al-Burhan and his deputy, Mohammed Hamdan Dagalo, staged a coup against civilian political groups affiliated with the TSC, effectively ending Sudan's democratic progress[5] (Ali et al., 2022; Nuhu, 2021).

On October 25, 2021, General al-Burhan and the Sudanese military staged a coup, arresting several civilian officials, MPs, activists, and journalists. The goal of this coup was to prevent civilian political parties from gaining control of the government. The dynamics between General Dagalo and General al-Burhan reveal profound regional and societal splits in Sudanese politics. Dagalo, who hails from Darfur, a region frequently overlooked by the political elite, has suffered prejudice and disparaging remarks about his rural background. As tensions rose, both generals mobilized their resources and power bases, resulting in a battle for supremacy that threatened to further destabilize Sudan (Makonye, 2023; Natsios, 2008; Peace, 2019).

The recent tension in Sudan has risen in response to rumors of General al-Burhan's instructions to disband and label the RSF a rebel group. With around 100,000 members, the RSF, led by Dagalo, strongly opposes this decision (Reuters, 2023). In reaction, the RSF allegedly fired rounds in public on April 15, intensifying violence around the country. While the specific location of RSF bases is unknown, their fighters appear to have migrated to densely populated areas. As a result, the Sudanese Air Force conducted bombings in the capital city, intensifying the war. This intensifying dispute poses a huge challenge to Khartoum's political elite and threatens to destabilize Sudan even more. As mentioned before, the upheaval in Sudan stems from a larger global power battle. The UK, the USA,

118   SONALI JHA

and the European Union have all urged for a cease-fire and peace talks to end the issue. However, Western countries now have limited clout because Sudan has been mostly isolated since the 2021 coup. The USA is looking into many options, but its capacity to affect the situation is limited. Sanctions against staff and RSF are being discussed, but they may be ineffective.

THE SOCIO-ECONOMIC CRISIS

Every country in the world has been affected by the global financial crisis that arises at various points in time. For example, the USA and many other countries faced a financial crisis in 1929, leading to a severe economic depression. Similarly, there was a global crisis between 2007 and 2009,[6] affecting every country. Sudan is not an exception at all after witnessing a long civil war. Nearly half of the population is unemployed, and the Sudanese pound's value has decreased by 50%. In Khartoum, industries, banks, stores, and markets have been robbed or vandalized, making it difficult for citizens to obtain goods, services, and money. Despite a long-term ceasefire, inflation is predicted to stay high in 2024, resulting in large-scale unemployment and deepening the economic crisis further. Children are particularly susceptible, with over 10,000 schools closed due to violence, leaving about 19 million children without education and at risk of abuse or exploitation (Berke & Sell, 2018; Sistovaris et al., 2020). Vidushy (2016) argues that people are pulled and trapped into trafficking with lucrative job offers and such conflict situations create a fertile ground for traffickers to easily exploit the people who are already vulnerable.

A financial crisis is a shock to the financial system that disrupts its normal operations. It could include debt, banking, stock market, and currency crises. In other words, a financial crisis occurs when the financial system, including banks, stock exchanges, and central banks, fails. South Sudan's secession in 2011 resulted in Sudan losing a large source of revenue, given the country is wealthy in oil. Following the split, Sudan lost 75% of its oil revenue, resulting in a dramatic surge in inflation.[7] Inflation rates surged from 15.7% in 2006 to more than 44.4% in 2014, with government borrowing and higher taxes contributing to the problem. By October 2019, inflation had reached 57.7% (Ehteshami & Murphy, 2013; Ibrahim & Mutiarin, 2020; Tradingeconomics, 2019).

Sudan's economy has been experiencing a serious and constant balance-of-payments crisis since 1978. As part of the IMF Stabilization Programs, the government has implemented several corrective measures such as monetary, fiscal, and exchange policies. Two major contributing elements to the crisis have been recognized. First, indicators of stagnation emerged in the 1960s, particularly in agricultural productivity. Furthermore, the bread-basket program and other increases in development spending put additional strain on the economy. While there have been imbalances since independence, the government's budgetary situation did not become severe until the 1970s (Brown, 1986; Umbadda & Shaaeldin, 1985).

However, the main reason for the economic crisis in Sudan majorly began, after the split with South Sudan, which holds most of the oil reserves. Sudan expected to benefit from oil profits by allowing South Sudan's oil to pass through its pipelines. However, the conflict led to the shutdown of oil production in the South, causing inflation and devaluation of the Sudanese pound. Currently, the official and black-market exchange rates for the Sudanese pound differ. Despite Sudan's efforts to increase oil production, the situation remains challenging. Recently, the two countries agreed on oil transit fees, with Sudan receiving $25 per barrel[8] (Ehteshami & Murphy, 2013; Patey, 2017). This agreement is expected to generate revenue, although it will take time to recover from the economic damage caused by the oil shutdown. The crisis hit hardest between June and July 2012, especially after an attack on Heglig, a major oil town. Inflation made basic goods expensive, leading to protests. Loans from Kuwait and China helped ease the immediate effects of the crisis. However, one significant impact is the large number of educated people leaving Sudan due to a lack of jobs and frustration with daily life. Many are seeking opportunities abroad in countries like Saudi Arabia, Dubai, Kuwait, England, and America.

The economy in Sudan is in a dire state due to corruption among government officials who manipulate pricing, product availability, and tax systems, causing frustration and protests among the people. It is mainly the unstable political unrest. Despite the challenges, the Trump administration lifted sanctions on Sudan as a reward for cooperation on human rights issues, which ironically worsened the Sudanese economy. With no external sanctions to blame, the government now faces accountability for its actions. On the positive side, Sudan boasts of natural forests rich in biodiversity, though human hunting remains within sustainable limits.

LEGAL FRAMEWORK AND RECOGNITION OF RIGHTS

Legal rights play an important part in tackling Sudan's current issues. Despite enforcement challenges, talks on legal rights have had unforeseen positive consequences, permitting immediate relief avenues such as access to food and education, even in authoritarian settings (Roychowdhury, 2019). Sudan's legal frameworks are molded by historical and institutional considerations, which influence the prominence of informal practices and the interpretation of rights and wrongs in humanitarian activities (Hilhorst & Jansen, 2012; Ledeneva, 2008). Sudan's legal framework has come under criticism, notably in terms of women's rights and economic empowerment. Furthermore, the Sudanese police's conduct and procedures reflect broader issues about the rule of law, human rights, and governmental corruption (Ibrahim, 2017).

Legal frameworks play an important influence both domestically and internationally. The International Criminal Court has the authority to investigate and prosecute human rights offenses involving people such as Sudan's Omar Al-Bashir, highlighting the worldwide implications of legal procedures for dealing with human rights abuses (Oktaviana, 2022). Furthermore, legal rights overlap with broader socio-economic issues such as land grabbing and communal rangeland disputes, both of which have legal repercussions for Sudanese local populations (Sulieman,

2015). In order to navigate legal difficulties and promote rights in Sudan, it is critical to address barriers faced by underprivileged groups, especially women and youth (Shah, 2021). A full understanding of Sudanese women and youth's legal rights to job possibilities is critical for promoting a more inclusive economy and reducing socioeconomic inequities (Etang et al., 2022; Oette & Babiker, 2014). Sudan can seek to ensure fair access to rights, improve accountability, and support socioeconomic development in the country by critically examining and reformulating legal structures. Furthermore, Sudan's legal systems overlap with socioeconomic dynamics, revealing a complicated relationship between the legal system and economic development. Legal initiatives that operationalize patients' rights or empower young scientists have a socioeconomic impact, demonstrating how legal frameworks can influence larger societal results (Abdalla et al., 2018; Brück et al., 2010). Furthermore, problems with establishing household food security in Sudan highlight the need for legislative frameworks in tackling major socioeconomic issues, notably in agriculture (Ibnouf, 2011; Oette & Babiker, 2014).

HUMANITARIAN CRISIS

Sudan was already in a state of a humanitarian catastrophe caused by harsh weather, social and political upheaval, and rising food costs, all of which are contributing to poverty, hunger, and displacement. And, with the independence from South Sudan, the situation has got worse, making life harder for people who need help. There's fighting and it's not safe for many aid workers to stay. Protecting civilians is the biggest problem right now, as security forces are split and unable to keep people safe. Such dire situations are leading to a rise in crimes against women and children and creating buffer zones for human traffickers to operate without any resistance from the authorities. Traffickers can use such situations to their advantage entrapping innocent people.

Sudan has long served as a transit point for individuals traveling from the Horn of Africa to North Africa, Europe, and other destinations. This trend has experienced significant growth in recent years. Eastern Sudan, in particular, is a favored transit route for migrants from Eritrea, Ethiopia, and Somalia who are seeking to reach Europe or Israel (Abdel Ati, 2017). However, the prevailing political unrest, economic crisis, and gender inequality in Sudan indirectly render its people susceptible to exploitation by traffickers. Increasingly, Sudanese individuals are turning to international networks in pursuit of better opportunities overseas. Between 2014 and 2015, the number of Sudanese migrants arriving in Italy by sea surged by over 250%, from 2,370 to 8,370 (Abdel Ati, 2017). The persistent demand for vulnerable individuals worldwide fuels the escalating human trafficking industry. Consumers' desire for affordable goods and services drives the demand for trafficked and exploited labor in today's competitive global economy. For instance, a 2014 report by Human Rights Watch reveals that hundreds, if not thousands, of Eritrean refugees have been abducted in eastern Sudan and sold to traffickers in Egypt's Sinai Peninsula. These victims endure torture until their relatives raise tens of thousands of dollars in ransom.

Research finds Sudanese and Egyptian security authorities turning a blind eye to this violent trade in men, women, and children and suggesting collusion with traffickers (Abdel Ati, 2017; Siegfried, 2014). The refugees are held captive in remote locations, and their captors demand a ransom from their relatives. If the ransom is not paid, the victims are subjected to further torture. Another example of refugee trafficking, akin to the situation in Sudan, is the trafficking in Sinai. Yohannes (2023) examines this tragic phenomenon and emphasizes that it is not a mere coincidence, but a deliberate politicization of certain lives, leaving them without the protection they deserve. Sadly, the lack of recognition by any state or non-state actors and the absence of punishment for traffickers in Sinai demonstrates that the victims have been reduced to mere "bare lives" due to their circumstances. Rescuing these trafficked refugees is a rarity, and even when they are fortunate enough to be rescued, the process of rehabilitation and reintegration in a state with similar circumstances poses significant challenges to their sense of safety.

Sudan is classified as a tier-2 country in terms of combating human trafficking, indicating that despite its conflicting situation, Sudan has made efforts to protect the human rights of its citizens. Sudan has effectively addressed this issue, recognizing the problem of human trafficking as early as the 1980s, specifically referring to the abduction of Dinka women and children by Arab tribes in South Kordofan and South Darfur. These abductions resulted in the El-Di'ayn Massacre, as documented by Mahmoud and Baldo in 1987. In the 1990s, abductions became a politically charged issue due to the conflict between the Sudan People's Liberation Army and the central government. The involvement of "Arab" tribal militias in the fight against the Sudanese government raised international concerns (Abdel Ati, 2017; Littman, 1996; Lumley-Sapanski et al., 2021).

Human trafficking is a complex and multifaceted issue that is defined differently in various countries. The definitions of human trafficking often depend on the legal frameworks and cultural contexts of each country (Pierce, 2014). It is a prominent example of the numerous transnational crimes that are increasing in scale daily. Each year, hundreds of thousands of individuals, including men, women, and children, are illegally transported across the globe. Human trafficking not only causes trauma to the victims trapped in its grip but also inflicts severe physical and psychological suffering on those left behind. This affects individuals of all age groups, with an estimated 27.6 million victims (U.S. Department of State, 2023). Similar to the trade of drugs and the illegal movement of weapons, human trafficking contributes to worldwide conflict, instability, and oppression by profiting from unlawful activities. Despite the nearly unanimous consensus that human trafficking is ethically indefensible, there remains a lack of clarity regarding the criteria that define human trafficking within the USA (Bonilla & Mo, 2019).

Therefore, in terms of combating human trafficking, early NGO reports on human trafficking in Sudan primarily attributed the phenomenon to the North–South conflict, with a focus on the involuntary conscription of youngsters into the rebel army. These reports, such as the US Department of State Trafficking in Persons (TIP) Reports,[9,10] concentrate on internal trafficking issues in Sudan. Furthermore, they highlight that the payment of ransoms by humanitarian and religious groups to secure the release of kidnapped victims has unintentionally worsened the problem by creating a profitable market for middlemen from other tribes. As the crisis in Darfur worsened, similar charges of abductions, forced labor, illegal conscription, and exploitation of women and children emerged from other armed factions participating. These organizations include the Justice and Equality Movement, Sudan Liberation Army, Popular Defence Forces, Janjaweed militia, Chadian resistance forces, Sudanese Armed Forces, and the Central Reserve Police. Sudan was categorized as a Tier-3 country in the US Department of State's annual TIP Report from 2001 to 2013 and again in 2016 and 2017. This designation signifies that Sudan was found to have made insufficient efforts to comply with the US Victims of Trafficking and Violence Protection Act of 2000 (Akech, 2020; Abdel Ati, 2017).

Sudan, as previously mentioned, serves as a transit route for numerous refugees. However, the country faces significant challenges, including prolonged political instability, high inflation rates, food insecurity, poverty, unemployment, and, most importantly, a lack of effective law enforcement, which hinders the protection of vulnerable individuals (Pierce, 2014; Worley, 2017). Nevertheless, in 2014, Sudan enacted the Anti-Trafficking Act and made notable efforts at the national level to address this issue. These efforts included publicly acknowledging the problem, collaborating with UNHCR and IOM, establishing an anti-trafficking section within the Ministry of Labour, and securing convictions based on trafficking-related arrests. Although the focus of these efforts primarily centered on internal trafficking, they were actively institutionalized, leading to Sudan being recognized as a tier-2 country.

Specific actions were taken by the Sudanese government to mitigate the vulnerability of refugees to exploitation, forced labor, and trafficking. For instance, work permits were issued to 30,000 migrants, predominantly from Eritrea, in Kassala state. This was a significant increase from the 180 permits issued in 2012 (Ati, 2017). Furthermore, in 2013, the Child Protection Unit of the Sudan Armed Forces (SAF) trained military personnel and initiated the demobilization of juvenile soldiers from its forces, People's Defense Forces, and other government-associated militias.[11]

Unfortunately, due to all the power dynamics play children and women are the most affected population (Shah, 2020). One-third of West African countries are badly affected by human trafficking (Akuni, 2013). Cross-border trafficking, enabled by agents, has been linked to a lack of social protection for vulnerable individuals, forcing them to seek alternative livelihoods outside their communities. Now, these conflicts increase the demand for child labor in domestic servitude, commercial sexual and exploitation. Children are trafficked to work as soldiers, adoption, sex slaves, forced marriage, organ harvesting, and many more. This crops the question of how looking at these atrocities, the international bodies failed to safeguard the vulnerable. As Akuni (2013) states four issues about its failure, first is the definitions of "child" and "childhood" are ambiguous globally. The Western-centric definition of "child" and "childhood" as anyone under 18 contradicts traditional and cultural conceptions in Sub-Saharan Africa. Second, the state's failure to incorporate human rights principles that safeguard victims' interests into national counter-trafficking law is mostly due to a conflict between human rights and "tradition." Third, what many scholars have quoted is the absence of a legal definition of human trafficking, along with structural weaknesses in judicial institutions, hinders counter-trafficking efforts (Cameron et al., 2023; Onur Arslan, 2023; Zimmerman et al., 2021). Lastly, countries transitioning from conflict to peace struggle to adopt Western-centered counter-trafficking and child protection legislative principles into national legislation. One reason that I assume does not allow the countries to effectively combat human trafficking is its inability to rehabilitate the victims and provide them the re-integration plans. It is not majorly due to a lack of funding internally or internationally and this funding affects the number of volunteers needed to help these victims and it is not an easy job.

Furthermore, the recognition or lack thereof of basic rights in Sudan has far-reaching consequences for the country's ongoing societal challenges. Legal institutions play an important role in protecting fundamental rights; yet issues in enforcement and implementation frequently impede their protection. The junction of legal frameworks and socioeconomic dynamics in Sudan complicates matters further, as legal systems both impact and are influenced by the country's socio-economic landscape.

The failure to recognize essential rights, such as human rights and access to justice, leads to the continuation of Sudan's socioeconomic problems. Issues such as human rights violations, social discrimination, and economic exclusion are worsened when legal systems fail to appropriately protect individual rights. The struggle for recognition by marginalized groups, such as persons living with HIV/AIDS, demonstrates how the absence of legal support can lead to social stigma and exclusion (DeJong & Mortagy, 2013). Similarly, the impact of conflict on women's rights in South Sudan highlights the negative consequences of insufficient legal protection for vulnerable populations (Hove & Ndawana, 2017).

The high prevalence and severity of violence against women and girls in South Sudan can be attributed to three interconnected factors. Firstly, there is entrenched gender inequality, which manifests in deeply rooted patriarchal norms such as child and forced marriage. These norms not only strip women of their rights and autonomy but also perpetuate gender-based violence. Secondly, the country has been plagued by a protracted conflict spanning several decades, resulting in extensive loss of life and widespread displacement among the population. This state of ongoing conflict has contributed to an economic collapse, exacerbating suffering and leading to famine.

Other contributing factors to violence against women include the breakdown of institutions and the rule of law, which were already fragile prior to the 2013 Crisis. Additionally, the normalization of violence and the emotional trauma and stress caused by the conflict and economic crisis play a role (Ellsberg et al., 2021; Shah, 2012, 2024b). Sudan has experienced violent instability, particularly in the western and southern regions, with Darfur being a focal point since the mid-2000s. The conflict between rebel groups, government forces, and militias has resulted in the deaths of approximately 300,000 people. Currently, over 3.5 million Sudanese are displaced, with over 2.5 million of them originating from Darfur alone (Franks, 2015; UN: Refugees from South Sudan cross 1.5 million mark, 2017).

Aid organizations have expressed deep concern regarding the surge in violent incidents, encompassing militia attacks and tribal confrontations, which have reached unprecedented levels. The previous year witnessed an uprooting of nearly 400,000 individuals from their homes due to the prevailing violence, with some of them already residing in displacement camps. The exacerbation of hostilities could be compounded by the escalating levels of poverty and hunger. Presently, Sudan hosts a staggering 1.1 million refugees, including those from South Sudan and Eritrea, as well as over 50,000 individuals displaced by the conflict in Ethiopia's Tigray region, which commenced in 2020. These refugees are accommodated in camps located in eastern Sudan, where political tensions and the specter of violence have witnessed an alarming escalation in recent years, with no sign of abatement in the foreseeable future.

FINDINGS AND CONCLUSION

The historical journey of Sudan until the tensions between General al-Burhan's and RSF arose to intensify in April 2023 is marked with colonization, internal regional conflicts, and subsequent separation into North and South Sudan, laying the ground for an intense path toward independence. The path eventually led to South Sudan's independence in 2011 which was manifested since the 1980s as both countries have been constantly indulging with each other in the form of a civil war, the conflict arose mainly because of differences in religious practices, ethnicity, economics, and politics (Collins, 2008). Due to its internal conflicts, humanitarian crisis arose with its continuous political unrest resulting in economic crisis and people seeking stability as they face humanitarian crises such as food insecurity, mass displacement, and healthcare services. The recent conflict between General al-Burhan and RSF in April 2023 has further worsened for people living in this region due to its extreme weather shock, increasing food prices that continue to escalate poverty and displacement.

The Sudan and South Sudan have always been struggling due to their religious and ethnic reasons at the local level being fueled by the conflict between SAF and RSF. The conflict has impacted the various regions of the country with mass killings and displacement. The International Refugee Committee reported that 5.9 million have been displaced, making it the largest internal displacement globally, and about 7 million people moving out of the country, which children comprising half of the population, making Sudan the largest child displacement crisis in the world. Additionally, the ethically motivated war has resulted in atrocities such as the RSF and its allies have devastated El Geneina, leaving at least 1,100 people dead. Furthermore, the healthcare systems such as hospitals and pharmacies have been dismantled, invaded, and destroyed, and within a month, about over 6,000 people have left El Geneina and sought safety in Chad, as reported by the Global Centre for the Responsibility to Protect.[12] As the conflict continued, sales of the third-largest producer of gold in Africa essentially stopped, depriving the nation of its primary source of foreign exchange revenue. Additionally, 40% of GDP and 80% of jobs and agriculture have also been negatively impacted by trade and financing; the value of the Sudanese pound has fallen by half since the conflict began intense. The IMF cautions that the effects of the violence may be long-lasting, and that reconstruction would probably take years, given that the value of the Sudanese pound has lost 50% of its value since April (IRC, 2023; Sin, 2023). The organization also speculated that a weaker Sudanese economy would also negatively affect North Africa and its neighbors.

The conflict which has continuously escalated has affected the children the most with children being homeless, stateless, in short being displaced multiple times in search of safety and security by its family. The conflict has displaced 5.5 million people, with 4.4 million internally displaced and 1.1 million seeking refuge in neighboring countries. The conflict has resulted in 1,265 fatalities, 8,396 injuries, and widespread disease outbreaks, limiting healthcare access for millions (Sin, 2023). Additionally, displacement has disrupted education, with hundreds of schools occupied by small regional groups. All these create a ground for urgent humanitarian intervention and conflict resolution to address the tragic loss of life and suffering among civilians caught in the crossfire.

Sudan, with so many of its ongoing issues, the continuous armed conflict and climate change in Sub-Saharan Africa, has been identified as a significant contributor to gender vulnerability, with causes including unjust resource exploitation, marginalization, unemployment, healthcare crisis, lack of education, and inequality (Okoyeuzu et al., 2023). In short, these underlying issues create a situational condition that makes individuals susceptible to trafficking, especially in conflict-affected regions like Sudan.

Moreover, it is not just the conflict that became more intense; with its historical political unrest and falling economic system, COVID-19 accelerated the pre-existing vulnerabilities in Sudan, impacting human trafficking dynamics as the country serves as a critical source, destination, and transit point for trafficking activities (Lijnders & Robinson, 2013; Lumley-Sapanski et al., 2021). The pandemic has disrupted social and economic systems, further marginalized vulnerable populations, and increased their susceptibility to exploitation by traffickers at a large scale. The lack of political will and ineffective governance structures have created an environment where traffickers can operate with impunity, exploiting individuals for profit (Malk Bahlbi, 2016). Hence, the causes of human trafficking in Sudan are multifaceted and interconnected, stemming from a combination of socioeconomic, political, and environmental factors. Addressing these issues requires a comprehensive approach that tackles problems such as conflict, climate change, governance failures, and transnational criminal networks to combat human trafficking and protect vulnerable populations effectively.

With the given factors and their circumstances, the Sudan government has failed to recognize that children and youth are the ones suffering the most and end up becoming or identifying as stateless in the process of seeking refuge and falling into the trap of traffickers; Children and youth are the ones who need the most safety, care and a safe environment to grow to not have a traumatic childhood, but are involuntarily becoming displaced and suffering from triple losses, loss of home, loss of community, and the loss of governmental protection. Additionally, the mass killing is losing families as well which goes unnoticed by international civil bodies and the state. This brings to the argument of Hannah Arendt who advocated for people's rights.

Arendt (2017) presents her argument for the existence of rights based on the historical backdrop of the Holocaust and the forced displacement resulting from World War II. This argument regarding the "right to have rights" remains applicable in the case of children and young people in Sudan who find themselves ensnared in the complex situation of being compelled to become refugees due to political crises such as the Israeli-Palestinian conflict or human trafficking in the Sinai Peninsula, to cite a few examples. Moreover, within South Sudan itself, approximately 3.5 million individuals have experienced displacement, with over 2 million displaced within the country's borders and an additional 1.5 million seeking refuge in neighboring nations like Kenya, Sudan, and Uganda (UN: Refugees from South Sudan cross 1.5 million mark, 2017; Franks, 2015). Furthermore, other instances worth considering include the severe devastation suffered by Malakal, South Sudan's second-largest city, due to ongoing warfare, resulting in its abandonment and destruction (Okeke et al., 2021). Consequently, this extensive displacement, coupled with the high number of casualties resulting from the ongoing conflict, has led to depopulation, the weakening of the government, and the erosion of the state's capacity to function effectively. Furthermore, the scale of child fatalities and exploitation is staggering.

The humanitarian crisis is major due to the failure of Sudan's economic, cultural, legal, and gender structures. Additionally, the ineffective support and advocacy of the internal organization and civil bodies to advocate for peace and provide support to its residents. Hence, the failure of society puts its residents into a position of becoming stateless and feeling alien as a refugee in a foreign land with no rights but relying on the refuge rights which are limited and always fearing the unknown atrocities coming there, and this results in making the children and youth fearful or get pulled by traffickers for their benefit which is another complex root to free oneself (Brooks, 2005; Eizenstat et al., 2005; Jaspars, 2023). Hence, the factors of the crisis of pushing the children and youth into the web of homelessness and rightlessness are not limited to the ongoing political unrest, crimes, and society failing both at the state and the international level get more on their list to solve, such as during crises like humanitarian emergencies, the poor or those already marginalized suffer the most. They often have few options or become part of the crossfire decisions, and the innocent victims including children and youth become victims seeking limited resources like food, jobs, or justice (Canavera et al., 2016; Shah, 2019; Strohmeier & Panter-Brick, 2022). This creates a fertile ground for people in power to take advantage of by stealing or manipulating things like land, livestock, or labor. In these situations, the inequalities become more prevalent, and corruption of the government is more to control people, which could be accurate due to the complex history and bond of the current power play in the context of Sudan.

Furthermore, the failure of the Sudan state has created a humanitarian crisis more severe is due to its weak judicial systems (Akuni, 2013; Nyadera, 2018; Rotberg, 2002), and the existing laws to be not implemented properly such as the laws whose amendment made Sudan become in tier-2 country but has not severed it purpose effectively. Hence, the economic crisis and ethnic war at the regional level have made people marginal people even more vulnerable to being mistreated or exploited, such as being trafficked with fraudulent employment opportunities or psychologically manipulated for sex work, organ trade, or domestic servitude (Ehteshami & Murphy, 2013; Strohmeier & Panter-Brick, 2022). This also adds the frame of families being forced to sell their belongings, split up, push their children to another country, agree to forced marriages another form of human trafficking, or leave their homes, which can break apart communities or find a different home being uprooted from their homeland (Jaspars, 2023; Okeke et al., 2021). Okeke et al. (2021) in their research explain the concepts of failure of states, the fragility of states, and the prospects of peace by focusing on South Sudan. Additionally, concluding that if a country fails, it can cause a significant crisis for the whole world. Hence, as functionalism speaks, each part of society should be doing its role so minor problems do not become big disasters. Hence, with so much to cover to provide justice to the vulnerable and provide the children and youth their home the international bodies should be working toward peacebuilding and advocating for human rights in countries with intranational ties to bring effective legal reforms and implement them because it will eventually lead toward peace and security, a stable state and try most importantly the civil societies should work at the regional level to limit the ethnic war that occurs frequently.

The international community, in this case, the international organizations, international civil societies, and state governments working together on different levels with mutual understanding to safeguard those becoming vulnerable with the continuous conflict, food crisis, and fear of becoming refugees in a different homeland which Arendt (2017) would argue that not only makes them homeless but also rightless. Sudan continues to fall short of satisfying minimal standards for eliminating human trafficking and providing basic human amenities and rights, particularly in the context of trafficking or the ethnic rights not holding the accused accountable and lacking funding and facilitating the sentencing, accountability for traffickers, and victim protection like rehabilitation protection. Although the government has identified more perspectives for victims, including trained officials, to understand the concept and spread awareness, it creates a gap and vulnerability, a waste of resources. Existing shelters are inadequate and lack skilled mental health specialists, which impedes victim care. While investigations into child army recruiting have improved, there are still worries about protecting vulnerable populations. Efforts to minimize demand for commercial sex are insufficient, and there is worry about corruption among governmental authorities. Ultimately, the ongoing issues have created nothing but inequalities and exploitation of hundreds of thousands of children childhood with no education or an environment to grow.

NOTES

1. https://www.chathamhouse.org/publications/the-world-today/2024-02/sudan-collapsing-heres-how-stop-it
2. https://www.bloomberg.com/news/articles/2024-01-17/suez-canal-traffic-drops-to-the-lightest-since-the-ever-given
3. https://carnegieendowment.org/2023/05/03/looming-danger-of-state-disintegration-in-sudan-pub-89673
4. https://www.bbc.com/news/world-africa-65297714
5. https://www.dw.com/en/unpacking-sudan-clashes-who-is-who-and-how-did-we-get-here/a-65336631
6. https://www.federalreservehistory.org/essays/great-recession-and-its-aftermath#:~:text=The%202007%2D09%20economic%20crisis,long%20but%20unusually%20slow%20recovery
7. https://sites.tufts.edu/reinventingpeace/2013/02/08/sizzling-south-sudan-why-oil-is-not-the-whole-story/
8. https://www.reuters.com/article/sudan-oil/sudan-demands-23-a-barrel-transit-fee-south-says-idUKL6E7IP14220110725/
9. HRW (Human Rights Watch) (1999). *HRW background paper on slavery and slavery redemption in the Sudan.* https://www.hrw.org/legacy/backgrounder/africa/sudan1.htm
   HRW (Human Rights Watch) (2002). *Slavery and slave redemption in the Sudan.* Human Rights Watch Backgrounder. https://www.hrw.org/legacy/backgrounder/africa/sudanupdate.htm
10. HRW (Human Rights Watch) (2014). *I wanted to lie down and die: Trafficking and torture of Eritreans in Sudan and Egypt.* Human Rights Watch. https://www.hrw.org/report/2014/02/11/i-wanted-lie-down-anddie/trafficking-and-torture-eritreans-sudan-and-egypt
11. https://www.dol.gov/sites/dolgov/files/ILAB/child_labor_reports/tda2013/chad.pdf
12. Global Centre for the Responsibility to Protect (2023, June 16). *Urgent alert on rising atrocity risks in Darfur, Sudan.* https://www.globalr2p.org/publications/urgent-alert-on-rising-atrocity-risks-in-darfur-sudan/#:~:text=Hospitals%20and%20pharmacies%20have%20been,targeted%20in%20ethnic%2Dbased%20attacks

REFERENCES

Abdalla, S. M., Mahgoub, E. A. A., Abdelgadir, J., Elhassan, N., & Omer, Z. (2018). Operationalization of patients' rights in Sudan: Quantifying nurses' knowledge. *Nursing Ethics, 26*(7–8), 2239–2246. https://doi.org/10.1177/0969733018787224

Abunafeesa, E. Y. A. (1985). *The post-1970 political geography of the Red Sea region with special reference to United States interests* [Doctoral dissertation, Durham University].

Akech, J. G. (2020). Exacerbated inequalities: Implications of COVID-19 for the socio-economic rights of women and children in South Sudan. *African Human Rights Law Journal, 20*(2), 584–606.

Akuni, B. A. (2013). *Child trafficking: A case of South Sudan* [Doctoral dissertation, University of Bradford].

Ali, H., Ben Hammou, S., & Powell, J. M. (2022). Between coups and election: Constitutional engineering and military entrenchment in Sudan. *Africa Spectrum, 57*(3), 327–339.

Abdel Ati, H. A. (2017). *Human smuggling and trafficking in Eastern Sudan* (Sudan Report SR 2017:2). Chr. Michelsen Institute.

Ati, H. A. A. (2017). *Human smuggling and trafficking in Eastern Sudan.* Sudan Report.

Berke, T. P., & Sell, J. (2018). Educational challenges in South Sudan. In E. Sengupta & P. Blessinger (Eds.), *Strategies, policies, and directions for refugee education* (Innovations in Higher Education Teaching and Learning, Vol. 13, pp. 101–116). Emerald. https://doi.org/10.1108/S2055-364120180000013005

Bonilla, T., & Mo, C. H. (2019). The evolution of human trafficking messaging in the United States and its effect on public opinion. *Journal of Public Policy, 39*(2), 201–234.

Bosworth, W., Huchon, P., & McClay, K. (2005). The Red Sea and Gulf of Aden basins. *Journal of African Earth Sciences, 43*(1–3), 334–378.

Breidlid, A. (Ed.). (2014). *A concise history of South Sudan: New and revised edition*. Fountain Publishers.

Brooks, R. E. (2005). Failed states, or the state as failure? *The University of Chicago Law Review, 72*(4), 1159–1196.

Brown, R. P. (1986). International responses to Sudan's economic crisis: 1978 to the April 1985 coup d'etat. *Development and Change, 17*(3), 487–511.

Brück, T., Beaudry, C., Hilgenkamp, H., Karoonuthaisiri, N., Mohamed, H. S., & Weiss, G. A. (2010). Empowering young scientists. *Science, 328*(5974), 17. https://doi.org/10.1126/science.1185745

Cameron, E. C., Cunningham, F. J., Hemingway, S. L., Tschida, S. L., & Jacquin, K. M. (2023). Indicators of gender inequality and violence against women predict number of reported human trafficking legal cases across countries. *Journal of Human Trafficking, 9*(1), 79–93.

Canavera, M., Lanning, K., Polin, K., & Stark, L. (2016). 'And then they left': Challenges to child protection systems strengthening in South Sudan. *Children & Society, 30*(5), 356–368.

Collins, R. O. (2008). *A history of modern Sudan* (pp. 6–9). Cambridge University Press.

DeJong, J., & Mortagy, I. (2013). The struggle for recognition by people living with HIV/aids in Sudan. *Qualitative Health Research, 23*(6), 782–794. https://doi.org/10.1177/1049732313482397

Ehteshami, A., & Murphy, E. C. (2013). *The international politics of the Red Sea* (Vol. 21). Routledge.

Eizenstat, S. E., Porter, J. E., & Weinstein, J. M. (2005). Rebuilding weak states. *Foreign Affairs, 84*(1), 134–146. https://doi.org/10.2307/20034213

Ellsberg, M., Murphy, M., Blackwell, A., Macrae, M., Reddy, D., Hollowell, C., ... & Contreras-Urbina, M. (2021). "If you are born a girl in this crisis, you are born a problem": Patterns and drivers of violence against women and girls in conflict-affected South Sudan. *Violence against women, 27*(15–16), 3030–3055.

Etang, A., Lundvall, J. M., Osman, E., & Wistrand, J. S. (2022). *Towards a more inclusive economy: Understanding the barriers Sudanese women and youth face in accessing employment opportunities* [Policy Research Working Paper No. 10244]. World Bank. https://doi.org/10.1596/1813-9450-10244

Franks, T. (2015, October 24). *Malakal: The city that vanished in South Sudan*. BBC News. https://www.bbc.com/news/world-africa-34571435

Gerenge, R. (2015). South Sudan's December 2013 conflict: Bolting state-building fault lines with social capital. *African Journal on Conflict Resolution, 15*(3), 85–109.

Global Centre for the Responsibility to Protect (2023, June 16). *Urgent alert on rising atrocity risks in Darfur, Sudan*. https://www.globalr2p.org/publications/urgent-alert-on-rising-atrocity-risks-in-darfur-sudan/#:~:text=Hospitals%20and%20pharmacies%20have%20been,targeted%20in%20ethnic%2Dbased%20attacks

Hilhorst, D., & Jansen, B. J. (2012). Constructing rights and wrongs in humanitarian action: Contributions from a sociology of praxis. *Sociology, 46*(5), 891–905. https://doi.org/10.1177/0038038512452357

Hove, M., & Ndawana, E. (2017). Women's rights in jeopardy: The case of war-torn South Sudan. *SAGE Open, 7*(4), 215824401773735. https://doi.org/10.1177/2158244017737355

Howell, J. (1978). Horn of Africa: Lessons from the Sudan conflict. *International Affairs (Royal Institute of International Affairs 1944), 54*(3), 421–436.

Ibnouf, F. O. (2011). Challenges and possibilities for achieving household food security in the western Sudan region: The role of female farmers. *Food Security, 3*(2), 215–231. https://doi.org/10.1007/s12571-011-0118-3

Ibrahim, A. H., & Mutiarin, D. M. M. (2020). The major factors behind the economic and financial crisis in Sudan. *Saudi Journal of Economics and Finance, 4*(12), 597–601.

Ibrahim, A. M. E. (2017). The police of the Sudan. *The Police Journal: Theory, Practice and Principles, 91*(3), 275–294. https://doi.org/10.1177/0032258x17726702

IRC. (2023, April 17). *Crisis in Sudan: What is happening and how to help*. https://www.rescue.org/article/fighting-sudan-what-you-need-know-about-crisis

Jaspars, S. (2023). Food and power in protracted crisis: How systems and institutions influence livelihoods, food security, and nutrition. *Food and Nutrition Bulletin, 44*(2_suppl), S23–S31.

Johnson, D. H. (2014). The political crisis in South Sudan. *African Studies Review, 57*(3), 167–174.

Kumsa, A. (2017). South Sudan struggle for independence, and its implications for Africa. *Вестник Российского университета дружбы народов. Серия: Социология, 17*(4), 513–523.

Ledeneva, A. (2008). blatandguanxi: Informal practices in Russia and China. *Comparative Studies in Society and History, 50*(1), 118–144. https://doi.org/10.1017/s0010417508000078

Lijnders, L., & Robinson, S. L. (2013). From the Horn of Africa to the Middle East: Human trafficking of Eritrean asylum seekers across borders. *Anti-Trafficking Review, 2*, 137–154.

Littman, D. (1996). The U.N. finds slavery in the Sudan. *Middle East Quarterly, 3*(3), 91–94.

Lumley-Sapanski, A., Schwarz, K., & Valverde-Cano, A. (2021). The Khartoum process and human trafficking. *Forced Migration Review, 68*, 46–48. Refugee Studies Centre. https://www.fmreview.org/externalisation/lumleysapanski-schwarz-valverdecano

Makonye, F. (2023). Political reflections on the Sudanese Civil War 2023: A qualitative study. *African Journal of Peace and Conflict Studies, 12*(3), 71.

Malk Bahlbi, Y. (2016). Human trafficking and human smuggling to and from Eastern Sudan: Intended and unintended consequences of States' policies. *Academic Journal of Interdisciplinary Studies, 5*(1), 215.

Middleton, N., & O'keefe, P. (2006). Politics, history & problems of humanitarian assistance in Sudan. *Review of African Political Economy, 33*(109), 543–559.

Morton, J. (1989). Ethnicity and politics in Red Sea province, Sudan. *African Affairs, 88*(350), 63–76.

Natsios, A. S. (2008). Beyond Darfur-Sudan's slide toward Civil War. *Foreign Affairs, 87*, 77.

Nuhu, M. B. (2021). The 2019 Military Coup in Sudan. In G. K. Kieh, Jr. & K. A. Kalu (Eds.), *Democratization and military coups in Africa: Post-1990 political conflicts* (p. 165). Lexington Books.

Nyadera, I. N. (2018). South Sudan conflict from 2013 to 2018: Rethinking the causes, situation, and solutions. *African Journal on Conflict Resolution, 18*(2), 59–86.

Oette, L., & Babiker, M. A. (2014). The Rule of Law and Human Rights in Sudan: Challenges and prospects for reform. *Institutional Reforms Series, 2*, 1–15.

Okeke, R. C., Idike, A. N., Akwara, A. F., Okorie, C. O., & Ibiam, O. E. (2021). Failure of states, fragility of states, and the prospects of peace in South Sudan. *SAGE Open, 11*(2), 21582440211020483.

Okoyeuzu, C. R., Ujunwa, A. I., Ujunwa, A., Nkwor, N. N., Kalu, E. U., & Al-Faryan, M. A. S. (2023). Interactive effects of armed conflict and climate change on gender vulnerability in Sub-Saharan Africa. *International Journal of Social Economics, 51*(3), 347–363.

Oktaviana, M. (2022). Yurisdiksi international criminal court (ICC) dalam penegakan pelanggaran hak asasi manusia berat oleh omar hassan al-bashir di darfur, Sudan. *Belli Ac Pacis, 7*(2), 59. https://doi.org/10.20961/belli.v7i2.59993

Onur Arslan, K. (2023). *Legal definition of modern slavery*. IntechOpen. https://doi.org/10.5772/intechopen.109994

Patey, L. A. (2017). *A belated boom: Uganda, Kenya, South Sudan, and prospects and risks for oil in East Africa* (OIES Paper: WPM No. 71). The Oxford Institute for Energy Studies. https://doi.org/10.26889/9781784670825

Peace, P. W. S. (2019). Safeguarding Sudan's revolution. *Africa Report, 21*(281), 1–37.

Pierce, S. (2014, November 18). The vital difference between human trafficking and migrant smuggling. *Open Democracy*. https://www.opendemocracy.net/beyondslavery/sarah-pierce/vital-differencebetween-human-trafficking-and-migrant-smuggling

Ramani, S. (2021). *Russia's growing ambitions in the Red Sea region*. Royal United Services Institute for Defence and Security.

Reuters. (2023, April 15). *Factbox: Who are Sudan's rapid support forces?* Reuters https://www.reuters.com/world/africa/who-are-sudans-rapid-support-forces-2023-04-13/

Rolandsen, Ø. H., & Daly, M. W. (2016). *A history of South Sudan: From slavery to independence*. Cambridge University Press.

Rotberg, R. I. (2002). The new nature of nation-state failure. *Washington Quarterly, 25*(3), 83–96.

Roychowdhury, P. (2019). Illicit justice: Aspirational-strategic subjects and the political economy of domestic violence law in India. *Law & Social Inquiry, 44*(2), 444–467. https://doi.org/10.1017/lsi.2018.13

Sawant, A. B. (1998). Ethnic conflict in Sudan in historical perspective. *International Studies, 35*(3), 343–363.

Shah, T. M. (2012). *Collective memory and narrative: Ethnography of social trauma in Jammu and Kashmir* [Doctoral dissertation, Kansas State University].

Shah, T. M. (2013). Chaos and fear: Creativity and hope in an uncertain world. *International Sociology, 28*(5), 513–517. https://doi.org/10.1177/0268580913496920

Shah, T. M. (2019). Social justice and change. In S. Romaniuk, M. Thapa, & P. Marton (Eds.), *The Palgrave encyclopedia of global security studies* (pp. 1–4). Springer Verlag.

Shah, T. M. (2020). Children of Kashmir and the meaning of family in armed conflict. In S. Frankel, S. McNamee, & L. E. Bass (Eds.), *Bringing children back into the family: Relationality, connectedness and home* (Sociological Studies of Children and Youth, Vol. 27, pp. 213–216). Emerald. https://doi.org/10.1108/S1537-466120200000027015

Shah, T. M. (2021). Women as "sites of gendered politics." In M. B. Marron (Ed.), *Misogyny across global media* (pp. 63–79). Lexington Books.

Shah, T. M. (2023). *Global patterns of decolonization and the right to self-determination: A comparative-historical analysis of East Timor and Kashmir* [Doctoral dissertation, The University of Utah].

Shah, T. M. (2024a). Decolonization and peacebuilding: The case of Timor Leste and Kashmir. In P. Pietrzak (Ed.), *Dealing with regional conflicts of global importance* (pp. 262–278). IGI Global.

Shah, T. M. (2024b). Emotions in politics: A review of contemporary perspectives and trends. *International Political Science Abstracts, 74*(1), 1–14.

Shay, S. (2019). *The Red Sea region between war and reconciliation.* Liverpool University Press.

Siegfried, K. (2014, February 14). *Africa: Sudan and Egypt implicated in human trafficking.* All Africa. http://allafrica.com/stories/201402131267.html

Sin, M. A. (2023). *The cost of war in Sudan over six months: April–October.* blnews. https://blnews.net/2023/10/the-cost-of-war-in-sudan-over-six-months-april-october/

Sistovaris, M., Fallon, B., Miller, S. P., Birken, C., Denburg, A., Jenkins, J., Levine, J., Mishna, F., Sokolowski, M., & Stewart, S. (2020). *Child welfare and pandemics.* University of Toronto.

Strohmeier, H., & Panter-Brick, C. (2022). Living with transience in high-risk humanitarian spaces: The gendered experiences of international staff and policy implications for building resilience. *Disasters, 46*(1), 119–140.

Sulieman, H. M. (2015). Grabbing of communal rangelands in Sudan: The case of large-scale mechanized rain-fed agriculture. *Land Use Policy, 47*, 439–447. https://doi.org/10.1016/j.landusepol.2015.04.026

Tradingeconomics (2019). *Sudan inflation rate – Trading economics.* https://tradingeconomics.com/sudan/inflation-cpi

Umbadda, S., & Shaaeldin, E. (1985). IMF stabilization policies: The experience of Sudan 1978–82. In A. Ali (Ed.), *The Sudan economy in disarray* (pp. 102–138). Khartoum.

U.S. Department of State. (n.d.). *About human trafficking.* U.S. Department of State. https://www.state.gov/humantrafficking-about-human-trafficking/

Vertin, Z. (2019). Red sea rivalries. *Foreign Affairs, 15*, 1–21.

Vidushy, V. (2016). Human trafficking in India: An analysis. *International Journal of Applied Research, 2*(6), 168–171.

Wassara, S. S. (2014). Political history of Southern Sudan before independence of the Sudan. In R. Bereketeab (Ed.), *Self-determination and secession in Africa* (1st ed., pp. 53–68). Routledge. https://doi.org/10.4324/9781315762906

Worley, W. (2017, February 11). 'The Death Road': A young Syrian mother's journey smuggled from Sudan to Egypt. *Independent.* http://www.independent.co.uk/news/world/africa/death-road-smuggledsudan-egypt-cairo-syria-people-trafficking-refugee-crisis-a7493126.html

Yohannes, D. (2023). Chapter 10: Peace and security. In U. Engel (Ed.), *Yearbook on the African Union* (Vol. 3, pp. 159–206). Brill. https://doi.org/10.1163/9789004683082_011

Zimmerman, C., Mak, J., Pocock, N. S., & Kiss, L. (2021). Human trafficking: Results of a 5-year theory-based evaluation of interventions to prevent trafficking of women from South Asia. *Frontiers in Public Health, 9*, 645059.

CHAPTER 7

BEYOND THE FRONTLINES: A CASE FOR GENDERED PEACEBUILDING AND INTERVENTION IN KASHMIR

Aksa Jan[a], Lakshya Kadiyan[b] and Sanjoy Roy[a]

[a]*Department of Social Work, University of Delhi, India*
[b]*School of Social Work, University of Illinois Urbana-Champaign, USA*

ABSTRACT

This chapter reviews existing literature to discuss the intersection of gender and armed conflict in Kashmir, with a specific focus on social work interventions. It gives an overview of the history of conflict in Kashmir, the various types of violence experienced by women, men, and people who identify as gender non-conforming, and talks about how gendered norms and expectations shape resistance and resilience in Kashmir, as well as the difficulties people face in peacebuilding initiatives. The chapter concludes by highlighting how crucial it is to treat gender issues seriously in social work interventions in Kashmir and how policymakers, practitioners, and academics must strive to support gender equity and peacebuilding in the area.

Keywords: Armed conflict; gender; Kashmir; violence; social work; intervention

---

Children and Youth as 'Sites of Resistance' in Armed Conflict
Sociological Studies of Children and Youth, Volume 34, 133–144
Copyright © 2025 by Aksa Jan, Lakshya Kadiyan and Sanjoy Roy
Published under exclusive licence by Emerald Publishing Limited
ISSN: 1537-4661/doi:10.1108/S1537-466120240000034008

INTRODUCTION

The history of conflict in Kashmir has had a significant impact on the lives of local people, especially women and gender non-conforming individuals (Malik, 2019). The intersection of gender and conflict has been recognized as a critical area of study in understanding the social, economic, and political dynamics of conflict-affected regions (Chinkin & Kaldor, 2013). Both men and women in Kashmir have been subjected to various sorts of violence, including sexual assault, domestic abuse, and enforced disappearances, which have had a long-lasting impact on their physical and mental health, social standing, and economic conditions and opportunities (Roy, 2016).

Despite the difficulties they have encountered, women in Kashmir have demonstrated incredible strength and defiance in the face of violence and persecution. They organized and mobilized protests for justice and peace, breaking patriarchal expectations and gender conventions in the process (Malik, 2019). The participation of women in such peacebuilding efforts is recognized as critical for the success of their actions in the face of violence and conflict (Tripp, 2013).

CONFLICT IN KASHMIR: AN OVERVIEW

Conflict is referred to as antagonism, opposition, or disagreement between people, groups, or nations. It is characterized by a conflict of interests, values, or goals that causes discord and frequently involves various levels of hostility or violence. Conflicts can occur in a variety of settings, such as interpersonal relationships, workplaces, communities, and international affairs. Conflict, in general, refers to a wide range of situations and contexts in which there is a clash or divergence of interests, goals, or values. It can manifest at various levels, from interpersonal relationships to global affairs, and understanding the nature, causes, and dynamics of conflicts is critical for effective conflict resolution and peacebuilding efforts.

Skaperdas et al. (2009) argue that conflict arises whenever two or more parties choose expensive inputs that are negatively coupled with one another and don't produce any positive externalities for other involved stakeholders. The constructed environment in conflict zones is one of gradual violence. Any disagreement disturbs the tranquil environment and fosters a fear that gradually permeates the entire web of interpersonal relationships and general mental wellbeing. As a result, people who live in conflict zones see a significant impact on many aspects of their lives (Rashid, 2019).

This brief introduction to the conflict in Kashmir provides a comprehensive overview of the Kashmir conflict, covering key historical events from the establishment of the princely state of Kashmir in 1846 to the Indian government's revocation of the region's special status in 2019. The history of the conflict in Kashmir is deeply entwined with the complex dynamics of colonialism, partition, nationalism, and geopolitical rivalries. The conflict in Kashmir is primarily the result of ongoing tensions between India and Pakistan, with both countries claiming sovereignty over the region.

The princely state of Kashmir was established in 1846 because of the Treaty of Amritsar, which transferred control from the Sikh Empire to the Dogra dynasty led by Gulab Singh (Sum et al., 2013). However, when British India was partitioned into India and Pakistan in 1947, resulting in communal tensions and territorial disputes, the Maharaja of Kashmir, Hari Singh, found himself in a quandary, as both India and Pakistan sought to incorporate the princely state into their respective territories (Kaul, 2018). In 1947, the Maharaja signed a treaty of accession with India, which triggered hostility between India and Pakistan over Kashmir. As a result of hostilities between India and Pakistan over control of Kashmir, the dispute turned into the first Indo-Pakistani War (Schofield, 2003).

Afterward, India raised the issue in United Nations Security Council, where a commission for India and Pakistan was established, named as United Nations for India and Pakistan, followed by the enactment of Resolution 47 on April 21, 1948, which (i) called for an immediate cease-fire, (ii) urged Pakistan's government to secure the withdrawal from the state of Jammu and Kashmir of tribesmen and Pakistani nationals not normally resident therein who have entered the state for the purpose of fighting, (iii) requesting the Indian government to reduce its forces to minimum strength, and (iv) the condition for holding a plebiscite on the question of the future status of the State of Jammu and Kashmir be put in place (Rai, 2004).

The United Nations brokered a ceasefire between India and Pakistan, resulting in a ceasefire line known as the Line of Control (LoC). The LoC became the de facto border, with Pakistan taking control of Azad Kashmir and Gilgit-Baltistan while India retained control of Jammu, Kashmir, and Ladakh (Qadeer, 2017; Westcott, 2020). The geopolitical complexities of the Kashmir conflict were heightened in 1962, when China defeated India in a brief war over the Aksai Chin border area in eastern Kashmir, consolidating its control over the region and creating further complexities in the Kashmir issue (Gupta & Lüthi, 2016). This added a new dimension to the geopolitical conflict, with China still controlling a significant portion of the region.

A second war erupted between India and Pakistan in 1965, primarily over Kashmir, resulting in a ceasefire but leaving the fundamental issue unresolved (Ganguly et al., 2019). The Shimla Agreement, signed in 1972 between India and Pakistan, attempted to formalize the ceasefire line as the LoC, reflecting a renewed commitment to dialogue and peaceful negotiations (Kousar & Bhadra, 2023). However, the rise of Kashmiri nationalism became another significant factor in the conflict, leading to the formation of the Jammu Kashmir Liberation Front with the goal of establishing an independent state through the reunification of both Indian-administered and Pakistan-administered Kashmir (Bose, 2005).

Since the political annexation of Kashmir to India in 1947 (Puri, 1995), it has consistently been at the center of security and political disputes on both the domestic and international fronts. However, during the 1980s and 1990s, there was a significant increase in opposition to Indian rule, which resulted in armed insurgency, large-scale demonstrations, and the emergence of militant organizations in Kashmir. This period was marked by widespread violence, human rights violations, and a high number of casualties (Rai, 2004).

In 1990, the Armed Forces Special Powers Act (AFSPA) and the Jammu and Kashmir Disturbed Areas Act were enacted by the Indian government in Kashmir. The AFSPA accords the Indian armed and paramilitary forces broad authority for arrest and detention, custody, and extrajudicial executions, which strengthens the impunity of offenders who violate its provisions, including the right to shoot to kill (Zia, 2021). The Kashmir conflict remained unresolved despite periodic and sporadic diplomatic efforts to ease tension. To achieve this, India and Pakistan opened a trade route across the LoC in 2008, which allowed for the limited exchange of people and goods across the LoC of Kashmir after 60 years of restricted movement. This move was intended to facilitate confidence-building measures and improve bilateral relations (Mukherjee, 2009). The year 2010 saw widespread anti-India protests in Indian-administered Kashmir, resulting in numerous casualties among the youth and highlighting the Kashmiri people's deep-seated grievances and aspirations (Iqbal & Magill, 2022). The Kashmir conflict has since then remained a source of hostility, political instability, extremism, and economic malaise in the region, leading to increased mental distress in the valley (Housen et al., 2017).

INTERSECTIONS OF GENDER AND CONFLICT

In recent years, the intersection of gender and the conflict in Kashmir has drawn more attention, emphasizing the difficulties and hardships that women, men, and gender-nonconforming people face in the region. Research has shown that gender has a significant impact on how conflict-affected populations see the world. For instance, during conflict, women are disproportionately victimized by gender-based violence, including sexual assault, domestic abuse, and other kinds (Enloe, 2014; Henry & Higate, 2009). The traditional gender roles of protector and provider may be expected of men, which may render them more susceptible to targeted violence by adversarial forces. Additionally, conflict may induce increased marginalization and discrimination against those who identify as gender nonconforming individuals (Kimmel, 2017).

The gendered dynamics of conflict in Kashmir extend beyond the immediate acts of violence. Women often bear the brunt of the socio-economic and psychological consequences of conflict. Displacement, loss of livelihood, and limited access to resources exacerbate the vulnerabilities faced by women in conflict-affected areas (Siriwardhana & Stewart, 2013). The disruption of social structures and traditional support systems can further isolate and marginalize women, impeding their ability to rebuild their lives and contribute to the recovery of their communities (Rai et al., 2019).

In conflict settings, gender roles and expectations become more pronounced and rigid. Feminist studies have highlighted that during armed conflicts, gender relations experience disruptions, leading to the militarization of men's roles and traits, which become centered around soldiering and militancy (MacKenzie & Foster, 2017). This shift in gender dynamics leads to an increase in gender role conflict, where men may face challenges in reconciling traditional expectations with the demands of conflict situations (Cournoyer & Mahalik, 1995). For example, research has shown that rates of domestic violence against women escalate when men seek to reassert power and reaffirm dominant gender roles that are challenged by war or post-war circumstances (Goessmann et al., 2021).

Women's agency is constrained, as their participation in decision-making processes and public life is often limited. This exclusion from formal avenues of power can hinder the development and implementation of inclusive policies and initiatives that address the specific needs and concerns of women and marginalized gender identities.

GENDERED EXPERIENCES OF CONFLICT IN KASHMIR

The Kashmir has had substantial gender ramifications, affecting women, men, and gender-nonconforming people differently. Médecins Sans Frontières performed a study in 2017 and found that 11.6% of Kashmiri women were victims of sexual violence during the conflict. In addition, the study revealed that women who reported sexual assault had a significantly higher prevalence of posttraumatic stress disorder (PTSD), anxiety, and depression than those who did not (Iqbal, 2021). This presents a grim reality where such acts are not merely by products of conflict, but systematic tools employed to exert control and instill fear within communities. The significantly higher prevalence of PTSD, anxiety, and depression among these women points to a crisis that extends beyond immediate physical violence, embedding itself deeply within the social fabric of Kashmiri society. This dimension of the conflict is frequently understated, with the long-term psychological and societal impacts on survivors receiving scant attention from policymakers and the media.

Men in Kashmir are affected by conflict in unique ways and are frequently subjected to targeted violence because of their perceived responsibilities as guardians and providers (Connell, 2013). As a result, they are frequently victims of targeted violence. Men who are thought to be on either side of the conflict may be subjected to extrajudicial executions, torture, and arbitrary incarceration (Seema & Law, 2012). LGBTQ+ people and other gender-nonconforming people experience greater marginalization and discrimination during times of conflict (Kimmel, 2017). These experiences are seldom highlighted in discussions on the Kashmir conflict, rendering an already vulnerable population invisible. The lack of safe spaces and supportive mechanisms especially for LGBTQ+ people in conflict zones like Kashmir signifies a critical oversight in both humanitarian aid and human rights advocacy.

Furthermore, gender-based violence is frequently employed as a war and conflict tactic, with women's bodies used as locations of political power and dominance (Enloe, 2014). Sexual violence is used to dehumanize and demoralize communities, as well as to control and enslave populations (Henry & Higate, 2009). The consequences of conflict-related gender-based violence go beyond the acute physical and psychological trauma that victims suffer. It can also have long-term effects on families and communities, such as job loss, displacement, and social marginalization (Iqbal, 2021).

It can be said that gendered conflict experiences in Kashmir are manifold, affecting women, men, and gender-nonconforming people differently. The next section discusses gendered resistance and resilience in Kashmir, including how women in Kashmir have organized and resisted violence despite the challenges they face.

GENDERED RESISTANCE AND RESILIENCE IN KASHMIR

Women in Kashmir have organized and opposed violence in a variety of ways, despite the difficulties they encounter. Gendered expectations and conventions that specify women's roles as mothers, wives, daughters, and caregivers have greatly influenced women's resistance in Kashmir (Kazi, 2012). Violence against women during the Kashmir conflict has prompted them to mobilize and resist, resulting in a shift in their social and political standing. Women have created spaces in which to organize and advocate for their rights, thereby breaking gender norms and stereotypes and extending their political and social agency (Kazi, 2022a).

Gendered identities, as well as other overlapping identities such as religion and race, have affected women's engagement in resistance movements. Muslim women in Kashmir, for example, have used religious identification to legitimize their participation in resistance organizations (Kazi, 2022b), while Hindu women have utilized ethnic identity to oppose the predominance of Muslim-dominated resistance movements. As a result, gendered identities and expectations intersect with other social and political identities to determine women's engagement in resistance activities.

Furthermore, women play a significant role in maintaining social networks and community structures during times of conflict, showing that women's resistance has extended beyond organized activism (Kazi, 2012). Women have acted as peacebuilders by providing a voice of reason and advocating for non-violent resolutions to conflict. Women's engagement in resistance and peacebuilding initiatives, however, is not without difficulties. Women experience prejudice and violence based on their gender, both within and outside of their communities. They may face sexual harassment, threats, and intimidation because of their activism (Dar & Mehraj, 2018). Due to gendered norms and expectations that favor male activists, women's voices and perspectives are frequently excluded from peacebuilding processes (Swaine et al., 2019).

In conclusion, despite the problems they encounter, women in Kashmir have played an important role in rejecting violence and developing resilience in their communities. Their experiences highlight the necessity of understanding the interplay of gender and war in conflict zones. The following part will look at the role of women in peacebuilding efforts in Kashmir, including the problems they

Beyond the Frontlines 139

face and the possibility for gendered approaches to peacebuilding to address the root causes of conflict and violence in the region.

GENDERED PEACEBUILDING IN KASHMIR

Women have played an important role in peacebuilding efforts in Kashmir, although their participation is sometimes limited by gendered norms and expectations. Women are valuable actors in peacebuilding processes because of their personal experiences with violence and their understanding of their communities. Women's involvement and impact in attempts at peacebuilding, however, may be constrained by violence and discrimination based on gender.

Women in Kashmir have been involved in organizing and resisting violence in the region, in addition to enduring various forms of violence (Kaul, 2018). Understanding the gendered dynamics of conflict, therefore, becomes critical for effective social work interventions that promote peace and security in the region. Women's participation in peacebuilding initiatives has been emphasized as critical for long-term peace in the region (Neogi, 2022). Gender-based discrimination and violence, however, continue to impede women's participation in regional peacebuilding and decision-making processes (Chenoy, 2004).

Women-led initiatives have evolved in recent years to address varied problems in Kashmir, such as poverty, unemployment, and political marginalization (Chakraborty, 2021). Women have campaigned for the inclusion of a gender perspective in peacebuilding processes, highlighting the necessity of addressing gender-based violence and encouraging women's participation and leadership in decision-making (Kazi, 2022a).

Women's involvement in peacebuilding projects has been critical in fostering more inclusive and long-term peace processes in Kashmir. Women's organizations, for example, have played an important role in settling local disputes, assisting victims of abuse, and lobbying for the protection of women's rights (*Progress in Security Council's Women, Peace, Security Agenda Lacking, as Sexual Violence, Insufficient Protection, Absence in Peace Processes Continues | UN Press*, n.d.). However, due to gender discrimination and violence, women's participation in peacebuilding initiatives remains challenging. Women's voices and perspectives are often excluded from decision-making processes, and they may face threats and intimidation for their activism (Swaine et al., 2019).

To overcome these issues, a gendered approach to peacebuilding is required. A gendered perspective acknowledges that gender roles, identities, and expectations influence how women and men experience conflict and the coping techniques they employ (Seema & Law, 2012). It also emphasizes the significance of encouraging gender equality, women's engagement, and women's rights protection in peacebuilding activities (Swaine, 2019).

Despite the challenges they face, women in Kashmir have made significant contributions to peacebuilding initiatives, demonstrating the importance of understanding the intersection of gender and conflict in conflict-affected settings. A gendered approach to peacebuilding is required to address the root causes of conflict in Kashmir and promote sustainable and inclusive peace processes.

SOCIAL WORK INTERVENTION: NEED OF THE HOUR

Social work intervention is essential in addressing the gendered dimensions of the conflict in Kashmir for several reasons:

- *Protection and support for survivors*: Social workers can provide vital support services for survivors of gender-based violence, including counseling, medical assistance, and legal aid. They play a crucial role in ensuring the safety and well-being of survivors and helping them navigate complex systems to access justice and support.
- *Empowerment and agency*: Social workers can facilitate the empowerment of women and gender non-conforming individuals by creating spaces for their voices to be heard, promoting their participation in decision-making processes, and supporting their efforts to rebuild their lives. By fostering a sense of agency, social workers can help individuals regain control over their lives and contribute to the reconstruction of their communities.
- *Gender-responsive policies and programs*: Social workers can advocate for the development and implementation of gender-responsive policies and programs that address the specific needs and rights of women, men, and gender non-conforming individuals. They can work alongside policymakers to ensure that interventions promote gender equality, challenge harmful gender norms, and prioritize the well-being and empowerment of all individuals affected by the conflict.
- *Engaging men and challenging harmful masculinity*: Social workers can engage men in conversations about gender roles and expectations, challenging harmful notions of masculinity that perpetuate violence and discrimination. By promoting alternative, non-violent models of masculinity, social workers can contribute to the prevention of gender-based violence and the creation of more inclusive and peaceful communities.
- *Capacity building and community mobilization*: Social workers can build the capacity of local organizations and community leaders to address gender-based violence, promote gender equality, and facilitate peacebuilding efforts. They can provide training, resources, and technical support to enable communities to respond effectively to the specific challenges faced by different genders in the context of conflict.
- *Advocacy and awareness*: Social workers can engage in advocacy efforts to raise awareness about the gendered dimensions of the conflict in Kashmir and mobilize support for gender equality, women's rights, and inclusive peacebuilding. They can collaborate with civil society organizations, media outlets, and other stakeholders to amplify marginalized voices and promote a more gender-just and peaceful society. Therefore, it is crucial for social work interventions in conflict-affected regions like Kashmir to recognize and address the gendered dynamics. A comprehensive approach must encompass efforts to prevent and respond to gender-based violence, ensure access to justice and support services for survivors, and promote gender equality and women's empowerment. Engaging men and challenging harmful gender norms can also play a pivotal role in fostering peaceful and inclusive communities.

Beyond the Frontlines

- Social workers can facilitate safe spaces for women to share their experiences, providing emotional support, and empowering them to access resources and participate in decision-making processes. They can collaborate with local organizations and stakeholders to design and implement programs that address the specific needs of women, men, and gender nonconforming individuals. This may involve providing psychosocial support, livelihood opportunities, and educational initiatives that promote gender equality and challenge stereotypes. Furthermore, social workers can advocate for policy reforms and systemic changes that prioritize gender equality and women's rights in conflict resolution and peacebuilding processes. They can engage in community dialogue and awareness campaigns to challenge discriminatory attitudes and behaviors, promoting a culture of respect and inclusion.
- By understanding and addressing the gendered dimensions of conflict, social workers can contribute to the creation of more resilient and peaceful societies in Kashmir and beyond. Their interventions can foster empowerment, healing, and reconciliation, while promoting justice, security, and dignity for all individuals affected by conflict.

CONCLUSION

The history of the conflict in Kashmir is complex and multifaceted, which has influenced the region's political scenario for more than a century. The perpetual conflict in Kashmir has impacted almost all aspects of life in Kashmir, both directly and indirectly. Conflict in Kashmir has a layered impact on the lives of people living there. According to Human Rights Watch (1993), the people in Kashmir are frequently in danger of being detained, assaulted, humiliated, undressed, and interrogated. For Kashmiris, punishments in both public and private settings have become lessons about Indian power. Both combatants and civilians are subjected to extreme brutality and violence. To analyze the underlying causes and implications of these complexities, one needs a thorough understanding of the region's conflict. It also necessitates an examination of historical, political, socioeconomic, and cultural factors, as well as the aspirations and grievances of the Kashmiri people, to understand the different dimensions of conflict in Kashmir. There is hope for a peaceful and equitable resolution to this long-standing dispute through careful analysis, informed dialogue, and sustained diplomatic efforts.

Attempts to resolve the conflict have been made through diplomatic channels, bilateral dialogues, and international interventions. However, resolving the Kashmir conflict in a way that addresses the aspirations, grievances, and demands of all parties involved, including the Kashmiri people, continues to be a daunting task. As a result, the ongoing conflict in Kashmir has resulted in tension between local people and armed forces and incidences of periodic violence. Resolving this conflict requires sustained dialogue, empathy, and a comprehensive understanding of the historical and socio-political complexities involved. However, the underlying problems of political autonomy, self-determination, violence, and divergent national aspirations nevertheless continue.

This chapter has explored the intersection of gender and conflict in Kashmir. It has drawn attention to the ways in which conflict affects women, men, and gender-nonconforming individuals differently and has examined the role of gender in shaping experiences of violence, resistance, and peacebuilding in the region. The gendered experiences of the conflict in Kashmir have shown how crucial it is to take gender into account when analyzing and resolving conflicts. Women have been disproportionately affected by the conflict, suffering from enforced disappearances, domestic violence, and sexual assault. Men have been impacted by the conflict, both as aggressors and as victims of violence. People who identify as gender non-conforming have experienced specific types of discrimination and violence.

Despite these obstacles of gender-based violence and gendered expectations and norms, women in Kashmir have organized, opposed violence, and significantly contributed to peacebuilding efforts. A gendered perspective on conflict intervention and peacebuilding is required to address these issues. This method acknowledges that gender plays a significant role in influencing conflict experiences and coping mechanisms. In conflict intervention and peacebuilding initiatives, it emphasizes the significance of achieving gender equality, women's participation, and the protection of women's rights.

In addition, this chapter has highlighted how social work intervention is crucial in addressing the gendered dynamics of the conflict in Kashmir. By recognizing and responding to the specific challenges faced by women, men, and gender non-conforming individuals, social workers can contribute to the promotion of gender equality, the protection of human rights, and the development of sustainable peace in the region.

Lastly, it can be argued that gender must be seriously considered by policymakers, practitioners, and academics working in Kashmir. Recognizing the difficulties men, women, and gender nonconforming people encounter in conflict-affected areas is one aspect of this, as is striving to advance gender equality and women's involvement in peacebuilding initiatives. By doing this, we may work to develop inclusive and long-lasting peace processes in Kashmir and other areas affected by conflict.

REFERENCES

Bose, S. (2005). *Kashmir: Roots of conflict, paths to peace*. Harvard University Press.

Chakraborty, A. (2021, May 22). *Women professionals in Jammu and Kashmir*. https://www.jkpi.org/women-professionals-in-jammu-and-kashmir/

Chenoy, A. M. (2004). Women in the South Asian conflict zones. *South Asian Survey, 11*(1), 35–47.

Chinkin, C., & Kaldor, M. (2013). Gender and new wars. *Journal of International Affairs, 67*(1), 167–187.

Connell, R. (2013). *Gender and power: Society, the person and sexual politics*. John Wiley & Sons.

Cournoyer, R. J., & Mahalik, J. R. (1995). Cross-sectional study of gender role conflict examining college-aged and middle-aged men. *Journal of Counseling Psychology, 42*(1), 11–19. https://doi.org/10.1037/0022-0167.42.1.11

Dar, N. A., & Mehraj, B. (2018). *Sexual violence against women in an armed conflict*. Lesley University.

Enloe, C. (2014). *Bananas, beaches, and bases: Making feminist sense of international politics*. University of California Press.

Ganguly, S., Smetana, M., Abdullah, S., & Karmazin, A. (2019). India, Pakistan, and the Kashmir dispute: Unpacking the dynamics of a South Asian frozen conflict. *Asia Europe Journal, 17*, 129–143.

Goessmann, K., Ibrahim, H., Saupe, L. B., & Neuner, F. (2021). Toward a contextually valid assessment of partner violence: Development and psycho-sociometric evaluation of the gendered violence in partnerships scale (GVPS). *Frontiers in Psychology, 11*. https://doi.org/10.3389/fpsyg.2020.607671

Gupta, A. R. D., & Lüthi, L. M. (Eds.). (2016). *The Sino-Indian War of 1962: New perspectives*. Taylor & Francis.

Henry, D. M., & Higate, D. P. (2009). *Insecure spaces: peacekeeping, power and performance in Haiti, Kosovo, and Liberia*. Bloomsbury Publishing.

Housen, T., Lenglet, A., Ariti, C., Shah, S., Shah, H., Ara, S., Viney, K., Janes, S., & Pintaldi, G. (2017). Prevalence of anxiety, depression, and post-traumatic stress disorder in the Kashmir Valley. *BMJ Global Health, 2*(4), e000419.

Human Rights Watch. (1993). *The Humans Right Crisis in Kashmir* (pp. 1–190). Human Rights Watch.

Iqbal, S. (2021). Through their eyes: Women and human security in Kashmir. *Journal of Asian Security and International Affairs, 8*(2), 147–173.

Iqbal, S., & Magill, S. (2022, April). Feature: Women's resistance in Kashmir memory as resistance: Oral histories from Kashmir. *History Workshop Journal, 93*(1), 245–270.

Kaul, N. (2018). India's obsession with Kashmir: Democracy, gender (anti-)nationalism. *Feminist Review, 119*(1), 126–143. https://doi.org/10.1057/s41305-018-0123-x

Kazi, S. (2012). *Law, governance and gender in Indian-administered Kashmir*. Centre for the Study of Law and Governance, Jawaharlal Nehru University.

Kazi, S. (2022a). Conflict in Kashmir and Manipur: History, ethnicity, gender. *Journal of Aggression, Conflict, and Peace Research, 15*(1), 39–50.

Kazi, S. (2022b). Women, gender politics, and resistance in Kashmir. *Socio-Legal Review, 18*(1), 95–117. https://doi.org/10.55496/AUKX4646

Kimmel, M. (2017). *Manhood in America* (p. 173). Oxford University Press.

Kousar, R., & Bhadra, S. (2023). Jeopardizing children's future: Insincere reconciliation in Jammu and Kashmir. *Peace Review, 35*(1), 119–129.

MacKenzie, M., & Foster, A. (2017). Masculinity nostalgia: How war and occupation inspire a yearning for gender order. *Security Dialogue, 48*(3), 206–223. https://doi.org/10.1177/0967010617696238

Malik, I. H. (2019). The continuing conflict in Kashmir regional detente in jeopardy. In P. S. Gosh (Ed.), *Rivalry and revolution in South and East Asia* (pp. 161–186). Routledge.

Mukherjee, A. (2009). A brand-new day or back to the future? The dynamics of India–Pakistan relations. *India Review, 8*(4), 404–445.

Neogi, D. (2022). Women's struggles in the Kashmir Militancy War. *Journal of International Women's Studies, 23*(6), 4.

Progress in Security Council's Women, Peace, Security Agenda Lacking, as Sexual Violence, Insufficient Protection, Absence in Peace Processes Continues | UN Press. (n.d.). Retrieved July 15, 2023, from https://press.un.org/en/2023/sc15221.doc.htm

Puri, B. (1995). *Kashmir towards insurgency*. Orient Longman. http://manushi-india.org/test/pdfs_issues/PDF%20files%2079/Kashmir%20%20Towards%20Insurgency.pdf

Qadeer, M. A. (2017). United Nations resolutions on Kashmir and their relevance. *Journal of Strategic Affairs, 2*, 65–95.

Rai, M. (2004). *Hindu rulers, Muslim subjects: Islam, rights, and the history of Kashmir*. Princeton University Press.

Rai, S. M., True, J., & Tanyag, M. (2019). From depletion to regeneration: Addressing structural and physical violence in post-conflict economies. *Social Politics: International Studies in Gender, State & Society, 26*(4), 561–585. https://doi.org/10.1093/sp/jxz034

Rashid, Q. (2019). *Psychological disorders as a major catalyst for the damage of urban fabric in a conflict-ridden zone: A case study of old town Srinagar*. Planning Tank. https://planningtank.com/thesis-dissertation/psychological-disorders-catalyst-damage-urban-fabric-old-town-srinagar

Roy, S. (2016). Flexing soft power locally and globally: The Kashmir conflict in India's mediated tourism discourses. In A. R. Smith (ed.), *Radical conflict: Essays on violence, intractability and communication* (pp. 233–249). Lexington Books.

Schofield, V. (2003). *Kashmir in conflict: India Pakistan and the unending war* (pp. 143, 189). IB Tauris & Co. Ltd.

Seema, K., & Law, G. (2012). *Gender in India–Administered Kashmir* [Working Paper Series, CSLG/WP/20]. Centre for the Study of Law and Governance, Jawaharlal Nehru University, New Delhi.

Siriwardhana, C., & Stewart, R. (2013). Forced migration and mental health: Prolonged internal displacement, return migration and resilience. *International Health, 5*(1), 19–23. https://doi.org/10.1093/inthealth/ihs014

Skaperdas, S., Soares, R., William, A., & Miller, S. (2009). *The costs of violence.* World Bank Group.

Sum, H. K., Moorthy, R., & Benny, G. (2013). The genesis of Kashmir dispute. *Asian Social Science, 9*(11), Article 11. https://doi.org/10.5539/ass.v9n11P155

Swaine, A. (2019). Reshaping how political settlements engage with conflict-related violence against women. *Feminists@ Law, 9*(1), 1–25.

Swaine, A., Spearing, M., Murphy, M., & Contreras-Urbina, M. (2019). Exploring the intersection of violence against women and girls with post-conflict state building and peacebuilding processes: A new analytical framework. *Journal of Peacebuilding & Development, 14*(1), 3–21.

Tripp, C. (2013). *The power and the people: Paths of resistance in the Middle East.* Cambridge University Press.

Westcott, S. P. (2020). Self-determination and state sovereignty: The case of UN involvement in Jammu and Kashmir. In J. R. Avgustin (Ed.), *The United Nations: Friend or foe of self-determination?* (pp. 127–143). E-International Relations.

Zia, A. (2021). Behind occupation and surveillance: The armed forces special powers act and the right to privacy in Kashmir. In S. Hussain (Ed.), *Society and politics of Jammu and Kashmir* (pp. 243–260). Springer International Publishing. https://doi.org/10.1007/978-3-030-56481-0_12

CHAPTER 8

AI'S ROLE IN ENHANCING HUMANITARIAN EFFORTS FOR CHILDREN IN ARMED CONFLICT

Tamanna M. Shah[a] and Javed M. Shah[b]

[a]*Ohio University, USA*
[b]*University of Illinois, USA*

ABSTRACT

This chapter examines the transformative role of artificial intelligence (AI) in supporting children and youth affected by armed conflicts, focusing on the integration of AI with humanitarian aid and child psychology. While AI is predominantly recognized for its capability in logistical and analytical tasks, we highlight its potential to address the emotional and psychological needs of vulnerable populations in armed conflict. By employing an interdisciplinary approach, the study bridges the gaps between technology, psychological support, and humanitarian efforts. The discussion extends into the ethical dimensions of AI application in conflict environments, emphasizing the importance of developing international regulations and standards that ensure responsible technology use. AI has the potential to enhance traditional humanitarian operations and innovate the means of delivering emotional and psychological support to affected children. AI-driven tools, such as empathetic computing and Natural Language Processing, can amplify the voices of young individuals, facilitating better understanding and support by capturing and analyzing their experiences and emotional states. By influencing policymakers, technologists, and humanitarian workers, there is scope for thoughtful development and deployment of

---

Children and Youth as 'Sites of Resistance' in Armed Conflict
Sociological Studies of Children and Youth, Volume 34, 145–155
Copyright © 2025 by Tamanna M. Shah and Javed M. Shah
Published under exclusive licence by Emerald Publishing Limited
ISSN: 1537-4661/doi:10.1108/S1537-466120240000034009

AI technologies to improve the resilience and recovery of children in conflict spaces to ensure their psychological well-being and emotional safety.

Keywords: Children; youth; artificial intelligence; AI resilience; trauma; conflict

INTRODUCTION

In armed conflicts, the voices and experiences of children and youth are often ignored or silenced. Children are frequently among the primary victims of armed conflict, enduring physical and psychological trauma (Shah, 2019, 2020). According to the Office of the United Nations High Commissioner for Human Rights (OHCHR, 2023), approximately 8,630 children were reported as killed or maimed, with 4,000 left without access to humanitarian aid. The mortality rate among young children, especially those under the age of five, spikes during wartime (Carlton-Ford, 2004). The repercussions of conflict extend beyond immediate casualties, compromising the future life chances of these vulnerable groups.

Even amidst such challenging life experiences, these young individuals demonstrate remarkable resilience, agency, and creativity in navigating the obstacles of conflict-ridden environments. Recognizing these capabilities, and in response to their complex needs, the global community has begun to see the value in incorporating cutting-edge technologies. The integration of new technologies offers historically marginalized groups the opportunity to shape their own discourse. During times of crisis, digital technologies have played a critical role in facilitating decentralized information transmission and amplifying messages to garner international support in times of war. However, scholars acknowledge the human and non-human consequences that come with technological advancements (Jones et al., 2018). Specifically, armed conflicts and wars have severe implications for the survival and well-being of children and youth (Denov, 2008).

Amidst these crises, artificial intelligence (AI) can potentially enhance humanitarian interventions. Specifically, the convergence of AI with empathetic computing can provide tailored support to address the unique psychological needs of affected children. Empathetic computing in AI systems involves the development of algorithms capable of recognizing and responding to human emotions, which is crucial in addressing the psychological impact of conflict. By leveraging these advanced technologies, stakeholders can develop innovative strategies for delivering aid and providing emotional and psychological support, thereby fostering resilience among young victims of war.

Children in armed conflict exhibit resilience and agency, navigating their challenging environments with remarkable adaptability and creativity. However, their voices often go unheard within the broader geopolitical discourse (Shah, 2012, 2023). Through empathetic AI applications, it becomes possible to interpret the subtle expressions of children's emotions and design interventions that are sensitive to their psychological state, thus facilitating a more effective recovery process.

This chapter explores the intersection of AI, empathetic computing, and humanitarian efforts in conflict zones – an area that has received relatively little attention. It examines the applications of AI in providing emotional support through empathetic computing and logistical aid through data analysis and pattern recognition. Furthermore, it considers the ethical challenges and considerations associated with the use of such technologies in sensitive situations. By integrating AI with a deep understanding of its impact on young individuals, this chapter aims to highlight how digital tools can be utilized to improve the lives of children affected by conflicts, ultimately fostering a more inclusive and effective humanitarian response. The next section discusses how technological advancements are reshaping the delivery of humanitarian aid and how these tools empower the very children they intend to assist. By bridging the gap between the theoretical potential of AI and its practical application, a framework for action can emerge that employs technology as a catalyst for tangible change.

AI-driven storytelling platforms serve as repositories for the traumatic experiences of young survivors and play a crucial role in the processing and understanding of these narratives from a psychological perspective. This approach supports advocacy and awareness efforts and aids in the psychological healing process, showcasing the multifaceted benefits of AI in humanitarian crises.

ENHANCING CHILD ADVOCACY IN CONFLICT ZONES THROUGH AI

Technological advancements have altered the tactics and strategies employed by warring parties and influenced the broader socio-political context within which conflicts arise. In the contemporary era, digital technologies have become increasingly intertwined with the conduct and consequences of armed conflict. The widespread use of social media platforms, mobile communication devices, and digital surveillance systems has enabled unprecedented levels of connectivity and information dissemination, shaping public perceptions, influencing political narratives, and facilitating peaceful mobilization and violent extremism. In conflict zones, digital technologies have been utilized by both state and non-state actors for purposes ranging from propaganda dissemination and recruitment to intelligence gathering and remote warfare (Katagiri, 2024).

Despite the potential risks associated with the militarization of AI, digital technologies also offer opportunities for advancing humanitarian and peacebuilding efforts in conflict-affected regions (Panic & Arthur, 2024). AI-powered tools, such as predictive analytics and satellite imagery analysis, can enhance early warning systems for conflict prevention, facilitate humanitarian aid delivery, and support post-conflict reconstruction efforts. Additionally, digital platforms provide avenues for documenting human rights abuses, amplifying the voices of affected communities, and fostering dialogue and reconciliation (Kurian & Saad, 2024). At the core of empowering the voices of children in armed conflict is AI's capability for Natural Language Processing (NLP). NLP allows machines to understand and interpret human language, enabling them to capture the nuanced narratives of children's experiences. This technological approach is grounded in the theory of symbolic AI, which focuses on the manipulation of symbols to mimic human cognitive processes. By processing children's descriptions of their experiences, AI can help document their stories in a manner that is scalable and sensitive to the nuances of their expressions.

From a psychological perspective, understanding how trauma affects children and how they express these experiences is crucial. Theories of psychological resilience, such as those proposed by Grotberg (1995), offer a framework for understanding how children endure and overcome adverse conditions. AI tools can be developed to detect patterns of resilience and trauma in children's speech and written words, providing insights that are vital for designing targeted psychological interventions. The mental health of children and youth is a direct reflection of their environment. Children and youth are subject to "visible and invisible" injuries (Evans, 1996, p. 2). Amidst the turmoil and devastation of armed conflict, children and youth are among the most vulnerable populations, facing a myriad of physical, psychological, and socio-economic challenges. The World Health Organization identifies the challenge of delivering timely Psychological First Aid to victims of war as a critical component of humanitarian response efforts. Conflict also inflicts indirect effects on young lives, which involves a breakdown of services such as healthcare, education, and water and sanitation. These effects are not temporary, rather they translate into generational trauma with long-term implications for mental health.

Empathetic computing is crucially aligned with psychological theories of resilience that emphasize the importance of empathy in therapeutic contexts. Resilience theory suggests that understanding and responding to an individual's emotional states can play a significant role in helping them recover from trauma. Empathetic computing leverages AI to interpret emotional cues and respond in ways that foster psychological resilience. By integrating these theories into the development of AI systems, empathetic computing can be fine-tuned to offer responses that are not only contextually appropriate but also psychologically supportive. Such technology can effectively contribute to building resilience, offering consistent, understanding, and context-aware interactions that reinforce coping mechanisms in children experiencing trauma.

The principles of humanitarian aid, such as impartiality, neutrality, and humanity, are essential when applying AI in conflict zones. These principles ensure that the deployment of AI technologies does not exacerbate the sufferings of those affected but instead works to mitigate their suffering and uphold their dignity. By embedding these principles into the development and deployment of AI systems, developers can ensure that these technologies serve as tools for effective and ethical humanitarian assistance. The integration of AI holds significant promise in addressing the multifaceted needs of young individuals affected by conflict, offering innovative solutions to mitigate harm, promote resilience, and foster long-term recovery. AI is a useful tool for understanding the human brain, including its structure, functionality, and how it can be used to resolve or alleviate traumatic memories. AI's ability to solve complex problems and perform critical analysis offers a promising approach to helping children and youth affected by armed conflict (Amir & Ahmad, 2019).

Empowering Young Voices: Digital Storytelling and AI

Researchers have demonstrated the influence of childhood trauma on psychological well-being and its persistence into adulthood when not addressed and managed promptly (De Bellis & Zisk, 2014). Such traumatic experiences during childhood can contribute to the development of diminished self-esteem, negative outlooks, and rigid beliefs across various domains of life (Orth & Robins, 2014). These factors may gradually compound with other challenges individuals encounter, amplifying feelings of pressure and fear, thereby impacting their overall quality of life.

Digital storytelling and narrative analysis, driven by AI, offer a transformative space for amplifying the voices of children and youth within contentious spaces. Digital storytelling, when combined with generative AI capable of adapting to specific contexts, particularly cultural nuances, holds significant potential for conveying information effectively through narrative formats (Tarigan & Hasibuan, 2024). These programs capture the intricacies of their traumatic experiences that can be used as powerful tools to dissect and interpret the traumatic narratives shared by young individuals. They have the potential to empower individuals to express their emotions (Shah, 2024a, 2024b), which can be beneficial for their mental health and emotional well-being. In essence, through storytelling, people can articulate their thoughts, feelings, and experiences, which can lead to a sense of validation, catharsis, and empowerment, ultimately contributing to their overall mental health and emotional resilience (Addie et al., 2024).

AI technology goes beyond extracting themes; it delves into the emotional nuances and cultural contexts embedded in their stories. By harnessing AI, digital storytelling becomes a platform for these children and youth to express their resilience, agency, and diverse forms of resistance. AI's language translation capabilities ensure that these narratives transcend linguistic barriers, fostering a global understanding of the challenges faced by young individuals in conflict zones. Ultimately, the integration of AI in digital storytelling becomes a catalyst for fostering empathy, awareness, and meaningful engagement with the unique narratives of children and youth navigating the complexities of armed conflict.

Building on the concept of digital storytelling, the role of AI extends into the realms of NLP, which offers further sophistication in handling and interpreting the complex narratives shared by children in conflict zones. The next section examines how AI understands and responds to the needs of those it serves. Through NLP, we see AI's capacity to dissect vast amounts of unstructured data, extracting meaningful insights that can inform targeted interventions and support mechanisms.

Decoding Trauma: AI and Natural Language Processing

AI utilizes rapid probabilistic algorithms, trained on extensive datasets or big data, to perform various tasks. NLP represents one such technology, capable of discerning human speech and executing designated commands (Abadi & Andersen, 2016). Language, at an individual level, furnishes substantial data for analysis. Through NLP, the system comprehends natural human language and translates it into a format readable by computers, facilitating task execution. NLP methodologies are instrumental in operationalizing mental health conditions, facilitating diagnosis, risk assessment (e.g., psychosis, suicide, and violence), and monitoring treatment responses (Corcoran & Cecchi, 2020).

The capacity to comprehend and attribute significance to encounters with violence, and to adapt emotionally to such occurrences, can be crucial for mental well-being and even survival. Children who cultivate effective coping mechanisms are more adept at regulating their emotions compared to those who dwell on the challenges and feelings of despair (Evans, 1996, p. 8). Central to children's coping mechanisms is their resilience – an essential dimension in navigating and overcoming adversity. Grotberg (1995) defines resilience and elucidates its significance in shaping a child's life:

> Resilience is the human capacity to face, overcome, and be strengthened by or even transformed by the adversities of life. Everyone faces adversity; no one is exempt. With resilience, children can triumph over trauma; without it trauma (adversity) triumphs. (p. 10)

Grotberg (1995) also identifies a common set of self-beliefs that underpin resilience across countries. In overcoming adversity, children draw upon three sources of resilience: *I Have*, *I Am*, and *I Can* AI and machine learning (ML) can be utilized to analyze the narratives and stories shared by children and youth in conflict zones. NLP techniques can help identify common themes, emotions, and expressions, providing a deeper understanding of their lived experiences. Moreover, AI-driven voice recognition technologies can be employed to transcribe and analyze oral narratives, ensuring that the diverse voices of children and youth, who might not have access to traditional written mediums, are heard and understood.

AI can be applied to analyze digital art and creative expressions by children and youth. Emotion recognition algorithms can help understand the emotional impact of their artistic creations, providing insights into their coping mechanisms and forms of resistance through creative outlets (Muratbekova & Shamoi, 2024). AI-powered generative art tools (Sai et al., 2024) can be used to collaborate with children and youth in conflict zones, enabling them to create unique digital artworks that reflect their experiences, dreams, and aspirations. This process can serve as a form of agency and empowerment.

NLP offers more than just data processing; it can be an important tool for understanding the psychological impacts of trauma. According to psychological theories, trauma can significantly alter an individual's language use, affecting their choice of words, speech patterns, and narratives. NLP can detect these subtle changes, offering insights into the underlying psychological states. By integrating principles from trauma psychology, such as the concepts of intrusion and avoidance behaviors described in trauma response theories, NLP can be tailored to identify linguistic markers that signify trauma responses. This application not only helps in diagnosing and understanding the psychological states of affected children but also in tailoring interventions that are sensitive to the nuances of trauma expressed through language.

CRISIS COMMUNICATION AND HUMANITARIAN SUPPORT

The significance of the incorporation of AI into humanitarian support was recently highlighted by the Secretary-General in the Roadmap for Digital Cooperation. Propelled into action by the COVID-19 pandemic, the Secretary-General emphasized the need for AI to be in alignment with human rights (UN General Assembly, 2020). Pizzi et al. (2020) argue for a "proactive and inclusive" (p. 149) role in developing AI tools that further human development and help achieve the SDGs. There is also a need to proactively reframe policies and accountability mechanisms that protect human rights (Pizzi et al., 2020; Shah, 2021). ML techniques are already being deployed to further humanitarian action. Satellite imagery analysis through ML allows for instant recognition of infrastructural elements, streamlining the process of observing migrant movements and optimizing resource deployment during humanitarian emergencies.[1] In several underdeveloped regions, a variety of programs such as AtlasAI, EzyAgric, Apollo, FarmForce, Tulaa, and Fraym are deploying AI to offer foresight to agricultural workers, helping them avoid risks associated with arid conditions and harsh climates while increasing harvests through timely planting (Pizzi et al., 2020, pp. 150–151). AI applications facilitate the assessment of health issues such as malnutrition in areas with limited medical supplies. The roster of capabilities continues to expand daily.

Other applications can include setting up AI-enhanced crisis hotlines and support services, providing immediate assistance to children and youth in distress. Chatbots equipped with empathy algorithms can offer a responsive and understanding interface for those seeking help. AI can assist in the early detection of trauma by analyzing facial expressions, vocal tones, and other cues indicative of distress. Emotion recognition algorithms can provide insights into the emotional states of children, enabling early intervention and support. NLP can be applied to analyze text and verbal content during therapy sessions. This helps mental health professionals understand the nuances of children's expressions, allowing for more personalized and effective therapeutic interventions.

AI-driven virtual therapy programs can offer personalized interventions based on the specific needs and responses of individual children. These programs can adapt over time, ensuring that therapeutic approaches evolve with the child's progress and changing circumstances. Wearable devices equipped with biometric sensors, coupled with AI, can provide real-time feedback to therapists. This feedback can be used to tailor therapeutic activities and gauge the effectiveness of interventions, creating a more responsive and individualized treatment plan. AI models can be deployed to analyze patterns in communication and social media to identify potential risks and threats to children and youth in conflict zones, enabling proactive community-based interventions.

CHALLENGES AND SOLUTIONS FOR PSYCHOLOGICAL REHABILITATION

The long-term psychological development and rehabilitation of children from conflict zones represent complex challenges that can be addressed, in part, through the thoughtful application of AI and ML technologies.

Some common challenges that the incorporation of AI in humanitarian efforts can pose have been identified in the literature. AI decisions are often not easily detected and therefore are hard to audit for monitoring purposes or explain to the public (Buiten, 2019; Rudin & Radin, 2019). The complexity of AI technologies can prevent people from understanding whether and how their rights have been infringed, making it difficult for them to seek compensation for such breaches. Additionally, even if deciphering the system is feasible, it often demands a level of technical knowledge beyond what the average person has, which can hinder attempts to obtain redress for damages inflicted by AI systems (Pizzi et al., 2020). The lack of transparency in the data economy, coupled with its insufficient accountability for human rights, can hinder individuals from becoming aware of violations of their rights and from pursuing remedies when such violations occur (Shah, 2013, 2019). Additionally, this opacity can challenge even well-informed experts or investigators who try to audit these systems and identify faults. The intricate structure of most development and humanitarian initiatives can further exacerbate these issues (Andersen, 2019; Ebert et al., 2020).

Another risk factor is the use of information to train an AI model. If the information is flawed, such as being biased or incomplete, the system might generate decisions and results that are prejudiced or unjust. Several phases are susceptible to the introduction of these defects: during the problem's initial definition (for instance, selecting a proxy variable associated with racial or socioeconomic traits); throughout the data gathering phase (for instance, when a marginalized group is not adequately represented in the training set); and during the data preparation stage.

It is important to note that while AI and ML can be powerful tools in psychological development and rehabilitation, they should complement, not replace, human-centered and culturally sensitive interventions. Ethical considerations, transparency, and ongoing research are essential to ensure that these technologies are applied responsibly, respecting the dignity and privacy of the children involved. Additionally, collaborative efforts involving mental health professionals, technologists, and community stakeholders are crucial for the successful implementation of AI in the rehabilitation of children from conflict zones.

Data Reliability and Integrity

The deployment of AI technologies in conflict zones raises significant challenges concerning data reliability and integrity. In environments where data collection is hampered by ongoing conflict, ensuring the accuracy and completeness of the data becomes problematic. AI systems are heavily reliant on the quality of data fed into them; thus, poor data can lead to misinformed insights, which in turn can affect the decision-making process. Addressing these issues requires

AI's Role in Enhancing Humanitarian Efforts 153

robust methodologies for data collection and validation, which must be adapted to the chaotic environments of conflict zones. This might involve using cross-verification techniques with multiple data sources or developing AI systems that are specifically trained to handle and scrutinize data inconsistencies typical of conflict scenarios.

Infrastructure Dependencies

The reliance on sophisticated infrastructure for operating advanced AI systems poses another significant hurdle in conflict zones. These areas often suffer from unstable electrical power supplies, limited internet connectivity, and damaged technological infrastructure, which can severely restrict the functionality of AI applications. For AI technologies to be feasible and effective in such settings, they must be designed to operate with minimal infrastructure requirements. Developing lightweight, low-power AI solutions that can function autonomously or with intermittent connectivity could be crucial. Additionally, deploying mobile and solar-powered AI units might provide a workaround for the infrastructural challenges in these regions.

Operational Security

Operational security is another critical concern when implementing AI in conflict zones. The use of AI systems, especially those involving data transmission over networks, introduces vulnerabilities to cyber-attacks, which can be more pronounced in conflict situations where technological systems are targeted. Furthermore, the sensitive nature of the data being processed – often involving vulnerable populations – demands stringent security measures to protect against data breaches. Implementing advanced encryption methods, secure data transmission protocols and robust cybersecurity measures are essential to safeguard the information and the technology from manipulation or exploitation by hostile entities.

CONCLUSION

This chapter presents a crucial interdisciplinary exploration that effectively bridges the domains of AI, humanitarian aid, and child psychology. This synthesis is not only innovative but essential for advancing our understanding of how technology can be employed to address complex and pressing social challenges such as armed conflicts. By delving into the intersection of AI with the experiences of children in conflict zones, the research highlights a significant, yet relatively underexplored, area. It emphasizes AI's potential not merely as a tool for logistical and analytical tasks but as a pivotal asset in providing sensitive emotional and psychological support to affected youth.

Moreover, the discourse on the ethical implications of using AI in conflict settings contributes meaningfully to broader conversations about the responsible application of technology. This discussion is particularly timely, as it touches on the necessity for international regulations and standards that govern the deployment of AI, ensuring its alignment with humanitarian principles and ethical considerations. The insights provided here are intended to inform and influence ongoing policy debates and the development of guidelines that prioritize the welfare and rights of vulnerable populations, especially children.

The practical implications of this research are substantial. It has the potential to influence a wide range of stakeholders, including policymakers, technologists, and humanitarian workers, prompting them to re-evaluate and innovate the ways in which AI tools are developed and implemented. The goal is to foster deployments of AI that are not only technologically advanced but are also deeply informed by an understanding of the psychological and emotional needs of children affected by war. Thus, this chapter does not just add to the academic discourse but also acts as a catalyst for real-world changes that could enhance the resilience and recovery of young individuals living through the severe trials posed by armed conflicts.

In conclusion, by integrating AI with humanitarian and psychological insights, this research paves the way for more informed, empathetic, and effective interventions. These efforts are crucial for building systems that not only survive ethical scrutiny but also actively contribute to the healing and thriving of humanity's most vulnerable members amidst the chaos of conflict.

NOTE

1. UN Global Pulse's PulseSatellite project, available at: www.unglobalpulse.org/microsite/pulsesatellite/.

REFERENCES

Abadi, M., & Andersen, D. G. (2016). *Learning to protect communications with adversarial neural cryptography*. arXiv preprint arXiv:1610.06918.

Addie, Y. O., Fakunle, D. O., & Jeffrey, P. (2024). Narrative Rx: Storytelling's healing capacities in public health. In G. Bouchard & A. Mermikides (Eds.), *The Routledge companion to performance and medicine* (pp. 261–271). Routledge.

Amir, S., & Ahmad, F. (2019). Artificial intelligence and its prospective use in armed forces. *Electronic Research Journal of Engineering, Computers and Applied Sciences, 1*.

Andersen, L. (2019). Artificial intelligence in international development: Avoiding ethical pitfalls. *Journal of Public & International Affairs*.

Buiten, M. C. (2019). Towards intelligent regulation of artificial intelligence. *European Journal of Risk Regulation, 10*(1), 41–59.

Carlton-Ford, S. (2004). Armed conflict and children's life chances. *Peace Review, 16*(2), 185–191.

Corcoran, C. M., & Cecchi, G. A. (2020). Using language processing and speech analysis for the identification of psychosis and other disorders. *Biological Psychiatry: Cognitive Neuroscience and Neuroimaging, 5*(8), 770–779.

De Bellis, M. D., & Zisk, A. (2014). The biological effects of childhood trauma. *Child and Adolescent Psychiatric Clinics, 23*(2), 185–222.

Denov, M. (2008). Girl soldiers and human rights: Lessons from Angola, Mozambique, Sierra Leone and Northern Uganda. *The International Journal of Human Rights, 12*(5), 813–836.

Ebert, I., Busch, T., & Wettstein, F. (2020). *Business and human rights in the data economy: A mapping and research study* (p. 44). DEU.

Evans, J. L. (1996). Children as zones of peace: Working with young children affected by armed violence. *Coordinators' Notebook, 19*, 1–37.

Grotberg, E. (1995). *A guide to promoting resilience in children: Strengthening the human spirit.* Bernard van Leer Foundation.

Jones, E., Kendall, S., & Otomo, Y. (2018). Gender, war, and technology: Peace and armed conflict in the twenty-first century. *Australian Feminist Law Journal, 44*(1), 1–8.

Katagiri, N. (2024). Artificial Intelligence and cross-domain warfare: Balance of power and unintended escalation. *Global Society, 38*(1), 34 48.

Kurian, N., & Saad, C. (2024). Where technology meets empathy: Using digital storytelling, gaming, and AI to teach about peace and human rights. In M. J. O'Hair, P. A. Woods, & H. Dan O'Hair (Eds.), *Communication and education: Promoting peace and democracy in times of crisis and conflict* (pp. 148–163). John Wiley & Sons.

Muratbekova, M., & Shamoi, P. (2024). *Color-emotion associations in art: Fuzzy approach.* IEEE Access.

OHCHR. (2023). *End the killing of children in armed conflict, UN Committee urges.* https://www.ohchr.org/en/statements/2023/11/end-killing-children-armed-conflict-un-committee-urges

Orth, U., & Robins, R. W. (2014). The development of self-esteem. *Current directions in psychological science, 23*(5), 381–387.

Panic, B., & Arthur, P. (2024). *AI for peace.* CRC Press.

Pizzi, M., Romanoff, M., & Engelhardt, T. (2020). AI for humanitarian action: Human rights and ethics. *International Review of the Red Cross, 102*(913), 145–180.

Rudin, C., & Radin, J. (2019). Why are we using black box models in AI when we don't need to? A lesson from an explainable AI competition. *Harvard Data Science Review, 1*(2). https://doi.org/10.1162/99608f92.5a8a3a3d

Sai, S., Gaur, A., Sai, R., Chamola, V., Guizani, M., & Rodrigues, J. J. (2024). *Generative AI for transformative healthcare: A comprehensive study of emerging models, applications, case studies and limitations.* IEEE Access.

Shah, T. M. (2012). *Collective memory and narrative: Ethnography of social trauma in Jammu and Kashmir* [Doctoral dissertation, Kansas State University].

Shah, T. M. (2013). Chaos and fear: Creativity and hope in an uncertain world. *International Sociology, 28*(5), 513–517. https://doi.org/10.1177/0268580913496920

Shah, T. M. (2019). Social justice and change. In S. Romaniuk, M. Thapa, & P. Marton (Eds.), *The Palgrave encyclopedia of global security studies* (pp. 1–4). Springer-Verlag.

Shah, T. M. (2020). Children of Kashmir and the meaning of family in armed conflict. In S. Frankel, S. McNamee, & L. E. Bass (Eds.), *Bringing children back into the family: Relationality, connectedness, and home* (pp. 213–216). Emerald Publishing Limited.

Shah, T. M. (2021). Women as "sites of gendered politics". In Aikat, D., Beamer, B., Biswas, M. K., Bowen, B., Brost, L. F., Fatima, S., ... & Srivastav, S. (Eds.), *Misogyny across global media.* Lexington Books.

Shah, T. M. (2023). *Global patterns of decolonization and the right to self-determination: A comparative-historical analysis of East Timor and Kashmir* [Doctoral dissertation, The University of Utah].

Shah, T. M. (2024a). Decolonization and peacebuilding: The case of Timor Leste and Kashmir. In Pietrzak, P. (Ed.), *Dealing with regional conflicts of global importance* (pp. 262–278). IGI Global.

Shah, T. M. (2024b). Emotions in politics: A review of contemporary perspectives and trends. *International Political Science Abstracts, 74*(1), 1–14.

Tarigan, F. N., & Hasibuan, S. A. (2024). Application and challenges of digital storytelling based artificial intelligence for language skills: A narrative review. *SALTeL Journal (Southeast Asia Language Teaching and Learning), 7*(1), 1–8.

UN General Assembly, Roadmap for Digital Cooperation: Implementation of the Recommendations of the High-Level Panel on Digital Cooperation. Report of the Secretary-General, UN Doc. A/74/821, May 29, 2020 (Secretary-General's Roadmap), para. 6. Retrieved December, 2020, from https://undocs.org/A/74/821

Printed in the USA
CPSIA information can be obtained
at www.ICGtesting.com
JSHW050300251124
74138JS00004B/16